add

80E12.50

FEB 22 1995
042

THE AMERICAN CATHOLIC PRESS
AND THE
JEWISH STATE 1917-1959

THE AMERICAN CATHOLIC PRESS
AND THE
JEWISH STATE 1917-1959

by
ESTHER YOLLES FELDBLUM

KTAV PUBLISHING HOUSE, INC.
NEW YORK
1977

© Copyright 1977
Estate of Esther Feldblum

Library of Congress Cataloging in Publication Data

Feldblum, Esther Yolles, 1933-1974.
 The Catholic press and the Jewish State.

 Bibliography: p.
 Includes index.
 1. Zionism—Public opinion. 2. Israel—Foreign opinion, American. 3. Press, Catholic—United States. 4. Catholic Church and Zionism. 5. Public opinion—United States. I. Title.
DS149.F44 1977   070.4′49′95694001   76-58007
ISBN 0-87068-325-X

The publication of this book was made possible with the financial assistance of Hadassah and of the Center for Israel and Jewish Studies of Columbia University.

MANUFACTURED IN THE UNITED STATES OF AMERICA

Contents

	Esther Yolles Feldblum 1933-1974	vii
	A Tribute	ix
	In Memoriam	xi
	Foreword	xv
	Acknowledgments	xix
I	Introduction	1
II	Homeland Versus Holy Land: Early Responses to Zionism	17
III	Advance and Retreat: The Era Between the Wars	33
IV	Non Possumus: On the Eve of a Jewish State	55
V	New Realities: Israel in the Holy Land	71
VI	Reassessments: The Factors of Communism and Ecumenism	91
VII	Theological Reinterpretations and the State of Israel	107
	Abbreviations	120
	Notes	121
	Bibliography	171
	Index	195

Dr. Esther Yolles Feldblum
1933-1974
תנצבה

Esther Yolles Feldblum
1933-1974

Dr. Esther Feldblum, born in Atlantic City on Aug. 23, 1933, was the daughter of the distinguished chief rabbi of Philadelphia, Rabbi Ephraim E. Yolles, and his wife Pepi. Esther was graduated from the Beth Jacob High School in New York in 1950 and from its Teachers Seminary in 1952. In 1962 she received her B.A. magna cum laude from the City College of New York, having been elected to the Phi Betta Kappa Society. Three years later, working under an NDFL Fellowship, she completed her M.A. in Near Eastern Studies at Yeshiva University's Bernard Revel Graduate School. Subsequently she studied at Columbia University on a Danforth Foundation Fellowship, and in 1973 attained her doctorate. Her thesis, on American Catholic Responses to the Holy Land, was nominated by the Columbia University Department of History for the Bancroft Dissertation Award.

Dr. Feldblum taught at Bard College during 1971-72, and in 1973 she was appointed Assistant Professor of Judaic Studies at Brooklyn College in New York. She has published articles in the *American Historical Quarterly* and in the *Journal for Ecumenical Studies*. In addition, some of her archival research was included in *Guide for American-Holy Land Studies*, edited by Moshe Davis (Institute of

Contemporary Jewry, Hebrew University, Jerusalem, 1973).

Married in 1954 to Professor Meyer S. Feldblum, Esther was the mother of four children, Avinoam, Sholom, Chai, and Miriam. She died in an automobile accident on September 1, 1974, while returning from lecturing at a Yavneh college youth convention.

A Tribute

Rarely does one meet a person who, too ideal for this world, could inhabit perhaps only the literary realm—but Esther was just such a person. So blended within her were beauty, generosity, and scholarship that she was truly extraordinary, yet imbued with a modesty that let her forget her uniqueness.

Esther combined the demanding task of raising a traditional family with the exacting requirements of modern scholarship. But for her, cooking was artistry and lecturing a delight. Forever relaxed and composed, at home and at work, Esther brought an extra sparkle to whomever she met.

A selfless mother and a committed teacher, Esther was an inspiring model for others. She seldom was fully aware of what she meant to me, to her family, and to her friends, but she never forgot what everybody meant to her. As a teacher, she brought Jewish learning and scholarship lovingly and wholeheartedly to her students, regardless of their own ideology or creed. And as a friend—such is her legacy:

> "Her loveliness conveyed a brilliance tempered by an unassuming simplicity . . . She was a phenomenon—a splendid manifestation of ideal Jewish womanhood."

"What particularly touched our hearts, however, was an intuitive empathy she had for others and a generosity of spirit to help assuage their pains and burdens . . ."

" . . . lovely, lovely Esther taught all of us . . . to give of ourselves . . . I can rarely remember a time when I did not see Esther with a smile on her face, a smile that warmed us all . . ."

Such a disposition was G-d's gift to her, and she was G-d's gift to me. Sadly, she is now gone, but she has left me and our four wonderful children with rich and inspiring memories.

Meyer S. Feldblum
September 1, 1976

In Memoriam

For those of us who knew Esther Feldblum as a fellow graduate student in Jewish history at Columbia University, she was, above all, the dedicated and enthusiastic scholar with a keen interest in our work as well as her own. It was Esther who took time from her research and family responsibilities to review the vast field of Jewish history with us in preparation for our oral examinations. It was Esther who often initiated lively discussions about major historical issues. We delighted in her knowledge, her balanced judgments, and her rigorous opinions. She expressed her ideas in an intimate fashion which suggested that they also represented strongly held personal convictions. Esther always brought to our conversations a sparkle of wry insight, and we anticipated the pleasure of our animated discussions with her. She was, in short, a stimulating fellow student.

But Esther was not simply another bright and engaging student. She was a wife and mother of four children who had returned to school after years away. Esther made light of the burdens of combining scholarship with family responsibilities. Or, rather, she accepted them in a matter-of-fact way, expressing neither bitterness nor a sense of martyrdom. For many of us, she became a sympathetic guide to the special problems of women in the academic world. She willingly offered us not only scholarly insight but also practical knowledge of what women faced in their pursuit of scholarship. We peppered her with questions. Why did she choose to return to graduate school? How did she do it? What did it mean, in concrete terms, to be a wife, mother of four children, and scholar-in-training? What inner drive and discipline had to be yoked to lead to such success? Esther's answers enlightened us without overwhelming us. For Esther the dilemma of being a woman and a scholar no longer pressed her, since she had resolved it with the help of an extraordinary and supportive husband. Though she recognized the problems confronting any woman trying to synthesize career and family with integrity, she advocated the effort. Esther saw the inherent worth of both choices and she was willing to sacrifice leisure and material comfort for the sake of scholarship and family.

Still another dimension of Esther's life affected her relationships with friends and colleagues. Esther was not only wife, mother, and scholar. She was also an Orthodox Jew. In her education, upbringing, and personal life, traditional Judaism occupied the central position. Yet she was able to reach out to friends and fellow students whose Jewish commitments were far different from her own. Esther brought to our discussions of religion the same dispassionate ability to explain other Jews' choices and the varieties of Judaism with which she analyzed Jewish history. She had a fine sensitivity to the reasons for Jewish diversity, coupled with tremendous tolerance of the forms of Jewish expression. Esther's warm willingness to accept individuals for what they were and to welcome them as human beings regardless of their religious perspectives, enabled her to bring new elements of understanding to all whom she graced with her friendship.

The last year and a half of Esther's life suggested the professional fulfillment that she so richly deserved. Her dissertation received academic distinction and was nominated for a Bancroft Award. Esther went to Brooklyn College to teach in the Judaic Studies Department. She began to convey to us, still in the throes of our own dissertation research, what it meant to be a professor: teaching students, coping with departmental politics, publishing articles, preparing papers. During her last summer she finished two articles for publication. The future was filled with promise of more growth. The hardest years of struggle lay in the past.

IN MEMORIAM

On September 1, 1974 Esther was killed in an automobile accident.

We cannot repay Esther for what she gave of herself to us and to her other friends and colleagues. But bringing her dissertation to publication is perhaps the most fitting tribute to her memory, for it continues her giving, in this case to the larger academic community. Esther leaves behind an enduring and wide-ranging heritage for those who were touched by her presence and for those who can know her only through her intellectual accomplishments.

Deborah Dash Moore
Paula Hyman

Foreword

Quite apart from its intrinsic merit as a work of scholarship, this volume is both monument and witness—a monument to the author's sudden, tragic death on September 1, 1974, and witness to a felicitous turn of events *of* which, in some respects, this study is in itself a product and *to* which it makes its own contribution.

To focus, in the first instance, on its wider implications, Dr. Feldblum's work is an example of a relatively new spirit informing Jewish and Christian scholarly-theological circles, for it provides a fine instance of the type of study by Jew of Christian (and by implication, by Christian of Jew) of the other's history, beliefs, practices and patterns of organization that is increasingly displacing the genre of expression that long dominated the field.

Adherents of Judaism and Christianity have, after a fashion, been studying one another's religion for over nineteen centuries. Ever since the earliest Christian sects began to preach their new doctrines, Jews and Christians have sought to know something about the other's ideology in the hope of striking telling blows of refutation at their religious adversaries and of converting some to "the true faith." Each side perused or listened to bits of the other's beliefs and claims to legitimacy. What R. Eleazar had urged his disciples to do with regard to Epicurus ("Be diligent in studying the Torah so that you may know how to refute him," *Ethics of the Fathers*, 2.14), Jews and Christians have done with respect to each other's teachings.

However distasteful this form of study, more commonly known as "polemics," may be to our contemporary temper, it is important to bear in mind—particularly in our approach to the work before us—that is was the dominant posture pervading examination of one religious tradition by the adherent of another (not only between Judaism and Christianity; indeed, not only between different "religions," but even between contending sects within the same religion). Nor should this polemical literature be cavalierly dismissed as devoid of interest to any but the historian of polemics and apologetica. Many of these works are replete with valuable and authentic information about the religious communities they represent as well as those they are intended to deride and undermine. In many ways, they are the forerunners of our disciplines of comparative religion and the sociology of religion. But, however valuable, these works are justifiably suspect to us today, for the contemporary study of religious attitudes and behavior emerges from an entirely new point of departure, one eminently exemplified by the work being presented here to the student of contemporary religious history.

In contrasting the spirit underlying and pervading the study by Dr. Feldblum—and of many others like it—with those of earlier ages, I am not celebrating the spirit of "dialogue" that obtains between Jews and Christians, however much that new spirit merits applause and encouragement. What I am making reference to is the multidimensional significance of this work of scholarship, which indeed incorporates the spirit of religious "dialogue" but happily goes far beyond it.

In the first place, what must, it seems to me, strike anyone who is at all familiar with the history of Jewish and Christian studies of each other and with the intense feelings seething in many quarters on the issues surveyed in this work is Dr. Feldblum's achievement of a scholarly form and content on a sensitive subject of contemporary religious as well as political significance. To Jews as well as Christians, the questions and viewpoints discussed in this work are little less than explosive, and to have them researched and described systematically

FOREWORD xvii

and *dispassionately* represents an achievement that, unfortunately, cannot as yet be taken for granted.

The author's courage and accomplishment are all the more notable, for no one who knew Esther Feldblum will explain her dispassionate stance as the consequence of emotional detachment from the subject of her investigation. Quite the contrary: Dr. Feldblum was very much "involved" in the issues she studied, by which I mean that she was concerned and affected quite personally with the persons and viewpoints she traced and analyzed. Nevertheless, she managed to prevent her emotional, religious and ethnic commitments from intruding upon her quest for historical truth and for fairness in judgment and evaluation. Her very "involvement" provided the stimulus for her research, but her spiritual and scholarly integrity enabled her to desist from partisan judgment and evaluation.

Anyone conversant with the literature of the last two decades on the issues of Zionism, the State of Israel, the Arab refugees, and the Christian holy places of the Holy Land in which many scholars and theologians have unabashedly taken unequivocally partisan positions will, I believe, concede that the dispassion exemplified in this work is, alas, even now all too rare.

Apart from its contents, therefore, Dr. Feldblum's work must also be seen as a commentary on a relatively novel temper that has begun to become increasingly manifest in intellectual religious circles of the United States. This frame of mind has generated a new constellation of interests that can transcend deepseated prejudices and hostilities of longstanding in favor of intelligent examination and even friendly critical analysis of religious attitudes across denominational lines without becoming religiously polemical or defensive. That a study of American Catholic attitudes by an American Jew can be composed with the hope that its audience will include Christians, Jews and religiously unaffiliated is a tribute not only to the author but to the society that enabled her, nay encouraged her, to attain this level of "dialogue." While the posture has its analogues elsewhere, I believe it is fair to say that it remains a peculiarly American achievement, for only in this country has interdenominational conversation attained the level of maturity and sophistication that obtains in other areas of research. Dr. Feldblum's work constitutes one more voice in a conversation stimulated and fostered by notable theologians-scholars, such as Abraham Joshua Heschel, John Courtney Murray and Reinhold Niebuhr, to mention but three of the many Jews, Catholics and Protestants who cultivated the soil on which the present volume could come into being.

On a somewhat different level, the work is a reliable index of the extent and candor of the exchange between the adherents and spokesmen of different faiths in the United States—many of whom are quite removed from intellectual concerns and orientations—for it describes the shift within the American Catholic community from an almost monolithic hostility to Zionism to a variety of attitudes including sympathy and even support. As a sociological commentary on American society, the work must take its place alongside other studies of religion—of Roman Catholicism in particular—in contemporary America, for it provides fresh evidence on the upheaval within the Roman Catholic community of the United States in the last decade. As a commentary on American society, the work helps illuminate the importance that the State of Israel attained for American society at large and most specifically for the American Jewish community since 1948.

For all its significance and nobility, the work presented here is incomplete, for the author's life was cut short before she could revise and polish it as she would have liked. Killed in an automobile accident, Esther Feldblum's life was prematurely ended at the age of 41. However, she left a rich legacy among her peers and colleagues to which this work testifies, for it has been brought to press thanks to the efforts of her classmates and friends. As one of those privileged to be her teachers, I can testify that I learned much from her on many levels. A person committed to excellence in everything she pursued, she radiated exemplary personal traits which hopefully the discerning reader will detect even in the necessarily subdued atmosphere of a work of scholarship.

Gerson D. Cohen

Acknowledgments

"Walk with the wise and attain wisdom" (Prov. 13:20). I consider myself fortunate to have had the opportunity to study at Columbia University. I am especially grateful to a profound scholar and masterful teacher, Gerson D. Cohen. Professor Cohen's teaching opened for me the portals to Jewish history, and his guidance gave me a sure footing in its many paths. I am also indebted to Robert T. Handy, professor of Church history at Union Theological Seminary, for the time and effort he gave so graciously to my work on this thesis. For his guidance, critical but always encouraging, I am very grateful.

It is a pleasure to acknowledge the assistance of the many persons who have helped me with advice and information. Among the many, I would like to single out Rev. Karl Baehr, Claire Huchet Bishop, Fr. Edward H. Flannery, Fr. George Barry Ford, P'ninna Herzog, wife of the late Rabbi Yaakov Herzog, Msgr. Francis J. Lally, Msgr. John M. Oesterreicher, Abbot Leo Rudloff, O.S.B., Rabbi Marc Tanenbaum, Rev. Carl Hermann Voss, and Dr. Chaim Wardi.

Many thanks, too, are extended to the staffs of the archives and libraries for their ready assistance, and particularly to Harry J. Alderman of the American Jewish Committee Archives; Msgr. Edward Foster of the Catholic Near East Welfare Association; Fr. Edmund Halsey, O.S.B., of the American Catholic Historical Society Archives; and Sylvia Landress and Esther Togman of the Zionist Library Archives. Of course, the responsibility for errors, omissions, and viewpoints is solely mine.

My graduate-studies expenses were generously undertaken by the Danforth Foundation. The Memorial Foundation for Jewish Culture and the National Foundation for Jewish Culture contributed grants toward the research of this project.

אחרון אחרון חביב To my husband, Meyer Simcha, in whose devoted companionship I found intellectual sustenance and continual encouragement, and to my children, Avinoam, Sholom, Chai, and Miriam, for their cheerful endurance.

I

Introduction

We are unable to favor this movement [Zionism]. We cannot prevent the Jews from going to Jerusalem—but we could never sanction it. As the head of the Church I cannot answer you otherwise. The Jews have not recognized our Lord, therefore we cannot recognize the Jewish people and so, if you come to Palestine and settle your people there, we will be ready with churches and priests to baptize all of you.
(Pope Pius X to Theodor Herzl on January 26, 1904)[1]

It could seem that Christians, whatever the difficulties they may experience, must attempt to understand and respect the religious significance of this link between the people and the land (Holy Land). The existence of the State of Israel should not be separated from this perspective. . . . the history of Judaism does not end with the destruction of Jerusalem, but continues to develop in a rich spiritual tradition.
(Read by Cardinal Shehan of Baltimore from a working paper prepared by the Secretariat for Promoting Christian Unity. December 10, 1969.)[2]

Sixty-five years separate these two Roman Catholic reactions to modern Jewish nationalism. During that period Jewish nationalism was transformed from a mere idea into the political reality of the State of Israel in May 1948. The historical background was momentous. It saw two world wars, the Balfour Declaration of 1917, the breakup of empires, the British mandate in Palestine, and the Jewish Holocaust in Europe. The two statements portray a change of Roman Catholic attitude during this span of events. Moreover, they clearly indicate a shift on the part of the Church in its theological interpretation of the role of the Jews and the Jewish state.

Purpose and Scope

The activities of the Church in the political and diplomatic struggle for a Jewish state have not yet been researched, nor are the Vatican archives available for a definitive study. Neither has an extended survey of the attitudes of the Church in the United States (nor, to my knowledge, in any other country) been undertaken in reference to Zionism and Israel.[3] The purpose of this study is to chart, describe, and interpret the shifting attitudes and responses of various segments of American Catholic opinion to certain key events in the history of Zionism/Israel.[4] Though limited in scope, this study may contribute to an understanding of the larger political motivations and theological gropings of the Catholic Church regarding the Jewish state.

The historical period covered by this study ranges from the Balfour Declaration of 1917 to the eve of the Second Vatican Council in 1960. However, the study's final chapter looks beyond that year by evaluating the theological momentum initiated by Vatican II and the impact of the State of Israel on the new theological directions, particularly as reflected on the American Catholic scene. The events of the 1960s and the formulation of Church attitudes during that period call for a special study. This investigation, which has prepared the way, may hopefully lead to other definitive studies of the Roman Catholic Church and the Jewish state.

Description of Sources

At this time, when the full range of Catholic archival sources is still not available,[5] the Catholic press offers distinct advantages for charting the responses and shifting attitudes of the American Church.[6] Certainly the press is influential in shaping the opinions of its readers. Yet, at the same time, it responds to and reflects already existing attitudes of its constituency. Moreover, in the case of the Catholic press it is generally assumed that there is a correlation between the views expressed by the editor of a paper and that of his diocesan ordinary.[7] The assumption rests on the Church's definition of the role of the press and the manner in which the press interprets its own role.

In the eyes of the Church, the press has an Apostolate, that is, a mission to serve the Church. Pius XII, in his 1950 address to the International Congress of the Catholic Press, stressed the importance of the press in infusing in temporal matters the spirit and guidance of the Church. On another occasion, he instructed the press to give obedience to the bishops and to reflect the unity of the Church.[8] Pius XII was only reiterating what had long been policy in regard to Catholic periodicals and newspapers.[9]

For American Catholics, the guidelines were set down in the Third Plenary Council in Baltimore in 1884. The *Acta et Decreta* of the council clearly defined the qualifications for a Catholic paper: "Only those periodicals shall be considered Catholic which expose and defend the Church, describe the progress of the Church at home and abroad, and are prepared to subject themselves to the authority of the Church in all things."[10] A majority of the press complied with these exhortations, particularly during the years 1900–1945, the period of central concern in our study. According to the periodization suggested by John G. Deedy in his survey of the Catholic press, these years fall in the "middle phase" of Catholic journalism, during which the majority of the press was under clerical control and direction.[11] Even as late as 1957, 75 percent of the editors of the Catholic newspapers were clergy or religious.[12] Therefore, it is not surprising that when the press defined itself, it adhered closely to the guidelines of the Church. In the words of Msgr. Francis J. Lally, long-time editor of the *Pilot*, the purpose of a Catholic press is to instruct in matters religious and moral and "to apply as far as possible the message of the Gospel to the passing events of the days in which we live." The editor of another diocesan weekly, the *Catholic Standard*, maintained that for the "interpretation" of news, the Catholic editor should consult with his ordinary, and that the latter could rightfully silence controversial issues in the press.[13]

The degree of hierarchial control depends upon the nature of the paper. The diocesan press, many papers of which carry on their mastheads the words "official organ," can be expected to follow more closely the opinions of their ordinaries. And yet, even in that area of Catholic journalism there are considerable differences from diocese to diocese. In some papers, all editorial comments are approved by diocesan officials before publication. But in many others the editor works without supervisory interference, and the opinions expressed in the paper are wholly his own.[14] Independence and diversity of opinion are more marked in nondiocesan papers and are most pronounced in the small segment of the press that is owned and operated by the laity. When *Commonweal,* a lay journal of opinion, began publishing in 1924, it explicitly rejected the notion of serving as a mouthpiece of the Church. In the first issue the editors promised that *Commonweal* would be "definitely Christian in its presentation of orthodox religious principles and their application to the subjects that fall within its purview," but at the same time they emphasized that the opinions stated would be those of laymen and that the paper would open its pages to dissenting views, even those not of the Catholic faith.[15] But journals of *Commonweal*'s type were scarce in the first half of the twentieth century. For the most part, the Catholic press used in this study operated within the shadows of the Church.[16]

In 1917 there were over 300 American Catholic publications; by 1960 the number of publications had climbed to 575 and the total circulation had soared to over 23 million.[17] Obviously, selections had to be made to keep the study within manageable proportions. For systematic scrutiny and analysis, I selected representative papers from the following categories: diocesan, religious orders, organizational, and lay.

The guidelines for my choices were that papers be representative of the particular category and that they respond to news concerning Jews, Palestine, and Israel.[18] For my choices among the diocesan papers, I paid attention to the size and geographic position of the diocese. I gave preference to papers of larger dioceses because their potential for influence is greater. I also favored dioceses that contained sizable Jewish communities, in the expectation that proximity would provoke interest. Accessibility of the newspaper source was an additional factor which had to be taken into consideration.[19]

Among the various diocesan papers, I chose seven which conform to the above guidelines for intensive examination: the *Pilot* (Boston); the *Tablet* (Brooklyn); the *New World* (Chicago); *Michigan Catholic* (Detroit); *Tidings* (Los Angeles); and the syndicated weeklies, the *Register* (published in Denver) and *Our Sunday Visitor* (published in Huntington, Indiana). The combined total of dioceses served by the syndicated papers ranged from forty to forty-seven dioceses. To supplement the diocesan press, I made extensive use of the bulletins of the National Catholic Welfare Conference News Service, which have supplied news and editorials, since 1919, to Catholic weeklies across the country.

The diocesan papers researched were all established before 1917 and have continued publication to the present. This presents the opportunity of an unbroken line of investigation, as well as a more accurate measure for determining evolving attitudes. Furthermore, all of these papers were cited for their professional excellence by the Catholic Press Association.[20]

In choosing journals of religious orders, I was guided both by the prominence of the religious order and by the attention given in its journal to Zionism and the Jewish state. For example, while there would be no question regarding the importance of the over 6,000 Jesuits in the United States, the 800 Passionists might not have attracted our attention were it not for the interest evinced in Palestine in their journal. Size of circulation was not always an indicator of influence. For example, the Paulist Fathers' *Catholic World* averaged less than 10,000 subscribers in its circulation statistics, but historians of the Catholic press credit it with greater influence than many a periodical with far larger circulation.[21] While not all journals listed under publications of religious orders are necessarily official organs of the order, for the purposes of this study I considered them representative of the order if they were staffed and directed by its members. Though papers of other religious orders were consulted (and are included in the bibliography), the following were extensively examined: *America* (Jesuit); *Ave Maria* (Holy Cross Fathers–Notre Dame); *Catholic World* (Paulists); *Sign* (Passionists); and to a lesser degree because of difficulties of access, the *Crusader's Almanac* (Franciscans).[22]

Organizational journals fell into basically two categories, fraternal and institutional. The selections were based on two criteria: the importance of the respective organization on the American Catholic scene and the extent of nonorganizational news content in its journal. In the first category, *Columbia* and *Central-Blatt* were chosen. *Columbia* is the journal of the Knights of Columbus, the largest lay fraternal organization of Catholics in the United States. The Knights are a financial pillar of the Church and are active in numerous apostolic works and community projects. *Columbia* has an enormous circulation of over one million subscribers.[23] *Central-Blatt and Social Justice Review* is a publication of one of the oldest lay organizations of Catholics in the United States, the Catholic Central Verein (later Central Union).[24] The Central Verein was established in 1885 to represent the large body of immigrant German Catholics. Indicative of its importance, it was the first society ever given an official mandate for Catholic Action by the American bishops.[25] Its journal was valuable for this study because it was outspoken on both national and international affairs. Apart from its liberal stance on economic and industrial reform during the twenties and thirties, the paper served as a good example of conservative Catholic opinion in the United States.

Two publications of institutional organizations were regularly consulted. *Catholic Action* was the official bulletin of the National Catholic Welfare Conference.[26] The bulletin not only chronicled all the activities of the various departments of the organization, but it also provided editorial comments on current events. *CAIP News* was a monthly newsletter issued by the Catholic Association for International Peace. I consulted the newsletter because the organization occasionally served as a spokesman for the American bishops on matters relating to international affairs.[27]

The field of lay journalism was comparatively limited during much of the period from 1917 to 1960. The emergence of an exciting and vital lay press is largely a product of the 1950's and 1960's. Extensive use was made, however, of two outstanding lay journals which were founded in the first half of the twentieth century. *Commonweal*, founded by Michael Williams in 1924, was recorded in Baumgartner's 1930 survey of the Catholic press as an "interesting adventure."[28] It has surpassed that modest assessment to become one of the most influential journals of opinion, whose literary merit and independent liberal stance has gained for it a reading public far beyond the confines of the Catholic community. As one Catholic editor put it, *Commonweal* is "highly regarded by non-Catholics."[29]

Catholic Worker was founded in 1933 by two social agitators, Dorothy Day and Peter Maurin, whose economic and political philosophy veered sharply to the left. But its concern for the workingman and the welfare of discriminated groups in American society, areas often neglected by other Catholic papers, gave it a distinctive status in Catholic journalism. Of this paper it has been said, "the Catholic Church does not know what to do with it or what to do without it."[30]

There are a number of periodicals which do not fit in any of the above categories. They are primarily academic and theological journals. Their importance lies in the fact that they were read by intellectual and religious opinion-molders of the Catholic community. The following, in particular, were consulted:

American Ecclesiastical Review, a monthly which "has been a powerful influence in shaping the mind of the modern American priest."[31]

Catholic Biblical Quarterly, which is staffed by members of the most prestigious Catholic colleges and seminaries.[32]

Catholic Mind, in which each monthly issue contains an article on some question of the day "interpreted and enlightened by relevant statements of Catholic doctrine." A breakdown of subscribers in 1946 revealed that 68 percent of the subscribers were members of the hierarchy, priests, or religious.[33]

Homiletic and Pastoral Review, which addresses itself to issues of concern for the priest, to sermonic material, and to parish administration.

Priest, which is published by the editor of *Our Sunday Visitor* and is said to be one of the most widely read clerical journals in the world.[34]

Review of Politics was founded by Waldemar Gurian and is published under the auspices of Notre Dame University. It proclaims an interest in the "philosophical and historical approach to political realities,"[35] and has continually attracted the contributions of the leading intellectuals in the Catholic community.

Theological Digest, published by Woodstock, is a medium for original research in theology. America's most prominent theologians are represented in its pages.

In addition, *Catholic Digest* and *Theology Digest* were helpful for the later period of this study, in providing an overview of a larger segment of the Catholic press.³⁶

The Catholic Church in the United States

The twentieth century is considered the "adulthood" of the American Catholic Church. In 1908, Pope Pius X removed the Church in the United States from the jurisdiction of the Congregation de Propaganda de Fide.³⁷ No longer regarded as a missionary territory, in the United States the Church was placed on an equal footing with the long-established Churches of such countries as Spain, France, and Germany. An increasing number of American Catholics were represented in the offices of the Roman Curia and in the diplomatic service of the Holy See. By mid-century, Catholics from the United States were serving as apostolic nuncios and apostolic delegates. As Msgr. Ellis points out, "appointments of this kind clearly indicate the enhanced importance of Americans in the councils of the universal Church."³⁸

From the beginning of this century, the Catholic population in the United States increased from approximately twelve million to about fifty million. Its leadership was elevated from one cardinal to eight. Administratively, the American Church is divided into 132 dioceses, each headed by a bishop. A number of dioceses are large enough to have auxiliary bishops as well. The dioceses vary in population from fewer than 50,000 to more than a million. In area they range from approximately 540 square miles to 120,000.³⁹ In the New England States Catholics number nearly half of the population. Their largest single concentration, however, is found in the provinces of New York, Newark, and Philadelphia. The second largest concentration is in the industrial cities of the Northern Central States, such as Detroit, Chicago, Cincinnati, and Milwaukee. The Church is weakest in the South, where, except for centers such as Baltimore and Washington, D.C., most dioceses have to draw their priests, religious, and financial aid from outside the area. In the Midwest and West, Catholic strength is unevenly distributed.⁴⁰ Despite the vastness of the country and the ethnic diversity of the Church in the United States, a unity of Catholic communities and hierarchy has been achieved.

One of the distinguishing features of the American Catholic Church was the organization of the National Catholic Welfare Conference (hereafter NCWC).[41] It was established in 1919 as a coordinating agency for U.S. Catholic affairs. While as an organization it is purely advisory, the pronouncements which are issued by its Adminstrative Board of Bishops give it an aura of authority.[42] The NCWC operated eight departments divided into bureaus and sections which embrace almost every important area of Catholic interest and policy.[43] In my research I paid particular attention to the department concerned with the press, and to the influence of its releases upon the tone and direction of the diocesan press in the country.

Both Catholics and Jews in the United States share a number of similarities. They are religious-ethnic minorities in what was until recently a predominantly Protestant culture. Their histories on these shores are rooted in an immigrant past. Both, including the English-speaking Irish, passed through the crucible of the "triple melting pot."[44] The demographic patterns of both groups as they settled in the United States also have much in common. The immigrants clustered in the metropolitan centers of the North. In the closeness of urban settings, a certain degree of interaction was inevitable.[45] But as an authority on intercommunity relations has observed, "being neighbors does not mean necessarily neighborliness."[46] In religious communities a tension usually exists between more or less exclusivist doctrinal righteousness and modern humanistic universality.

During certain periods of their shared history in the United States, Catholics and Jews were thrown together in a struggle for common goals. This was especially true when both were targets of nativist prejudice. At other times, however, they were in opposite camps, both on domestic and foreign policy. The relationship between these two groups and their responses to each other's concerns are rooted in a long and painful history.

The Image of the Jew

We have witnessed in the 1950's and 1960's an attempt on the part of Christians and Jews to seriously reexamine their historical and contemporary relationships. However, the centuries-old popular and theological attitudes cannot be disregarded. Formed during the first centuries of the Christian era, these attitudes were reinforced and amplified down through the ages.[47] They were embedded in the Catholic reactions to the Zionist aspirations of the Jews, to the restoration of their "homeland," and to their acquisition of sovereignty over the Holy Land.

The starting point of attitude formation begins with the Gospels. As Augustin Cardinal Bea pointed out, "Christians continually read the New Testament and are therefore concerned with the facts as reported in the books they regard as sacred."[48] Beginning with Matthew,[49] the reader of the Gospels derives a sense of antipathy toward the Jews. In a description of John the Baptist, the narrative relates, "And seeing many of the Pharisees and Sadducees coming to his baptism, he said to them: Ye brood of vipers, who hath shewed you to flee from the wrath to come?"[50] A full-scale attack on the Pharisees is launched in the twenty-third chapter. This study is not concerned with the historicity of the narrative, nor with the veracity of the accusations leveled against the Pharisees.[51] However, it is important for our investigation to note that the graphic power of Matthew's imagery and the tone he set in this chapter remained vivid in Christian minds, particularly with the identification of post-Christian Jewry with the Pharisees of Jesus' time.[52] Matthew does not condemn the Pharisaic teaching as such, but rather the hypocritical practices among their teachers. This is clearly demonstrated by the opening verses of the chapter: "The scribes and the Pharisees have sitten on the chair of Moses. All things therefore whatsoever they shall say to you, observe and do: but according to their works do ye not; for they say and do not."[53] But the basic acceptance of the validity of the interpretation of laws by the high courts who sit "on the chair of Moses" is completely overshadowed by the following twenty-six verses, where even ostensible piety and good deeds are held in question and attributed to ulterior motives. "So you also outwardly indeed appear to men just; but inwardly you are full of hypocrisy and iniquity."[54] While not Matthew's intention, these allegations became the stock in trade of later anti-Semites, who needed but to read the twenty-third chapter to confirm their prejudices.

Among the writers of the Gospels, John is usually credited with having contributed most to the negative image of the Jews. Whereas earlier apostles had used the appellatives *Pharisees* or *temple priests* to designate the enemies of Jesus, John repeatedly used *the Jews*. Even Gregory Baum, the prominent Catholic theologian, who set out to lift the charge of anti-Semitism from the Gospels, was forced to concede that

> There can be no doubt that John's gospel has often served as a justification for the contempt in which the Jewish people were held and even for the injustices and violence with which they were treated. The hostile passages we find in the Church Fathers . . . have their literary origin in the Gospel of John. The same can be said of other myths regarding the Jews invented in later centuries.[55]

In the Middle Ages it was John's Gospel which provided the rationale for persecuting the Jews. And on Good Friday, the most dangerous day in the year for medieval Jewry, it was the Passion according to St. John that was read in the churches. Baum tried to extricate John from the charges of anti-Semitism. He pointed out that John's language is that of a Jew exhorting his brethren in the prophetic tradition and in the idiom of the pre-Christian Qumran community.[56] Literary history and historical context aside, our concern in this study is only with the resulting image and the fact that the theologian prejudices which grew out of the phraseology of the New Testament subsequently penetrated the mentality of Christians. These prejudices flourished in an atmosphere of Christian teaching which minimized the Jewish origins of its foundation. Even reading the Gospels one is not impressed with Jesus' identity as a Jew. Certainly, the facts that his family, his apostles, and the multitudes which supported him were Jewish are implicit in the text. But the lack of emphasis was misinterpreted by later Christians until finally, even the facts themselves faded.[57]

The trend of derogation of Judaism as a legitimate faith began with Paul. He introduced the concept that belief in Jesus was not an augmentation to the observation of the Law, but replaced the Law. When Paul instructed the Philippians, he forewarned them against the Jews and their religious practices. Of the Jews he said: "Beware of dogs, beware of evil workers"; of the laws he said: "[I] count them but as dung."[58] The expressions *dog* and *dung* may have contributed more to discrediting the Jews than can be balanced by Paul's lengthy and positive epistle to the Romans. In Romans 11, Paul made more felicitous comparisons and assigned to the Jews a significant role in Christian theology and eschatology.

> I say then, have they so stumbled that they should fall? God forbid. But by their offence, salvation is come to the Gentiles, that they may be emulous of them. . . . This partial blindness has come upon Israel only until the Gentiles have been admitted in full strength; when that has happened so all Israel shall be saved, as it is written: "There shall come out of Zion, he that shall deliver and shall turn away ungodliness from Jacob."[59]

At the conclusion of the chapter Paul affirmed that the Jews remain beloved of God and that His promises to them are irrevocable. But this theological perspective was long neglected by the Church, and only retrieved from oblivion by ecumenical theologians of today. The more prevalent and more deeply ingrained Pauline view of the Jews was his message to the Thessalonians.

> . . . for you also have suffered the same things from your own countrymen, even as they have from the Jews, who both killed the Lord Jesus, and the prophets, and have persecuted us, and please not God, and are adversaries to all men . . . for the wrath of God is come upon them to the end.[60]

The concluding phrase on the comprehensiveness and permanence of the retribution was further elaborated in the patristic literature.

The Church Fathers of the third and fourth centuries sprinkled their writings and sermons with vituperation regarding the Jews.[61] It is not our task here to examine the causes which gave rise to these attitudes in the early centuries of Christianity, though at the time they may have been rationalized as necessary to counteract the attractive rival religion of Judaism. Our interest is only in indicating the portrait painted.

In the first few centuries, when Christians themselves were being persecuted, or at best merely tolerated, their insecure position served as a psychological deterrent to unlimited denunciation of the Jews. When Christianity acquired influence and authority throughout the

Roman Empire, persuasive argument ceased. In the fourth century, sermons became increasingly shrill and ominous. The image of the Jew encountered in these sermons was hardly that of a human being at all. He was typified as a "monster . . . of superhuman cunning and malice, and more than superhuman blindness."[62] The association of the Jews and their form of worship with the devil was especially virulent in the sermons of John Chrysostom. "The synagogue is worse than a brothel . . . it is the den of scoundrels and the repair of wild beasts . . . the temple of demons devoted to the idolatrous cults . . . the refuge of brigands and debauchees, and the cavern of devils." According to Malcolm Hay, who researched 1900 years of the defamation of the Jews, the violence of the language used by Chrysostom "has never been exceeded by any preacher whose sermons have been recorded."[63]

The patristic literature is notable for what James Parkes calls its attempt at "falsification of Jewish history." Both theologically and historically Israel's past was given some ingenious twists. To provide Christianity with greater antiquity and legitimacy, all virtuous and righteous personalities from Abraham through the prophets were transformed into early Christian figures, while the villains of the Bible were presented as authentic Jews. The result of such typological interpretation was that even the reading of the so-called Old Testament would hardly enhance the image of the Jew or generate any appreciation for the monumental Jewish contribution to religion and ethics. The men of God were the precursors of Christ and the Jews were the obstinate unbelievers chastised by the prophets.

Typological interpretation presented an unreal picture of the biblical Jew, which was reinforced in medieval literature and art.[64] Most important, however, it blackened the image of the contemporary Jew. Whereas pre-Christian Jewry may have had its prophets and saints, post-Christian Jewry was an unredeemed race of the wicked and the devilish. As Parkes observed, "No people has ever paid so high a price for the greatness of its own religious leaders, and for the outspoken courage with which they held up an ideal and denounced whatever seemed to them to come short of it."[65]

Important in the understanding of attitudes is the emphasis given in the patristic literature to the charge that the Jews had a hand in the persecution of the early Christians, and that they continued to nurture a tenacious and malicious hatred of Christians. Again as Parkes points out, it is little consolation that the evidence, even from non-Jewish sources, indicates that the Jews took no active part in the great persecutions of the second and third centuries. It is not the historicity of the accusations which counts in popular thought, but the fact that Christian clergy and theologians could derive this erroneous picture from a reading of patristic literature.[66]

The most pernicious of all accusations, however, was the charge of a Jewish collective guilt in the crucifixion of Jesus. Summing up a history of anti-Semitism, Jules Isaac noted, "No idea has been more destructive and has had more deadly effect on the scattered Jewish minorities living in Christian countries than the pernicious view of them as the 'deicide people.'"[67] The concept of the "deicide people" developed in the spiritual climate of the early Church. Through Church preaching and teaching, through liturgy and the arts, the image of the Jews as a reprobate and accursed people became indelibly impressed. Worse than that, this image justified endless persecutions through the centuries.[68]

The guilt of deicide, coupled with the continuous rejection of Christ, led to a Christian interpretation of Jewish history which had direct bearing on Catholic responses to a Jewish state in Palestine. A theory evolved that the exile of Israel by the Romans in 70 C.E. was a divine punishment for the crucifixion and rejection of Jesus as the Christ. This belief was widely accepted, notwithstanding the fact that the dating of the dispersion in 70 C.E. was historically inaccurate. Long before the birth of Jesus, the great majority of world Jewry lived outside Judea. The diaspora was an accomplished fact by 586 B.C.E. as a result of the successive deportations following Nebuchadnezzar's conquest of Judea. From the fourth to the second century B.C.E. the diaspora expanded throughout the Hellenistic kingdoms. A particularly large and thriving community was situated in Alexandria. Toward the end of the first century B.C.E., when the Middle East was under the hegemony of the Romans, Jewish communities were scattered throughout most of the known world.[69]

No comparable mass exodus took place in 70 C.E. The number of captives was comparatively small, and the Jewish community in Palestine, despite heavy losses incurred during the war and in subsequent rebellions, maintained itself. Attempts of the Jews to recoup political independence attested to their self-cognizance as a nation, and the extensive and variegated literature emanating from the spiritual centers in Palestine attested to the vibrant quality of their religio-cultural life. Despite the fact that the Jews were impoverished and oppressed by the Roman and Byzantine emperors, Jewish communal life, with quasi-political autonomy, continued to exist for many centuries in Palestine.[70] Yet, under the influence of popular Christian theology, general Western literature and histories operated under the erroneous assumption that the end of Jewish history and the dispersion of the Jews dates from 70 C.E.[71]

Embedded in Christian literature is the idea that the ingathering of the Jews is unthinkable as long as they persist in the rejection of Christ. This belief may have been a key stumbling block for Catholics in coming to grips with the political realities of Zionism. Indicative of such convictions is an article which appeared in *Civiltà Cattolica* in 1897, the year of the first Zionist Congress.

> 1827 years have passed since the prediction of Jesus of Nazareth was fulfilled, namely, that Jerusalem would be destroyed. . . . That the Jews would be led away to be slaves among all the nations, and that they would remain in the dispersion until the end of the world. . . . according to the sacred Scriptures the Jewish people must always live dispersed and *vagabondo* [wandering] among the other nations, so that they may render witness to Christ not only by the Scriptures . . . but by their very existence. . . . As for a rebuilt Jerusalem which might become the center of a reconstituted state of Israel, we must add that this is contrary to the predictions of Christ Himself who foretold that "Jerusalem would be trodden down by the Gentiles until the time of the Gentiles is fulfilled" (Luke 21:24), that is . . . until the end of the world.[72]

This article was a plain warning that Zionism was on a collision course with the Catholic Church.

II
Homeland Versus Holy Land: Early Responses to Zionism

On November 2, 1917 the Balfour Declaration was promulgated, committing the British government to support and facilitate the establishment of a Jewish homeland in Palestine.¹ The publication of this document was greeted with rejoicing and celebration by Jews in Europe and the United States. In fact, even non-Jewish newspapers shared in the enthusiasm and voiced their approval.² A notable exception to the favorable response accorded to the Balfour Declaration by the general and religious press in America was the chilly silence maintained by the nation's Catholic press.

The Balfour Declaration did not come as a complete surprise. Extensive diplomatic activity, involving negotiations with various countries, preceded it. Even the Vatican was consulted. Nahum Sokolow, who had been selected by the Zionist Organization to obtain the approval of the French and Italian governments, was received in a private audience by Pope Benedict XV on May 10, 1917. Sokolow received words of encouragement from the Pope, who extended his moral support and concluded the audience with the assurance: "Yes, yes, I believe that we shall be good neighbors."³

As early as the spring of 1917 the American public had been alerted to the possibility of the Zionists' receiving British support. When Lord

Balfour visited President Wilson in April 1917, the press reported that their conference included a discussion concerning the establishment of a Jewish state in Palestine. Anticipating the declaration, many American papers offered their support.[4] "The Jews gave to the Christian Church its head. If now the arms of the Christian nations should give back to the Jews their state . . . a new fellowship would adorn a coming world of goodwill."[5]

In the Catholic press, however, Zionism elicited almost no comment, although the Arab Christians in the United States tried to make themselves heard. In September 1917, the *Bookman,* a monthly literary review with wide-ranging interests, published an article on the future of Palestine, entitled "The Holy Land: Whose to Have and to Hold?" The author, Ameen Rihani, a Lebanese Christian and an articulate spokesman for Arab nationalists,[6] commented on the various plans that were then being circulated in the international diplomatic community. He criticized British plans for a mandate over a Jewish homeland in Palestine as a smokescreen for selfish British imperialistic interests. Arab plans for control, under the religious rule of the sherif of Mecca, came under criticism for being undemocratic and politically reactionary. While conceding the Vatican's legitimate interest in the future of the Holy Land, Rihani rejected the idea of Vatican control, even indirectly by means of a protectorate by a Catholic country, on the grounds that it would be unrepresentative of the Palestinian populace, and as such, unjust. Zionist aspirations were rejected for being politically dangerous as well as economically impracticable. Rihani's criticism of Zionism was based on the following considerations:

    1. If a Jewish state were to be created in Palestine, the Jews, unable to defend themselves successfully, would be massacred by infuriated Arabs in an inevitable war.

    2. A land from which 600,000 Arabs barely managed to eke out an existence was obviously too barren to support a massive influx of Jews. The new settlements were located in the fertile areas; most of the remaining land was unproductive.

    3. A Jewish state would threaten the security of those Jews living elsewhere by raising charges of dual loyalty. This would inevitably trigger a new wave of anti-Semitism.[7]

Rihani's own ideas proposed a Greater Syria plan, which resembled a scheme later popularized by George Antonious in *The Arab Awakening*.[8] It is difficult to determine the impact of Rihani's article on Catholic thinking at the time, since no subsequent editorial in any Catholic periodical betrays direct evidence of his influence. However, a decade later, the political and economic impracticality of Zionism became a favorite argument in the Catholic press, though it is possible that this was due to other factors.

As noted before, the Balfour Declaration was virtually ignored by American Catholic periodicals. When questioned on the reasons for this silence, Catholics now explain that their papers at the time were so preoccupied with internal Catholic problems and concerns that they could hardly have been expected to focus upon an event of primarily Jewish interest.[9] This explanation is surely justifiable, yet theoretically speaking, a question still remains. Would not such news about the future of the Holy Land have been of prime interest to Catholics, especially when it foreshadowed a Jewish return to that land?

Taking theological implications into consideration, the silence of the Catholic press may be attributed to another cause. In November 1917, there was apparently no clear directive from the hierarchy either to approve or to disapprove the declaration. To most Catholic editors, the safest course probably seemed to be to ignore it. It was not until a full year later, on November 10, 1918, that the leading member of the American hierarchy finally issued an authoritative statement. Responding to a request from the Zionist Organization of America for a statement in honor of the first anniversary of the Balfour Declaration, Cardinal Gibbons replied: "It is with pleasure *that I learn* [emphasis added] of the approval accorded by his Holiness, Benedict XV, to the plan providing a homeland in Palestine to the members of the Jewish race."[10]

The promulgation of the Balfour Declaration was followed by an event in Palestine which, in contrast, aroused immediate and ecstatic enthusiasm in the Catholic press. Only a few days after General Allenby made his victorious entry into Jerusalem on December 10, 1917, diocesan editors were already interpreting the conquest's importance to their Catholic readers. Ignoring the military import of the victory they focused almost exclusively on the religious significance of the event, which they interpreted as a triumph for Christianity. Their readers were treated to visions of restored Christian rule in the Holy Land, and the Allied troops, as the so-called Christian armies, were compared to the Crusaders, who had been able to "wrest this truly Christian inheritance from the dominion of the Moslem." Moreover, the Allied victory was seen as even more conclusive than the Crusades. The editors assured their readers that this time the Holy Land would remain under a lasting Christian rule.[11]

The Catholic periodicals, such as *America, Catholic World,* and *Ave Maria,* joined the diocesan weeklies in celebrating the "Christian victory." For example, one article in *America,* captioned "Crusaders in Khaki," maintained that the reconquest of Jerusalem served to restore self-respect to Christians, who had felt humbled and disgraced as long as the Holy Land was under Moslem rule. Now that Jerusalem rested safely in Christian hands, the writer insisted, no other guardianship would ever be tolerated.

> Over the Mosque of Omar, the crescent has been lowered before the Cross. A sigh of relief and a hymn of gratitude have gone up from the nations that still worship Christ. . . . They can sing their *Te Deum,* for Bethlehem and Gethsemane, Calvary and the Holy Sepulcher are once more in Christian hands. Never again should the Turk be allowed to keep guard over the holiest spot in all the world. No statecraft, no game of shifting world politics should ever be tolerated by which these hills . . . will ever pass out of the power of the last of the Crusaders, who have just entered the portals of the Sacred City.[12]

Father Godfrey Hunt expressed regret, in the *Ecclesiastical Review,* that the "redemption by a Christian army" of Palestine was not effected by a united Christian world, but added that this did not diminish the jubilation among the Catholic nations. The Easter issues of the popular missionary journal *Extension* featured regularly, for several consecutive years following the conquest, photographs of Catholic religious activities in Palestine. One picture of a Franciscan leading a procession of pilgrims was typically captioned: "Palestine Under Christian Rule."[13]

The contrast between the Catholic disregard of the Balfour Declaration and the subsequent warm response to the Allied victories in Palestine is significant. The two attitudes complement each other and contribute to our understanding of the Catholic position on the Holy Land's status. Christian claims and bonds to the Holy Land were vigorously reasserted. Within the perspective of the "rescue" of the Holy Land from the clutches of the "awful Turk," the Jewish aspirations in Palestine appeared marginal. As will be shown later in detail, from the point of view of contemporary demographic statistics and preconceived notions concerning the Jews' inability to mount an intensive colonization effort, the Balfour Declaration did not seem to pose an immediate problem with which the Church had to cope. Even when Zionist programs were deemed viable, the Catholic press persisted in its assumption that the Jews would remain subservient, and amenable to Christian interests in the area. Finally, the Balfour Declaration, viewed in conjunction with a "Christian victory" in Jerusalem, could become part of a larger, divinely ordered, millennial scheme. Not all Catholic papers focused on every one of these perspectives; examples of each, however, are scattered in the periodical literature.

The assertion of Christian ties to the Holy Land can be found in the published responses to the capture of Palestine. Indirect effects of this renewed emphasis are also discernible. For instance, the Brooklyn *Tablet* used its November 10, 1917 issue to highlight the discovery of the ancient church of Gaza. The same week, the Los Angeles *Tidings* featured a selection of prophecies from St. Malachy,[14] some of which referred to Palestine. Though the author did enter a pro forma demurral that this may not be the correct interpretation, St. Malachy was said to have forecast that the seat of the Papacy would move to Jerusalem at the end of days. In that apocalyptic era, the Mohammedan world would submit to the Holy See and a Pope of Turkish descent would reign. Though the *Tidings* probably did not intend this popular folklore to be taken seriously, the very publication of these prophecies at such an auspicious moment may have played a role in shaping the attitudes of its less sophisticated readers.[15]

Another side of the same coin was the portrayal of Palestine as still suffering from the wrath of God's vengeance upon the Jews. A midwestern periodical, *Ave Maria,* published a pilgrim's description of contemporary Palestine which supplied a graphic, first-hand attestation to the immutability of the scriptural prophecies of doom. Yet another midwestern publication, *Our Sunday Visitor,* ruefully noted that the desolation of Jerusalem was the most complete "vengeance for the murder of the Son of God."[16]

The conviction that Zionism did not loom as a real threat to Christian interests was bolstered by the belief that Zionism had only remote chances for success. As early as 1900, *Catholic World* confidently editorialized that Zionism would never be able to command a substantial following among the Jews in the Western democracies, such as America, England, and France. A full year after the Balfour Declaration, Zionism was still regarded by the periodical as merely an "interesting" scheme, but with no hope of eventual success. Similar questions of practicability and viability were raised by the *Tidings,* which considered Zionism a lesser evil than Arab nationalism. Outside the United States, this lack of immediate concern was expressed by a London (Jesuit) periodical, the *Month,* which shunted off the possibility of the Balfour project's successful realization to a very distant future. "Until its ancient fertility is restored, it is not likely that Palestine will be able to support a larger population than its present million."[17]

Various editorials in the diocesan papers of 1917–18 indicated a prevalent conviction in some Catholic circles that despite anticipated concessions to the Jews, ultimately it would be Western Christendom which would be ensconced as the ruling authority in the Holy Land. As such, it would be the Christians who would dispense favors and grant toleration to the various peoples of Palestine. Only after the editor of the Chicago *New World* had assured his readers that "whatever fate awaits the Holy Land, of this we have a surety, never again will it depart from Christian control," did he permit himself to continue, without any direct reference to the Balfour Declaration,

> The Jew will most certainly be welcome in the country of his forefathers. He will have a country of his own. He will be a citizen of it. But neither Jew nor gentile shall ever be able more to make the place hallowed by the life and death of Christ a place of persecution for his followers.[18]

The Los Angeles *Tidings*, too, voiced the "general international determination that Jerusalem in the future must be under the rule of a Christian Power," and added that even the Jews throughout the world preferred a Christian, rather than a Moslem, mandate in Palestine. The Los Angeles paper was openly distrustful of Arab nationalism, fearing that it could not be curbed by Christians, whereas it deemed Jewish nationalism, in contrast, far more tractable and relatively innocuous.[19]

An entirely different perspective on the Zionist future in Palestine was put forward by Henry O'Keefe, C.S.P., in an article entitled "Zionism and the New Jerusalem." O'Keefe placed the Balfour Declaration into the larger eschatological scheme.[20] He approved the international recognition Zionism had received because the fruition of the Zionist dream was bound to lead to the glorious culmination of history in the "new Jerusalem." O'Keefe was almost lyrical in his enthusiasm:

> . . . now by a sudden twist in history, Jerusalem is free. Is this freedom to unravel the racial and religious entanglements of Jew and Gentile? Is Zionism, exclusive of its sociological purpose, to react to the significance of the Mosaic Covenant and the Messianic Idea? . . . Is Zionism an adumbration of some historic religious boon to be vouchsafed to modern Judaism?

The Holy Land would become the meeting ground for all religions.

> This world-wide constituency will perforce break the racial and religious conflict. The fundamental religions will be drawn to one center; comparisons will be drawn within the area of Golgotha, where was lifted up He who would draw all nations unto Himself. . . . In that hour the Jew will take up the golden thread of his portentous history.[21]

One article which is crucial in any survey of early Catholic responses to Zionism appeared in 1918 in the *American Catholic Quarterly Review*. Intriguingly titled "Christ's Attitude toward the Politico-Religious Expectations of the Jews," it espouses a unique view on an entirely different dimension. The bulk of the article does not even deal with the Jews, but is directed against the Protestant churches. Although there is no reference to Zionism or contemporary events, both the title and the opening pages themselves are significant in their point of emphasis. Asserting that the Jews' nationalistic aspirations are intimately intertwined with their religious beliefs, the author depicts the Jewish messiah, whose arrival was expected in the time of Jesus, as a political figure who would brutally crush all opposing kingdoms. "Revengeful as the Jewish character was, the complete destruction of their enemies was one of the great moments in the national expectations, and in the satisfaction of their vindictiveness many Jews saw parts of the glory of their future happiness." To prove that the Jews maintained such expectations to this day, the author cited four blessings of the Amidah, recited daily by Jews throughout the world.[22] The discerning reader could hardly fail to grasp the warning implicit in this interpretation.

If the bulk of the American Catholic press dismissed the prospect of a Jewish state in the Holy Land in a cavalier manner, this attitude was not evident in Europe and the Middle East. On the contrary, it was treated with the utmost seriousness.

Almost immediately after the conquest of Jerusalem, Benedict XV began to have qualms about the eventual consequences of the Balfour Declaration. In December 1917, the Pope conveyed his concern to Count DeSalis, the British representative to the Vatican, that the Jews might gain direct control over Palestine, to the detriment of Christian interests.[23] Sir Mark Sykes, an English Catholic who was chiefly responsible for gaining Vatican receptiveness to the idea of a Jewish homeland in 1917, was disturbed by the marked change in attitude which he encountered when he revisited Rome in 1918. His subsequent talks with the Franciscan custos and the Latin patriarch, upon his arrival in Palestine, proved equally discouraging.[24]

Confirming and even heightening the Pope's fear of Zionist activity were the negative impressions communicated to the Vatican by men of stature, such as Cardinal Bourne, the archbishop of Westminster. After a tour of the Middle East from December 1918 to March 1919, Bourne recalled that on the eve of his departure for Palestine, the Pope was "full of anxieties" over the disposition of the Holy Land. Upon his return, Bourne reported to the Pope that the Zionists indeed were bent upon gaining political control. Adding fuel to the fire were reports from the Latin patriarch, Msgr. Louis Barlassina, alleging that atheism, communism, and immorality were rampant among the recent Jewish immigrants.[25] In a consistorial allocution of March 10, 1919, the Pope expressed dismay over the situation in Palestine, and stated, "It would be a great grief to the Holy See if in Palestine the preponderating position were given to infidels. . . ."[26]

Verbal remonstrances against Zionism were translated into action by Catholics and other Christians living in Palestine. Moslem-Christian associations were formed for the express purpose of bringing about a renunciation of Balfour's pledges. In December 1920, these associations convened the Third Arab Congress in Haifa, where a resolution was passed demanding the mandate's revocation and the immediate establishment of a national (i.e., Arab) government in Palestine.[27]

Prior to 1921, the American Catholic press confined its reports on Palestine to the work of the Catholic missions and institutions in the area, with virtually no notice being taken of the agitation of the Moslem-Christian associations or the shift in Vatican sentiment. To be sure, considerable publicity was accorded the visits of the Melchite and Maronite archbishops in 1920 and 1921, but it focused primarily on their fund-raising objectives for the continuing relief work on behalf of the Syrian Christians.[28]

The American hierarchy issued no public statements on the political disposition of Palestine, and Cardinal Gibbons, in a personal note to President Wilson, pleaded only for measures safeguarding the holy places.[29] If Catholics had misgivings about a Protestant mandatory, few papers voiced this concern. One of the few periodicals to argue, at the close of the war, for a Catholic mandatory was the *American Catholic Quarterly Review*. It editorialized that by right of precedence and moral preponderance, and as "her reward for a thousand years of the apostolate," France should be awarded the dominant role in Palestine. While the *Tidings* also urged that France be retained in its traditional role as Protector, its position was motivated more by fear of British submission to Arab demands than by worries over British assistance to Zionism. Only two days before Palestine was awarded to Britain as a Class "A" mandate, the *Tidings* reiterated its warning against accommodation with the Arabs in settling the future of Palestine. It remarked pointedly that a British mandate which recognized Palestine as the "homeland" of the Jews was a preferable alternative to any Arab domination.[30]

By the spring of 1921, rumblings of discontent in Palestine began to emerge in the news summaries of the American Catholic press. Citing a *New York Times* report on the turbulence in Palestine, the *Catholic Historical Review* commented that the land was "full of dissatisfied people except [for] the Zionists." *Ave Maria* drew the attention of its readers to the deterioration of Catholic religious activity in the Holy Land by quoting at length from a letter of the archbishop of Galilee to *Les Missions Catholiques*. In that letter, Mgr. Haggear complained that since the war the land had become the site of religious and national rivalries, and that the schools had been turned into the "mightiest organs of propaganda," in which Jews and Protestants, supported by large funds, were working diligently. "Catholic missionary progress in the Holy Land has been hampered during the year by unusual difficulties, and now the situation is even worse. . . ."[31]

It was not, however, until the Papal allocution of June 14, 1921 that the U.S. Catholic press finally adopted an unequivocal anti-Zionist stance. In that allocution, ostensibly precipitated by the May riots of 1921, the Pope declared:

> The situation in Palestine not only is not improved, but has been made worse by the new civil arrangements which aim, if not in their authors' intentions, at least in fact, at ousting Christianity from its previous position to put the Jews in its place. We, therefore, warmly exhort all Christians, including non-Catholic Governments, to insist with the League of Nations on the examination of the British mandate in Palestine.[32]

The allocution's authoritative request galvanized the American Catholic press into action. Across the United States, a number of Catholic papers responded. In July 1921, the National Catholic News Service (hereafter NC-NS) released a report on the dismal situation in Palestine. Warnings that the "Christians are Menaced by Jews" and that the "Zionist Movement Threatens to Gain Complete Control of Institutions in Palestine" headlined the Brooklyn *Tablet*'s front page, which carried the report. Not only were readers informed that Zionists were swamping all other groups in the country, but emigration statistics were cited to prove that many Christians were leaving Palestine because they were "tired of Jewish interference." The report concluded with the hope that the counter-Zionist movement of the "Palestine Congress" would be effective in rallying a "united body of Christian opinion" against the Zionist encroachments.[33] Besides the NC-NS report so prominently featured in the diocesan press, national periodicals, such as *Catholic World* and *Catholic Historical Review*, also carried articles whose tenor echoed the spirit of the Papal allocution.[34]

The flurry of Catholic press opposition to Zionism lasted only a few short weeks. However, a year later, during the summer of 1922, the campaign gained further momentum. By then the problem was compounded both by the U.S. congressional resolutions favoring the establishment of a national homeland for the Jews in Palestine and by the release of official Vatican memoranda sharply criticizing the objectives of a Jewish national homeland. As late as June 1922, the League of Nations still had not ratified the draft of the mandate, and this delay was attributed to the objections that had been raised in many quarters, including the Vatican.[35] The objections were debated not only in the council, but also in the legislative chambers of England and America. On both sides of the Atlantic, the question of the mandate, with particular reference to its pledges to the Jews, was widely aired and discussed.

American public opinion was favorably disposed to the Zionist idea. In a New Year's greeting to the Jews on August 31, 1918, President Wilson publicly acknowledged his approval of a Jewish homeland in Palestine. In 1919, under the sponsorship of the Zionist Organization of America, a volume containing expressions of congressional support appeared. It contained statements of several hundred U.S. senators and representatives endorsing the intent of the Balfour Declaration.[36]

Shortly afterwards, a massive effort was mounted by the Zionist Organization of America to obtain a formal congressional resolution in support of the establishment of a Jewish national home in Palestine. To secure its passage, the Zionists launched a lobby whose organizational efficiency and aggressive articulation were unmatched by any counter-group, and which succeeded in persuading the legislators that the majority of Jews shared their convictions.[37] The high points of that campaign were the passage of the Senate resolution on May 3, 1922 and the House resolution on June 30. Its culmination came when President Harding formally signed the joint resolution in September. Though the resolution's final text was couched in carefully guarded terms and hedged with reservations, it still reflected a positive attitude toward Zionist endeavors.

> Resolved by the Senate and House of Representatives of the United States of America in Congress assembled, That the United States of America favors the establishment in Palestine of a national home for the Jewish people, it being clearly understood that nothing shall be done which may prejudice the civil and religious rights of Christians and all other non-Jewish communities in Palestine, and that the holy places and religious buildings and sites in Palestine shall be adequately protected.[38]

In Europe the debate that raged on this question was far more acrimonious. Pro-Zionist sentiment clashed with many opposing interests and pressure groups. The British, who were to bear the burdens of the mandate, were naturally more sensitive to the objections raised by the delegations of the Moslem-Christian associations and the other spokesmen for the sundry Arab, French, and Vatican interests in Palestine. Of particular interest to Catholics was the pleading of the Arab Christian case by Msgr. Barlassina, the Latin Patriarch of Jerusalem, who made a special journey to London to influence British opinion.[39] This heavy pressure for the renunciation, or at least the modification, of the Balfour Declaration brought the entire question of the mandate under review in both houses of Parliament. The adversaries of Zionism were triumphant when, on June 21, 1922, the House of Lords passed a resolution declaring the present terms of the mandate contrary to the wishes of Palestine's inhabitants. Shortly thereafter, Winston Churchill, the colonial secretary, issued a White Paper which drastically reinterpreted the mandate and sharply restricted the political future of the Zionists in Palestine.[40]

The American congressional resolution, the British retreat, and Vatican notes to the League of Nations[41] were recorded in the Catholic papers during the summer of 1922, but in a pattern surprisingly different from what might have been expected. The national periodicals, which usually reported international news, hardly touched upon the Palestine question. Instead, it was the more parochial diocesan weeklies which provided the fairly sustained coverage.

Diocesan editors selected their material from the news bulletins distributed by the NC-NS, which regularly received cables from its overseas correspondents. London dispatches, especially those of Montgomery Watts, tended to take a jaundiced view of Zionist activities. In Watts's opinion, the Zionists were a body of schemers "who are determined to carry out their plans at all costs."[42] Dispatches from Rome eschewed all forms of polemic. They concentrated on two major items of concern: fear of Jewish political ascendancy in the Holy Land, and fear of losing a position of privilege with respect to the holy places. The single dispatch from Washington was a report on the passage of the pro-Zionist congressional resolution. It was accompanied by editorializing: "If the dreams of the apostles of the Zionist movement are realized, the last [Jews] will come back to its [sic] dwelling place, the national home of the Jews." It even mentioned the "eventual establishment of a Jewish regime." On the whole, the dispatch was impeccably courteous, with only the barest suggestion of mild reproof. No inkling was given of Vatican displeasure with the proposed "Jewish regime."[43]

With the exception of a rare editorial on Palestine, the attitude of the various Catholic papers can best be described as carefully selective in the treatment of news dispatches. Thus, the Boston *Pilot* printed only Vatican releases, yet discriminated in its choices. For instance, it omitted the report on Cardinal Gasparri's memorandum of May 15, 1922 to the League of Nations, in which he detailed Rome's objections to Jewish "preponderance." On the other hand, a later memorandum dealing with the holy places was fully reported. Rounding out the Vatican releases were occasional items featuring Catholic organizational and institutional work in Palestine. Zionism, as an issue, was largely ignored.[44]

On the other hand, the Brooklyn *Tablet* relied primarily on the London dispatches. Jubilant that the House of Lords had finally taken action that "checks Zionist ambitions," it pointed out that this parliamentary resolution had closely followed upon the Vatican's protest to the League. It also noted that the "continental" Catholic journals were generally gratified with Britain's latest move. Scornfully, the Zionists were depicted as "infuriated" and as interested in seeking a "curtailment" of the Vatican's political power. Another London dispatch took sharp issue with the attacks directed by the *Jewish Chronicle* (London) against Vatican intervention. This report launched into a full-scale diatribe against the political power of the Zionists, whose recriminations against the Vatican were said to betray their continuing hatred of the Catholic Church. Although the *Tablet* did print the Washington release on the congressional resolution, the editor followed it up a fortnight later with a London release which contended that the Jewish settlement in Palestine was disruptive, unspiritual, and crassly materialistic.[45]

The attitudes of the other diocesan weeklies fell somewhere between the above viewpoints. No paper responded to Zionism with outright sympathy, and none endorsed editorially the congressional resolution. Nevertheless, with a few scattered exceptions, the press was not vituperative in its opposition. A number of editors were careful to distinguish between the Zionists, whom they opposed, and the American Jews, with whom they enjoyed tolerably good relations. For example, the editor of *New World,* undoubtedly aware that his critique of Zionism could be construed as an expression of anti-Semitism, made sure to preface his indictment with a paragraph deploring racial prejudices against the Jews. When the same editor sought to justify the Vatican objections to Zionism in June 1922, he not only claimed that the Pope was motivated by purely humanitarian concerns (aid to Moslem Arabs and Christians who were now being "dispossessed"), but he also maintained that American Jews, as well, were at variance with the Zionist movement.[46]

The differences in response between the national periodicals and the diocesan press may be attributed to the difference in their status in the community. The former,[47] because of their wider audience, were more aware of and attuned to the mood of the country at large. Therefore, they may have chosen to withhold comment during the summer of 1922. The latter, because of local diocesan control, usually reflected more faithfully the traditional Catholic point of view, modified by the prejudices prevalent within local hierarchial circles.

Though rarely explicit in the press, theological premises existed in assessing the Palestine question. According to the Church's interpretation of Genesis 49:10, the scepter of dominion had passed from Jewish hands ever since the coming of Christ. Medieval legislation prohibited Jews from assuming positions of authority over Christians.[48] When Benedict XV had originally given his assent to the establishment of a Jewish homeland, he had reason to believe that Jewish sovereignty was not contemplated. Prior to his audience with the Pope, Sokolow had emphatically denied, in his conversation with Cardinal Gasparri, any plans for a Jewish state. Hence, the Pope could countenance a return of the Jews to their "home," but, as was noted by the London *Tablet*, he could not approve the creation of a Jewish state.[49] A review of the Vatican pronouncements during these years reveals an apprehensive vigilance against Jewish sovereignty in the Holy Land. When the Churchill White Paper of June 30, 1922 removed the possibility of Jewish political domination, the Dubuque *Witness* could confidently expect that the Vatican objections to the mandate were withdrawn.[50]

In 1923, with the mandate firmly in English hands, the Palestine problem receded from the consciousness of the non-Jewish world. It was not until the riots of 1929 that the attention of the Catholic press was again riveted on Palestine.

III

Advance and Retreat: The Era Between the Wars

The era between the wars was a period during which the political promises of the Balfour Declaration were steadily whittled away through a succession of White Papers. Under article 6 of the mandate, the Palestine government was bound to facilitate Jewish immigration and to encourage close settlement by Jews on the land. Both instructions were subjected to increasing modification. In the Churchill Paper of 1922, regulated immigration supplanted unrestricted immigration, and a pledge of non-domination by the Jews was added. In the Passfield Paper of 1930, restrictive land-transfer measures as well as tighter immigration control were proposed. The progressive change in British policy culminated with the issuance of the MacDonald Paper of 1939, in which the establishment of a Jewish state was ruled out in unequivocal terms.[1] Counterbalancing the decline in the political fortunes of the National Homeland was the steady growth of its Jewish population, and the concurrent emergence of quasi-official political, economic, and educational institutions.[2]

While the minor fluctuations in Zionist development in Palestine occasioned little comment in the outside world, moments of crisis, such as the riots of 1929 and the White Paper in 1939, did stir the attention of the international press. In the United States, the Catholic press also reacted to these events, but its responses fluctuated and did not flow from any consistently formulated attitude toward Zionism. At times they reflected a specific kinship between Catholic and Jews in the United States because of manifestations of Protestant bigotry during the 1920s. At other times they were influenced by peripheral Catholic concerns. And on some occasions their tenor reflected Vatican views appearing in news stories from Rome. However, by 1939 these trends had been transmuted and a clearly discernible anti-Zionist bias emerged.

After World War I, Catholics in the United States embarked on a program of national and religious consolidation. Prior to the war, American Catholics were fragmented along ethnic lines. A typical example of the atomization of Catholic organizational activity was the Central Verein, which concentrated primarily on the needs of German Catholics. Even the broader-based Knights of Columbus was restricted as an official, authoritative Catholic agency because of its lay fraternal structure. An earlier attempt made at the turn of the century to organize a Federation of Catholic Societies quickly floundered.[3] To meet the exigencies of the war in 1917, the clergy and the laity united in a combined effort to form the National Catholic War Council. Spurred by its success, the idea of a peacetime council was broached and specifically urged by Archbishop Cerretti, secretary of the Vatican Congregation of Extraordinary Affairs. The National Catholic Welfare Council,[4] or NCWC as it became popularly known, was established in 1919 and included departments ranging over a wide spectrum of interests, such as legislation, education, social, and economic problems, lay organizations, and the press.[5] During this period, the religious life of American Catholics took on a greater degree of uniformity as a result of the implementation of the new Code of Canon Law, which went into effect in 1919. The new code's pressure upon Catholic parents to send their children to Catholic schools gave added impetus to the expansion of the parochial-school system. Closer ties with the Church also were effected by the growing postwar practice of frequent and daily Communion, especially among the urban Catholics. Religious pride reached a climactic point when the International Eucharistic Congress was held in Chicago in 1926.[6]

As gratifying as the progress of the Catholic Church in the United

States appeared to native Catholics, their satisfaction was marred and their sense of security jolted by the strong resurgence of anti-Catholicism in the twenties. The sharp rise in nativist sentiment and the growth of the Ku Klux Klan in the postwar period touched off a disquieting number of attacks on Catholics.[7]

The Catholic press waged a campaign to expose and refute the canards of the various hate-groups. Since the nativists frequently linked Jews and Catholics together as undesirable aliens, and since the counterattack of the Catholic editors emphasized that bigotry was un-American, the editors often found themselves staunchly defending Jews as well as Catholics. Moreover, the insecurity Catholics felt in the face of these attacks brought about cooperative efforts with the Jews in common defense against the calumniations.[8]

While Jewish assistance in the fight against bigotry was acknowledged and appreciated, there may have been an undercurrent of jealousy regarding the success which crowned purely Jewish efforts. For example, when the *Dearborn Independent* was barred from circulation in St. Louis in 1921 because of its publication of anti-Semitic material, *Ave Maria* commented that "while the few Jews in the country can have periodicals banned and publications refused admittance to public libraries when articles reflect upon the race," the far larger community of Catholics are unable to prevent their being maligned in U.S. publications. The *Tablet* queried why the *Menace,* an anti-Catholic paper, was not likewise barred in St. Louis. The editor contended that "even if it should be held that the criticisms against the Jews which are appearing in Mr. Ford's paper are defamatory, they are not indecently vituperative and abusive," as in the *Menace.* Peevishly, the editor posed the question why St. Louis should offer more protection for Jews than for the Catholics, who had founded the city and had largely built it up.[9]

Notwithstanding occasional malicious remarks, such as those in the *Tablet,* the thrust of most editorials was: If Jews can do it, why can't Catholics? Anti-Semitic nuances generally were eschewed, and the question was raised primarily to goad Catholics into emulating Jewish efforts. With the same reasoning, Catholic papers culled examples of Jewish philanthropy,[10] Jewish pursuit of higher education,[11] and Jewish unity in times of crisis.[12] The emphasis in most of the papers was Catholic emulation, rather than resentment. Smarting under prejudices directed against them in the twenties, Catholics generally shied away from employing the same tactics against another minority. When blatant anti-Jewish remarks were printed in two midwestern Catholic papers, the Chicago diocesan weekly, *New World,* squirmed uncomfortably and called it a solitary attempt among Catholic periodicals to stir up anti-Semitism.[13]

From the time the mandate was ratified in 1923 until the riots of 1929, there was little reason for the press to comment on the Palestine situation. The quiet even encouraged a sense of optimism concerning the future of the Holy Land. *America* reprinted Cardinal Bourne's impressions on the occasion of his second visit to the Holy Land in 1924. Bourne found that there was no longer "the same unwise insistence on an untenable domination on the part of the Zionists," and concluded that the "Mandate, reasonably interpreted, reasonably applied, reasonably accepted, may contain within it, by patient application, the long-sought solution of the government of the Holy Land, so as to satisfy both the Palestinian population and the rightful claims of Christendom. . . ."[14]

With the same sense of equanimity, *Catholic World* reported a literary debate between a Palestinian Arab and an English Zionist. Reading the report, one could quibble that the Arab case was made explicit, while the refutations of the English Zionist were only implicit; nevertheless, *Catholic World* did concede: "It must be said that the show of statistics in this [Zionist] rebuttal is just as convincing as those in the first [Arab] paper." Any urgency to discredit the Zionists was apparently lacking at this time.[15]

The Church was actually experiencing a period of growth and prosperity in Palestine. The Jesuits opened a Jerusalem branch of the Biblical Pontifical Institute. Hospitals, schools, and hospices were being built in Haifa, Nazareth, and Jerusalem by the Discalced Carmelites, the Salesians, and other religious orders. The Franciscans, who still outstripped the other orders in their activity, were responsible for building a number of imposing churches, monasteries, and a boys' school in Jaffa.[16]

An editorial in the *Pilot* expressed particular satisfaction with the growth of the Roman Catholic Church in Jerusalem. This success was attributed to two factors: a decline in the influence of the Greek Orthodox Church, and the attraction of Catholicism for many of the new settlers who had renounced other religious affiliations.[17] Indeed, this latter point was suggested by other papers as well. *Catholic World,* quoting from an English Catholic monthly, called attention to the new possibilities of conversion among Jews in Palestine, since the "emancipated" Zionist Jews were deemed less intransigent than their Orthodox forebears.[18]

Pilgrimage was another topic of perennial interest. Advertisements for Catholic pilgrimages to both Rome and the Holy Land dotted the papers, though frequently the Holy Land tour was labeled "optional." Pilgrimage literature, too, saw a revival. Meistermann's classic *Guide to the Holy Land,* reprinted in a revised edition, even took note of the numerous "Jewish colonies" scattered throughout the country.[19] Cardinal Bourne's introduction to this revised edition urged:

> It is indeed much to be hoped that they [the pilgrims] will undertake this sacred journey in ever-increasing numbers, for it is only by the presence in the Holy Land of Catholics of every race and language that the rights of Christendom therein can be safely and adequately safeguarded.[20]

One of the most widely read authors in Catholic America was the English writer, G. K. Chesterton. A description of his own pilgrimage to the Holy Land was set down in *The New Jerusalem.* In the last chapter, he dealt with the "problem" of Zionism. Superciliously, he commended Zionism as a worthwhile experiment in regenerating and reeducating the Jews to make them "normal,"[21] but he shared the Arabs' fear of Jewish domination. To resolve the conflict between Arab and Jew, he proposed a system of cantonization, wherein each group would have quasi-independent and autonomous enclaves. Unlike later proposals for partition, the appeal of Chesterton's plan to the Christian reader was his insistence upon the ultimate suzerainty of Christians over the Jews.[22]

Peace in the Holy Land was shattered on August 23, 1929. Actually, the sudden eruption of violence can be traced back a year earlier to the end of the summer of 1928. A screen temporarily erected for prayer services at the Western Wall became the casus belli. The Wall, a venerated remnant of the Jewish Temple, is also part of the exterior of the Haram-es-Sherif, the sacred Moslem area containing the Mosque of Omar. To an overconscientious British official, the screen appeared to be an "infringement of the status quo ante." British police officers rushed to dismantle the screen, and did so at a most inauspicious time, in the midst of the solemn services of the Day of Atonement. Arab religious leaders, who had earlier voiced their indignation at the sight of the screen, mistook British zeal for pro-Arab sympathies and used it to their own advantage. To accentuate Moslem legal and religious rights to the Wall area, the Arabs built an extension above the northern part of the Wall. A muezzin was stationed on a nearby roof to call the faithful to prayer five times daily. In the summer of 1929, a passage was opened from the Haram to the pavement, so that the place before the Wall was converted into a thoroughfare. All these alterations, "infringements" of the "status quo ante," were vehemently protested by the Jews. Concurrently, Arab nationalists, led by the mufti, engaged in inflammatory propaganda accusing the Jews of planning an assault on the Mosque of Omar itself.

In this tinderbox of rising tension, a minor pretext was sufficient to set the area aflame. During Jewish observances of the Fast of Ab, a Zionist demonstration was held at the Wall. The next day, the Arabs, presumably instigated by the mufti,[23] began rioting, but were quelled by the police. A week later renewed rioting broke out with greater fury and spread to the countryside. The British, who had insufficient forces in the country, were unable to maintain order. Arab rioters swooped down on defenseless Jewish colonists, indiscriminately murdering men, women, and children.[24]

American Jews immediately reacted to the riots. The dominant mood was one of "marked solidarity for their fellow-Jews in Palestine."[25] Funds were quickly raised for projects of relief, and massive protest demonstrations were held in a number of cities. A Madison Square Garden rally in New York City drew over 25,000 persons. Even such prominent non-Zionist Jews as Felix Warburg, Julius Rosenwald, and Herbert Lehman expressed grave concern and offered their unstinting support.[26]

A number of Catholic papers also reacted to the tragic events. Again a difference can be discerned between the immediate reaction of the national periodical press and the general reaction of the local diocesan weeklies. Those periodicals which had hitherto encouraged the cooperation of Catholics with Jews against their common detractors during the trying decade of the twenties, and had thereby opened the door to more friendly relations between the two groups, responded with indignation. Expressions of outrage at the massacre of the Jews were accompanied by sentiments of sympathy, even when the Jews were not fully exonerated from their share in provoking the feud.[27] *Commonweal* carried a full report on the brutal massacre at Hebron, and a message of condolence sent by New York's Cardinal Hayes to Jewish organizations.[28] *America* editorialized: "We hope that our Jewish brethren will secure ample protection for their rights. We trust we do not intrude when we express our sincere sympathy with the family and friends of the slaughtered men."[29] *Commonweal* further urged that Jews be given the explicit right to worship at the "Wailing Wall," since the Jew's right was "anterior to the Moslem's in history; and speaking as Christians, we hold that his right is spiritually superior, as well."[30]

In Boston, the *Pilot* shared in this sympathetic response. The anglophobia of the Boston Irish was reflected in the scathing denunciation of the British as inefficient and grossly negligent in protecting the Jews. The paper had just as little liking for the Arabs, who were depicted as "menacing."[31] As for the Jews, the editor had this to say: "To the unfortunate victims of the uprising in Jerusalem go the condolences and sympathy of their friends throughout the world. The popular mind associates the Jewish people with Jerusalem because of the tradition of the past and the Old Testament Christian people applauded the Zionist movement."[32]

Most of the diocesan weeklies, however, reviewed the tragedy from a different perspective. The syndicated *Our Sunday Visitor* was typical in that it confined its attention to the Christian casualties and to the relief work of the Catholic religious orders, particularly the Franciscans, who offered shelter to all Christians during the tumultuous days of the rioting.[33] A few diocesan papers also touched on the background of the riots, using a news dispatch from Rome to set the tone. The dispatch, quoting from the *Osservatore Romano*, deplored the violence, but noted that the Vatican had forewarned the British of the rising tensions early in August and even recommended that "certain changes in policy" be made in order to avert a bloody conflict. Although the recommendations were only hinted at, the trouble was clearly defined as one of "economic injustice" stemming from the Jewish immigration. The informant for the Vatican was identified as Msgr. Barlissina, the Latin patriarch of Jerusalem. He was specifically quoted as saying that both Christians and Moslems concurred in their opposition to continued Jewish immigration.[34]

Editorials and articles following the Rome dispatch amplified the reasons for the hostility felt toward the Zionists. As one NCWC correspondent from Jerusalem pictured it, the Jews were militantly arrogant in demanding supremacy: "We want [a] . . . Jewish police force; Jewish defense force; Jewish administration."[35] Reinforcing the negative attitude toward Jewish immigration and political control was the widespread belief that communism and atheism were rampant in the new Jewish settlements.[36] Palestinian Christians were also bitter and disappointed with their minority position in a Christian mandatory government; so much so that one Catholic editor dared to suggest that the former Turkish rule was more just to Christians than the present British rule.[37] The Balfour Declaration, which had been largely ignored by the Catholic papers when it was first promulgated, was now pointed out as the villain of the Palestinian tragedy. The causes of the riot were justified as political grievances resulting from inequitable conditions created by the declaration, and not mere outbursts of religious intolerance. Charges of Arab intolerance were curtly dismissed by the editor of the *Tablet,* who reminded his readers that "there was once a religious warfare in the Holy Land. The papers said nothing about it. It was when Christ was crucified."[38]

Diocesan interest in Palestinian events was not sustained. After the initial reports and comments on the rioting, the papers turned to problems closer at hand, and no follow-up on the commissions of inquiry and the ensuing recommendations was made. Some national periodicals, however, continued to evince a lively interest in the aftermath. But their spontaneous outburst of sympathy, expressed in September 1929, slowly turned to reserve and to critical review.

From the first report on the "Wailing Wall" riot to the final report on Ramsey MacDonald's letter reinterpreting the Passfield White Paper, *America* published over twenty news items. All were generally impartial in their coverage, and yet, as time elapsed, a friendlier interest was evoked in the Islamic world and the paper sought more and more frequently to "explain" the Arab position. At the high point of the trials in the wake of the Shaw Commission,[39] a news report in *America* quoted at length from an editorial in an Arab daily which flatly blamed the riots on Zionist "usurpation" of the land.[40] When the Shaw Commission report was made public, *America* sympathetically noted Zionist displeasure, but in the same breath spoke of Zionist "aggrandizement" of economic control.[41] In the opinion of the paper, the Simpson report clearly showed that "Jewish settlers have every advantage—capital, science, and organization."[42]

Symptomatic of the new regard for the Arabs were occasional essays on Arab culture and religion. John LaFarge, an associate editor who authored a weekly column under the pseudonym of "The Pilgrim," devoted two of his columns to the virtues of the Arabs in the modern world. A converted Moslem teaching in the Pontifical Oriental Institute of Rome was quoted as saying that the "good features" of Islam could combat the "evils of our age. Islam occupies an intermediate position between doctrines of bourgeois capitalism and Bolshevist communism."[43] Nonetheless, there was never outright condemnation of Zionism, and a review of John Haynes Holmes's *Palestine, Today and Tomorrow* maintained that even though Holmes's idealistic picture of Zionism was not recognizable in the current situation, the "spiritual idealism" of Zionism could offer a basis for future peace.[44]

Commonweal also continued to review developments in Palestine through background articles which explored contemporary conditions in Palestine. The first of a series of such articles was prefaced by the editors as "admittedly . . . not a case either for or against Zionism." Unquestionably it was not a case for Zionism. The author, a journalist who had visited Palestine, flatly repudiated the validity of the Balfour Declaration. Zionism was described as a "creation of the Jews of Northern and Eastern Europe whom it chiefly benefits," and the Jewish immigrants were stigmatized as a "pampered minority" which was fed by a "stream of gold" pouring into the country. The only positive statement in the article was the refutation of the then prevalent argument of economic distress as the cause of the riots.[45] The article drew a variety of comments from the readers, but they generally confirmed the author's opinions.[46]

The second article was more subtle. It was written by a man who was assumed to have expert knowledge of the Middle East. Pierre Crabites, who served many years as a judge on the Mixed Commission in Cairo, approached the "Palestine Problems" with kid gloves. Without impugning the "purity of motives" which inspired the Balfour Declaration, he maintained that it was phrased in complete disregard and ignorance of the Arab temperament. British policy in implementing the pledge, also pursued in ignorance of the Arab mentality, was doomed to disaster and would bring ruin to every religious group and shrine in the Holy Land. "American Catholics are interested in the preservation of the holy places; so are American Protestants. So are American Jews. If these three elements will but realize the common danger a way can be found to delete the Balfour Declaration from the Mandate for Palestine."[47] Crabites assured his readers that if the declaration were "deleted," peace would be restored, and since the Arabs were "the most tolerant of men," they would see to it "that the spirit back of the Balfour Declaration is made a living reality."[48]

Another article was written by a journalist, Vincent Sheean, who had been in Palestine during the 1929 riots as a foreign correspondent for the North American Newspaper Alliance. Reporting on the recommendations of the Shaw Commission, he commended them as the first positive step in a fair policy for the Arabs. He noted with some satisfaction that the recommendations would also toll the death knell of Zionism. According to Sheean, Zionism was a "profound and disastrous mistake." In a telling sentence, Sheean remarked, "Even a race whose history is one long disappointment can hardly be expected to go forever putting its money on such a doped horse."[49]

Commonweal's editorial opinion was never as hostile as the articles which it published, though the editors began cautiously to suggest compromises and modifications. Several months after the riots, an editorial highly recommended a "bi-national" Palestine as the only feasible plan in the face of the opposition.[50] In a later editorial, the editors conceded that the Balfour Declaration would have to be somewhat modified, even though they still believed that Britain was responsible for the protection and establishment of a Jewish national home.[51] When the Passfield Paper was made public, the editors penned a condolence on the demise of Zionism:

> We have expressed before this our sense of the tragic *impasse* in Palestine. The peculiar need of the Jews for a geographical home, the peculiar historic and spiritual appropriateness of locating that home in Palestine, are beyond question. Beyond question, too, are the facts of the solemn invitation and guarantee extended to the Jewish race by the Balfour document, and that race's overwhelming response in dollars and men. On the other hand, the resentment of the Palestinian Arabs at what they feel to be an alien invasion, is as little to be conjured away; and when we consider the homogeneity of the whole Moslem body, and the 75,000,000 Indian Mohammedans who at any moment may take up actively the cause of their Arab co-religionists, we can understand Britain's present minimizing of their undertaking.[52]

With the restrictions of the Passfield Paper, the "Zionist experiment," as *Commonweal* was fond of calling Zionist activity, struck a stone wall. "And fairminded opinion seemed to agree, with regret, that the stone wall was more or less inevitable."[53] In the zigzagging pattern of British policy, *Commonweal*'s opinions were ambivalent—they always bogged down on the difficulty of arriving at a satisfactory solution.

Until a new crisis erupted in 1939, most papers were content to ignore events in distant Palestine. In the meantime, despite the economic havoc wrought by the depression in the early thirties, American Catholics were beginning to feel more confident and more "at home" in America. Manifestations of anti-Catholicism subsided after the apex was reached during the ugly presidential campaign of 1928.[54] With the decline of overt bigotry came a growing confidence among American Catholics in their strength as a religious and social force in the United States. The National Catholic Welfare Conference, which had a fitful start in the twenties, grew by leaps and bounds, and became fully established in U.S. Catholic life by the thirties.[55] There was less reticence and less apologetics in expressing an exclusively Catholic point of view. Pastoral letters which were issued in the name of the hierarchy addressed themselves to contemporary social and economic problems in the United States and boldly offered "Christian" solutions.[56]

No longer preoccupied with anti-Catholicism at home, U.S. Catholic concern focused on the plight of co-religionists in other countries. While Freemasonry and Modernism were the bogeys of the nineteenth century, the success of communism in the twentieth century elevated this new ideology to the status of a major threat. To Catholics in the thirties, it appeared that wherever members of their faith were being persecuted—whether in Mexico, Russia, or Spain—the forces of oppression were invariably socialist or communist.

The Church had spoken out against communism as early as 1854,[57] but in the thirties it undertook a more zealous campaign to combat the spread of "bolshevism."[58] From 1929 to 1932 there was virtually a total liquidation of the Catholic hierarchy in the Soviet Union and an unprecedented rise in anti-religious propaganda.[59] Abhorrent as the conditions of the Church were in the USSR, Catholics comprised only 9 percent of the total population, and so the foci of Catholic concern more naturally gravitated to persecutions in the predominantly Catholic countries of Mexico and Spain.

The festering sores of the Mexican revolution erupted in the thirties with renewed violence. The revolution, which began in 1910, went through sanguinary periods of rebel activity and civil war, frequently led by anti-clerics who in their programs of social and agrarian reform were determined to strip the Church of its power. The situation worsened in 1934 when Lázaro Cárdenas instituted a new program of reform with Marxist socialism as its guiding doctrine. Churches and church property were confiscated, clergy were deported, and religious orders were harassed and persecuted.[60]

In Spain, too, the Second Republic of 1931–36 was inspired by a program of socialist reforms, which brought in its train an onslaught of attacks on the Catholic clergy. In May 1931 churches were burned by mobs in Madrid, Valencia, and southern Spain, and the primate, Pedro Cardinal Segura y Sáenz, was expelled. The new constitution of December 1931 disestablished the Catholic Church and enacted restrictive legislation affecting religious orders. When new waves of riots broke out in February–July 1936, General Francisco Franco led a mutiny which developed into a civil war, lasting until 1939. Franco's army of counterrevolutionaries, who called themselves "Nationalists," claimed to have risen in defense of religion and to restore traditional values. Foreign aid to the Nationalists came mainly from Fascist Italy and Germany through the supply of combatants, matériel, and technicians. Aid to the Republicans came primarily from the USSR and Mexico, but volunteers for the International Brigade streamed from many countries, including the Abraham Lincoln Brigade from the United States.[61]

Observing U.S. responses to the upheavals in Russia, Mexico, and Spain, American Catholics were alarmed by the seeming governmental and public support of the leftist regimes.[62] Catholics resentfully felt that the news media never adequately or fairly represented the Catholic position in these countries.[63] When, in 1935, the Knights of Columbus demanded an investigation of religious persecutions in Mexico, their request was turned down by President Roosevelt.[64] The only countries which seemed to take the threat of communism seriously were the Fascist countries. Moreover, to many Catholics it appeared that while their protests were rebuffed or unheard, while they were consistently unable to elicit any mass support for their concerns, the Jews were uncannily successful in drumming up public support and sympathy for the persecuted Jewish community of Germany. Such response to the Jewish plight was all the more vexing since many Catholics sincerely believed that statistically the number of Catholic victims of persecution far exceeded the number of Jewish victims. Invidious contrasts were drawn in the Catholic press.

> The papers, led by the N.Y. *Times,* have played up the German persecutions day in and day out, all over their columns. Just try to get them to do the same for Mexico.[65]

> The sad note is here: while the press and public officials bitterly denounce the attack on ten synagogues in Germany . . . the protest has not been widened to include the far worse crimes committed against Catholics in Spain.[66]

For some papers, the most judicious response to Jewish persecution was silence.[67] When S. A. Baldus, the managing editor of *Extension*, wrote an editorial unreservedly condemning persecutions of Jews in Germany and Italy, he was constrained to postscript his editorial with a reminder to his readers that the editorial "we" used in the essay was stylistic and not to be taken literally. The opinions expressed were wholly his. In a later editorial, again denouncing manifestations of anti-Semitism, Baldus abandoned the editorial "we" in order that he "may write with greater freedom."[68]

Mulling over the disproportionate news on Jews and the corresponding apathy toward Catholics, Catholic papers raised the charge of Jewish ownership of the press and news media.[69] Compounding the allegations against the "Jewish monopoly" was the stigmatizing presumption that Jews were Communists or, at least, leftist-oriented. Even when Stalin began a series of anti-Jewish purges in 1937, *America* quoted the *Osservatore Romano* as saying that it was the "Vatican belief that Stalin's external policies are in close cooperation with the Jews."[70]

There were, of course, exceptions to this widespread notion. *Commonweal,* which generally took a markedly independent position,[71] tried in January 1930 to blast the myth that "sovietism is the creature of the Jews, who use it as a weapon against Christianity."[72] Likewise the *Catholic Worker* dissociated Jews from Communists, and depicted Jews and Catholics as brothers in suffering under Communist regimes.[73] Unfortunately, this perspective did not prevail, and more profuse examples of uncompromising dislike of the Jews began to appear.

Spearheading the anti-Semitic agitation among Catholics was the popular radio-priest, Father Charles Coughlin. He translated the struggles of the Christ and the Antichrist into contemporary terms, in which Chistianity and America represented Christ, and Communists and bankers represented the Antichrist. And conveniently, the two evils were linked together in the Jewish race. Though a number of the hierarchy were displeased with Coughlin's ravings, he, nevertheless, found a receptive and supportive audience in the diocesan press.[74] One of his key supporters in the eastern press was the *Tablet*. In a typical defense of Coughlin's anti-Semitism, the editor remarked, "Fr. Coughlin has fearlessly and courageously discussed the Jewish problem that others would pass by in cowardly silence . . . [no Catholic can honestly criticize] Fr. Coughlin's very temperate reference to the part that a Jewish *Weltanshaung* contributed to the untoward world conditions."[75]

Some Catholic papers not only vilified the Jews as subversives, but charged them with warmongering as well. As international tensions rose and rumors of war began to fly, Jews were suspected of enlisting American intervention against the Fascist countries. Moreover, the papers implied, the Jews were responsible for creating an indiscriminately negative image of *all* Fascist countries.[76] Though most Catholic papers were unsympathetic to Nazi Germany after 1935, when the Vatican openly protested the violations of the Concordat,[77] they believed that the Fascistic governments of Italy and Spain were nonoppressive and even beneficent. Along with most Americans, Catholics took a firm noninternventionist stand in European affairs and, in addition, resented the aggressiveness of Jewish opinion.[78]

In the emotionally charged atmosphere preceding the Second World War, Britain reneged on the Balfour promises by promulgating the White Paper of 1939. In brief, the paper severely curtailed Jewish immigration to Palestine; it made further land transfers dependent solely on the opinion of the high commissioner; and it envisioned the establishment of an independent Palestinian state in which the Jews would be a permanent minority. Implicit in the paper was Britain's conviction that her obligations under the Balfour Declaration were fulfilled, and that she was now at liberty to treat Palestine as an ordinary Class "A" mandate.[79]

The crystallization of British policy as expressed in the White Paper resulted from a sequence of crises, punctuated by almost continuous Arab unrest and violence. An aggressive and organized Palestinian revolt began with the general strike of 1936. The immediate grievance which touched off the strike was the British veto of a proposed legislative council,[80] although the roots of dissatisfaction lay in the continued British support of the growth of a Jewish National Home. When Parliament opposed the council scheme, in the conviction that it would only serve as an additional irritant in Arab-Jewish relations, the Arabs were outraged at what they considered proof of Jewish backstairs influence in mandate policy. Strikes and demonstrations, then being successfully employed by Egyptian and Syrian Arabs in their own nationalist struggles, were seized upon by the Palestinians as their pattern of protest. The strike was directed by Haj Amin al-Husaini, the mufti of Jerusalem, who earlier had gained notoriety for his involvement in the 1929 riots and was now ensconced as president of the newly formed Supreme Arab Committee.[81] The strike was marked by violence, terrorism, and destruction of property. Its objectives, in order of priority, were: (1) stoppage of all Jewish immigration; (2) prohibition of land transfers to Jews; (3) establishment of an independent national government under a representative legislative council.[82]

Giving the strike the form of an ultimatum, the Arabs refused to negotiate with the British unless Jewish immigration was totally suspended. British offers to send a Royal Commission to investigate the grievances and mediate a settlement were rebuffed until the coercive persuasion of neighboring Arab rulers, coupled with the dampening of native enthusiasm in face of progressive economic exhaustion, helped grind the strike to a halt. The termination was agreed upon by the strikers in the hope that a conciliatory British government would acquiesce in the demands of the Arabs.

Under the chairmanship of Earl Peel, a Royal Commission arrived in Palestine on November 11, 1936, and after a thorough investigation into the general situation, concluded that the British policy based on a concept of equal obligations to Jews and Arabs was untenable and unworkable. It was untenable because the mandate's primary purpose was "to promote the establishment of the Jewish National Home," and unworkable because Jewish and Arab interests were really irreconcilable, despite well-intentioned British attempts at compromise. The commission suggested a partition of the country into separate Arab, Jewish, and mandate-controlled states.[83] This scheme was resisted with an uproar of protest by Moslem and Christian Arabs, and only grudgingly conceded by Parliament, the League, and the Jews, in terms of a limited agreement on the principle of partition.[84] The vigorous opposition, uncontested by the lukewarm approval, prepared the way for the eventual demise of the plan. In the words of the Woodhead Report, written by a second commission dispatched by the British government to deal with the technical details of the partition, "we have been unable to recommend boundaries which will afford a reasonable prospect of the eventual establishment of self-supporting Arab and Jewish states."[85]

Open Arab rebellion was again raging, ever since the truce of October 1936 ended with the publication of the Peel Commission Report in July 1937. Most unsettling to the British, however, were statements made by Arab leaders at conferences held in Bludan in 1937 and in

Cairo in 1938, which threatened Arab cooperation with the Axis powers if their demands were not met.[86] British prestige in the Middle East was seriously impaired by the Italo-Ethiopian War, and German and Italian designs in the Levant were increasingly evident in the anti-British propaganda beamed to the Arab countries by Fascist radio.[87] With the prospect of war imminent, the friendship of the Arab states appeared more vital to the British than did that of the Zionists, who would have no choice but to side with England. Therefore, when a last-ditch effort to arrive at a compromise solution at the London Conference in February–March, 1939 failed, it seemed politic that compromise should take the form of the largest concessions to Arab demands.

Though the British predicament was politically understandable, many Britishers condemned the moral bankruptcy of the ultimate decision. Mr. Winston Churchill, then colonial secretary, branded the White Paper a "plain breach of a solemn obligation." Harshly criticized in Parliament, the paper was passed by only a small majority in the House of Commons, and then was sent to the Permanent Mandates Commission for review. After a brief four-day session, the commission unanimously rejected the new policy as "not in accordance with the interpretation which . . . the commission has always placed upon the Palestine Mandate."[88]

It is unreal to assess the reactions to the White Paper without reference to the plight of European Jewry, which loomed in the background. Confronted with legal disabilities, economic ruin, and physical assault, the mere existence of the Jews in Germany and many East European countries was in question. The need for escape and refuge was so urgent that it sparked the convening of an international conference. Held in Evian, Switzerland, on July 6–15, 1938, the conference attempted to coordinate efforts in saving the victims of persecution. That the Evian Conference arrived at no adequate solutions did not lessen the problem—if anything it served to heighten the despair evoked a year later when the White Paper of 1939 practically shut the door to the only remaining haven.[89]

Clamors of protest against British policy in the White Paper arose not only from Zionist circles, but from Jews who were earlier indifferent or even antagonistic to Zionism. With the advent of Hitler and the pressure to save their kin trapped in Europe, Jews could hardly afford to maintain a negative attitude toward Jewish immigration to Palestine.[90] Popular reactions in the United States echoed the Jewish distress. Newspaper editorials in the major cities throughout the country condemned the British policy in acrimonious terms—"a colossal sellout," "a breach of faith," "a Black paper," "A Munich for the Holy Land," and so on.[91] Though there was no official reaction on the part of the White House, fifteen of the twenty-five members of the House Foreign Affairs Committee and twenty-eight senators publicly protested.[92]

In view of the prevalent Catholic state of mind in America toward the Jews when England reneged on her promises, Catholic press reactions to the event were not surprising. To the White Paper itself, there were few direct responses. *Central-Blatt* offered the same cryptic remark with which it had reacted to anti-Semitism: "wise men are silent." Essentially agreeing with the necessity for the British move, but sensing its unpopularity with American audiences, the editor counseled his readers to remain silent on the issue.[93] *Catholic World* and *America* both praised the White Paper unreservedly. *Catholic World* espoused the drastic cutback in immigration as the only measure that would effectively avert the outbreak of a serious conflagration in the Middle East, which could involve the United States as well. The opinion of *Catholic World* was in agreement with its editorial policy of isolationism. Moreover, the argument had been adumbrated in 1936 and in 1937 in two lengthy articles, both harping on the inevitability of violence and bloodshed if Britain continued the policy of Balfour.[94] *America* praised the new British policy as an attempt to act justly in a difficult situation. It did not even mask its annoyance with the Jewish reactions to the White Paper.

> One phase of the Palestine problem that is impressive is the force and the vehemence of the attack of international Jewry. The union of sentiment, the similarity of method, the use of propaganda, the moral pressure of Jews in every nation, particularly in the British Commonwealth and the United States, all manifest that Jewry is an international power, and it is aggressive and may be ruthless, and that it is determined to champion its interests against all and any who would question its aims. The problem of Palestine may pro-

voke a new orientation of ideas in regard to the place of the Jewish race in world affairs.

In the United States, likewise, there is in process a new Jewish consciousness, characterized by militancy and acumen. This, also, requires a new American evaluation and orientation.[95]

A clue to *America's* underlying position in regard to *any* policy decision on Palestine can be found in an editorial published during the strike of 1936.

> The British Mandate has so far been a failure. Not, however, for lack of goodwill on the part of the Mandatory Power; but rather perhaps for more goodwill than a real understanding that religious conditions in Palestine are rooted in something vastly more fundamental than the *laissez-faire* idea that one religion is as good as another. The overpowering interest in the future and welfare of the Holy Land is neither Jewish nor Islamic. It is Christian. And as its soil was trodden by the Incarnate Word Who founded His Church there, the welfare of Palestine is inextricably bound up with the Catholic and Apostolic Church of Christ.[96]

The White Paper of 1939 may have appeared as one attempt to redress the balance.

Other Catholic papers totally bypassed the news of the White Paper, even though some of the same papers had reported and commented fairly regularly on the Palestine situation since the Peel Report of 1937. It seems that without being as blunt as the *Central-Blatt*, there was good reason, now that British policy was finally crystallized in the White Paper, for "wise men to remain silent." To have some idea of how these papers would have expressed themselves in May–June 1939, it is necessary to turn back and see how they reviewed the events leading up to that date.[97]

We may single out *Tablet* and *Sign* during the few years preceding the White Paper as the most vocal exponents of the dominant attitude, and *Commonweal* as an exponent of another attitude, which though not as prevalent in the press, did exist. In the former publications the vulgar portrayal of the Jew as an atheist and Communist was carried over in the evaluation of the Zionists in Palestine.[98] It was not unusual to hear, at this time, that "one can expect more from the Moslem Arabs than [from the] atheistic Bolshevik Jews."[99] *Tablet* and *Ave Maria* further blackened the prospect of a Jewish Palestine by painting a sinister image of Jewish greed and insidious influence.

Arab opinion, which received considerable publicity in the *Tablet*, played upon these fears, and the Arab National League, headquartered in New York City, provided the *Tablet* with letters and appeals. An excerpt from one letter, written by the Executive Committee of the Arab National League, will suffice to indicate the tenor of these communications: "The wandering Jew, the apostle of unbelief, is appealing to the American Christians to sustain him against a hundred thousand Christian Arabs. . . . our American children, yours and mine, are bartered on a Jewish counter."[100]

Sign, while taking the same anti-Zionist stance as *Tablet*, weighted its position with the denial of any inherent rights of the Jews to the Holy Land. This denial was inextricably tied up with the devotion peculiar to the publication's sponsors and their veneration of the Holy Land as the land of the Passion.[101] To permit control of the Holy Land to the people whose responsibility "for the death of Christ is incontestable"[102] would have appeared sacrilegious. Any site other than Palestine was acceptable to the Passionists for the settling of a Jewish colony, but "Palestine is not and never will be a national home for the Jew."[103]

In contrast to these papers, *Commonweal*'s position on Jews in Palestine was distinctly favorable. And yet, upon closer examination, it was a position which was bobbing in a sea of ambivalences and could easily turn in either direction. On one score, however, there were no ambivalences, and that was *Commonweal*'s forceful repudiation of the canards publicized by other papers in their discussions on Jews. In *Commonweal* there was no anti-Semitic rationalization on which to peg editorial opinion.[104] Basically, the journal was open to hear all sides of the Palestine question. On the one hand, a glowing article on the Jewish colonies was printed, on the other hand, a persuasive article urged placation of the Arabs, and then, still another article placed the onus for all the troubles on British imperialistic interests in the area.[105] Yet with all the variety of background reports and authoritative opinions, editorially it did not seem to reach any clear-cut decision on what its position on Palestine should be.

Editorial opinion tended to conclude that the situation had reached an impasse. Unlike other Catholic papers, *Commonweal* was not willing to solve the impasse by declaring that the Jews should look for another haven, nor, like others, did it seek to invalidate the Balfour Declaration.[106] Significantly, the editors recognized the link between sentiments of anti-Semitism and anti-Zionism. In an essay on fighting anti-Semitism, the paper referred proudly to a telegram sent to President Roosevelt by the National Council of Catholic Men urging him to "cooperate in a solution of the Palestine problem which will not deprive Jews of an asylum in their traditional home."[107] There is little doubt that *Commonweal* comprehended the need for a haven for Jews and even the logic of the haven being in Palestine, but the paper was not committed to the degree that it would maintain its position in face of continued disturbances, violence, and contrary British policy.[108] Avoiding an editorial on the White Paper, *Commonweal* submitted, a full six months after its promulgation, an article which attempted to rationalize British policy in light of strategic necessity in event of war.[109]

In conclusion, the differences in the Catholic responses to events in 1929 and 1939 can be summed up as follows:

1. Catholic papers which began to oppose Zionism in 1929 became more firmly entrenched in their opinions by 1939; Catholic papers which had supported the Zionists in 1929 were now either opposed or reserved comment. There was no evidence in 1939 of any genuinely warm feeling toward Jewish settlement in Palestine, such as that which had spontaneously welled up immediately following the 1929 riots.

2. During the twenties there did exist a feeling of kinship between Catholics and Jews, which was largely built up as a result of their common experience as targets of nativist bigotry. The relationship altered in the thirties with the lessening of anti-Catholic prejudice in the United States and the consequent growing concern about Catholic persecution in other countries. Catholics now saw themselves as an unequally beleaguered group, more so than the Jews, and their indignation was heightened by the public apathy accorded to their problems in contrast to the sympathy evoked for Jewish problems. Catholic-Jewish relations cooled considerably, and there was a greater incidence of anti-Semitism in Catholic writings. Attitudes toward Zionism underwent corresponding changes.

3. For the first time, and not soon to be repeated, Catholic papers

were frank in positing their positions on theological considerations. For example, *Sign* claimed that the Jews had forfeited their rights to the Holy Land, presumedly because of the crucifixion of Christ and rejection of the new covenant; *America* claimed that the Holy Land is Christ's land and it is in the Catholic interest to maintain this identity; and the *Catholic Worker* posited that following the advent of Christ, Jews were no longer a nation and so could have no legitimate nationalist aspirations.

With the onset of World War II, general interest in the specifically Jewish problem of Palestine abated. It was not until the close of the war that the Palestine issue again jumped into the forefront of world attention. By then, the intensity of the Holocaust gave the problem a new perspective and posed a particular challenge to Catholic attitudes.

IV

Non Possumus: On the Eve of a Jewish State

There is a prevalent notion that the Holocaust was a catalyst which stirred Christian sympathy for the Jews and increased the readiness of the Christian world to accept a Jewish state. In reference to U.S. Catholics, this assumption must be hedged with many reservations. Catholic press reactions to the Holocaust during and after the war did not lay the groundwork for a sympathetic appreciation of the urgency of Zionist demands. In fact, once plans for the establishment of a Jewish state began to materialize, lack of sympathy turned to outright hostility.[1]

A Jewish state in Palestine presented a hornet's nest of problems to Catholics. Theological, psychological, and pragmatic political considerations converged to shape Catholic attitudes. As one factor or another became more relevant, there were corresponding fluctuations in intensity of response. Immediately following the war, the most visible factor was the Zionist interlinking of the refugee problem with Palestine. The Zionists did not reckon with the fact that U.S. Catholics had a serious refugee problem of their own. A great many of the "displaced persons" were Catholics from Eastern Europe, who refused repatriation because their countries were now under atheistic governments. Catholics called for the opening of America's gates to the refugees; Jews clamored for the opening of Palestine to their refugees. While each group vied for public sympathy and official action, Catholics attempting to project their demands effectively experienced a growing frustration vis-à-vis the successful campaign of the Jewish groups.

Another factor, which played no minor role, was the theological state of mind among Catholics concerning Palestine. The very name, Holy Land, evoked an image hardly consonant with secularization, modernization, and settlement by Jews. The possibility of Jewish dominion in the land of the Passion aroused theological concern. While the holy places were in the forefront of the Catholic argument, the wellsprings were hidden in the fear of the inevitable transformation of the Holy Land.

A final factor loomed alarmingly in the background. The threat of spreading communism was a serious concern to U.S. Catholics viewing postwar alignments. Apprehensions over Communist penetration in the Middle East were reinforced by the suspicion of left-wing tendencies rife among the Jews in Palestine and by the rationale that Western acquiescence to Zionism would provoke the Arab world to ally itself with Soviet Russia. These three—refugee rivalries, Holy Land image, and the threat of communism—were the main factors around which Catholic opposition to Zionism crystallized from World War II until May 1948.

Disclosures of the magnitude and cruelty of the Nazi persecutions of the Jews in Europe began reaching the American press in 1942, and by 1944 informed Americans knew, in broad outline, of the existence of a Jewish catastrophe.[2] Shocked and incensed, many Jews perceived in the totality of Hitler's success the complicity of Christian Europe. Shadows of accusation extended to the Vatican, for its passivity if not outright collaboration.[3]

U.S. Catholic newspapers and periodicals defensively began to direct their attention to the Jewish tragedy. Papal pronouncements which denounced racial intolerance were reprinted.[4] Stories of individual Catholic efforts to rescue Jews in Europe were publicized. *Our Sunday Visitor,* a syndicated diocesan weekly which had hardly exhibited interest in the persecutions during the early war years, buffeted its readers with one item after the other in the spring of 1944.[5] Expressions of Jewish gratitude to the Pope made the headlines and served as particularly strong arguments against allegations of Papal indifference or collusion with the Nazis.[6]

As the Boston *Pilot* explained to its readers, it was necessary to publicize protests of Catholic authorities in Europe at the time of the persecutions so that no impression be given that Catholics were remiss in their Christian duties to their fellowmen. The *Pilot* worried that the impressions currently received suggested that the protests and interventions of Catholics in authority had been too rare, too limited, and too timid.[7] Other papers attributed the negative impressions of Catholic efforts in Europe to a Communist conspiracy aimed at discrediting the Church by implicating the Vatican and the hierarchy in the Nazi atrocities. Less circumspect papers, such as the *Tablet,* accused the Jews themselves of deliberately framing the Catholics.[8]

There were exceptions to this pattern of apologetic interest in the plight of European Jewry. *Commonweal* and *America* stand in the forefront as papers which continually and consistently denounced anti-Semitism and decried persecutions of Jews *throughout* the war period.[9] As early as 1942, both papers informed their readers of the grim facts and statistics of the Nazi extermination policies. They urged their readers to join in prayer for the deliverance of the Jews from their suffering.[10] By and large, however, the tenor of the Catholic press response to the Holocaust was more defensive than anguished.

The close of the war forced upon the world's attention not only the full horror of the Nazi atrocities, but also the immediate problem of resettling the refugee survivors of those horrors. American Catholics, along with other Americans of every denomination, were shocked and appalled by what had happened, and most were sincerely sympathetic to the plight of the displaced persons. However, as indicated earlier, the Catholic response was complicated by another concern. East European Christians who were interned in the Nazi labor camps were not systematically annihilated, as were the Jews, and, therefore, made up the majority of the DP's after the war. In an official report presented by the State Department to Congress, Jews accounted for 193,332 displaced persons out of a total number of 794,735.[11] Of these, a considerable proportion were Catholic.[12]

Weighing these statistics, U.S. Catholic newspapers were indignant that the attention of the United States was focused on the smaller percentage of Jewish refugees, while relatively ignoring the urgent needs of the overwhelming number of Christian DP's. As in prewar days, Catholics again felt that the Jews unjustly monopolized the stage. Their papers loudly protested that "the problem represented by these people [DP's] is largely a Christian problem." And while most non-Catholic Americans were still regarding Russia as our erstwhile ally, Catholics had never forgotten, even during the war, the dangers of a Soviet regime. Therefore, Catholics could not entertain repatriation to Communist-controlled countries as a possible solution for their co-religionists. Since the only haven was in the Western democratic world, the hue and cry raised by the Catholic papers was for unrestricted immigration to the United States.[13]

American Jews also rejected any suggestion of repatriation for Jewish DP's, but they advanced a solution different from that of the Catholics. Immigration to Palestine had always been the plea of the Zionists. Their demand gained a wider hearing in the United States with the onrush of mounting catastrophe, and during the war it won adherents even among non-Zionist American Jewry. No longer was immigration to Palestine a mere desideratum; it became an imperative need.

The knot of refugees and statehood was tied at an Extraordinary Zionist Conference convened in New York in May 1942. The conference adopted an eight-point program, subsequently known as the "Biltmore Program," which concluded with the joint aim of open immigration and Jewish statehood.[14] The American Zionist Emergency Committee (AZEC) waged an intensive campaign to mobilize Jewish and non-Jewish opinion behind the Biltmore Program. Pressing for official action, local committees deluged their representatives with letters and telegrams.[15] Congress was moved to act, and the congressional resolutions of 1944 breathed the spirit of the Zionist program.

> Resolved that the United States shall use its good offices and take appropriate measures to the end that the doors of Palestine shall be opened for free entry of Jews in that country, and that there shall be full opportunity for colonization so that the Jewish people may ultimately reconstitute Palestine as a free and democratic Jewish commonwealth.[16]

Later in 1945, President Truman called for 100,000 certificates for Jewish refugees to emigrate to Palestine. The ensuing Anglo-American Committee of Inquiry on Palestine unhesitatingly included the Jewish DP problem in its terms of reference.[17] Inevitably, the questions of the refugees, immigration to Palestine, and even the establishment of a Jewish state blended together in a seemingly logical fusion.

Catholics resisted succumbing to this logic. They felt that the already distorted popular impression of the refugee problem as being solely a Jewish concern became even more twisted out of focus by the Jewish clamor for immigration to Palestine. They apparently felt that the insistence upon Palestine deprived them of massive Jewish support for their own campaign to open U.S. immigration, and, at the same time, that the Palestine scheme provided no relief for Christian DP's. If the Zionists had not joined the two issues—refugees and the Jewish homeland—the refugee question would be clearly seen as a problem apart; and if the Jews would press for opening U.S. doors instead of Palestine, the Catholics could ride on the crest of American sympathy for the Jewish refugees to resettle their own DP's.

Fulminating against the nexus of refugees and Palestine, *Sign* warned its readers to separate the humanitarian issue from the political one. *Catholic World*'s editor feared that American efforts to relocate Jewish refugees in Palestine would precipitate another major war. *America*, too, was apprehensive over the consequences of such a policy.[18] *Commonweal* adopted its usual puzzled stance in reference to Palestine and confided to its readers that it was in a dilemma.

> We have never been able to make up our minds on the subject of Jewish immigration into Palestine. We fully recognize the desperate need of Europe's remaining Jews for a homeland in which they can be reasonably confident of living unmolested. We are likewise aware that the Jewish colonies in the Holy Land have in fact proved a great economic asset to their Arab neighbors. We are aware that the question has been used by Arab nationalists as a means to arouse passions which need never have been aroused. But we are likewise and equally suspicious of Zionist nationalism and we cannot withhold our sympathy from the natives of Palestine, who, however shortsightedly, seem to prefer to keep their country for their own use. Americans, of all people, can with the least grace criticize others for attempts to restrict immigration. And hence, we cannot

make up our minds, especially since we believe that the first duty of our own country is itself to provide a haven of refuge to the harborless.[19]

There were but few exceptions in the Catholic press to the generally negative attitude toward Jewish immigration to Palestine.[20] Whatever hesitant sympathy did exist was later stifled by acts of terrorism committed by a militant segment of Palestinian Jewry.[21]

Ever since the beginning of the war, British obstructionist policies regarding the refugees had aroused bitter resentment among the Jews. The Palestinian Jewish community watched with inconsolable grief as British officialdom turned back shiploads of refugees to a fate that was uncertain at best. Cumulatively, these and other incidents of British insensitivity hammered away at Jewish patience. When, finally, the tragic proportions of the Nazi extermination plan seared the consciousness of the free world, Jews confidently expected Britain to change its policy. But when neither the British nor the Allied governments offered any tangible help to the victims, the disillusioned Palestinian Jews undertook operations of rescue on their own.[22]

The desperate efforts of the *Bricha,* the Jewish underground rescue organization, were necessarily pitted against the unrelenting policies of the White Paper. British obduracy continued even after the war—again for reasons of political expediency. Arab loyalties had to be won over, this time to forestall Russian expansion in the Middle East. Jewish survivors of the Holocaust were turned back to DP camps or rerouted to Cyprus. The "official" Jewish military, the *Haganah,* could no longer control the anger unleashed by the dissident Irgun and Stern groups. Despair led to terrorism, which in turn led to reprisals and ever more repressive British policies.[23] Faced with an inflammable situation, the British responded with the usual ploy of an investigating commission.

The Anglo-American Committee of Inquiry began its work in January of 1946 with the assurances that its recommendations would be accepted if they were unanimous. Four months later the committee submitted its report, including among its unanimous recommendations the entry of 100,000 Jewish refugees to Palestine. In a surprising about-face, the British foreign secretary, Ernest Bevin, reneged on his earlier promise and flatly rejected the report as unacceptable. Viable alternatives did not replace the discarded recommendations, and terrorist action intensified. Unable to maintain the upper hand in a rapidly deteriorating situation, Bevin finally announced that he would submit the Palestine question to the United Nations.

On April 28, 1947, a special session of the United Nations was convoked to find a way out of the imbroglio. Proposals flew back and forth during the agitated debates in the General Assembly. An all-Arab state, an all-Jewish state, a trusteeship government, a partitioned state were among the suggestions. To resolve the debate, the General Assembly appointed a Special Committee on Palestine (UNSCOP) to prepare a conclusive report. The eleven members of UNSCOP emerged from their deliberations with a majority report and a minority report. The former recommended a partition plan, with special status reserved for Jerusalem; the latter supported the creation of a federated Palestinian state. Ultimately, the majority report was favored in the historic United Nations decision of November 29, 1947.[24]

How did the Catholic press respond to this intensive diplomatic activity and to the variety of proposals suggested in the United Nations? For those who look for Vatican directives behind every Catholic response, it would be just as well to dispense with this question forthrightly.

The Pope did not make any explicit public statement on Palestine until his May 1948 encyclical, *Auspicia Quaedam*.[25] U.S. Catholic papers did not print Vatican releases on the subject, nor was the *Osservatore Romano* quoted. Only the reports on new Egyptian-Vatican ties and the publicity given to a Papal audience arranged with Arab representatives in August 1946 lent some coloring to the otherwise neutral tones emanating from the Vatican.[26] However, in a private memorandum to Myron Taylor, U.S. representative to the Vatican, Archbishop Amleto G. Cicognani, the apostolic delegate to the United States, set forth, in no uncertain terms, the Vatican position on Palestine. Cicognani attached to his letter a Vatican *Aide Memoire* of June 4, 1922 to the League of Nations and an explanatory note of Cardinal Gasparri. This correspondence strenuously objected to the eventual preponderance of Jews in Palestine and called for drastic modification of the Balfour pledge.[27] In his own letter Cicognani openly stated:

Catholics the world over are piously devoted to this country [Palestine], hallowed as it was by the presence of the Redeemer and esteemed as it is as the cradle of Christianity. If the greater part of Palestine is given to the Jewish People, this would be a severe blow to the religious attachment of Catholics to this land. To have the Jewish People in the majority is to interfere with the peaceful exercise of these rights in the Holy Land already vested in Catholics.

It is true that at one time Palestine was inhabited by the Hebrew race, but there is no axiom in history to substantiate the necessity of a people returning to a country they left nineteen centuries before.

If a "Hebrew Home" is desired, it would not be too difficult to find a more fitting territory than Palestine. With an increase in the Jewish population there, grave, new international problems would arise. Catholics the world over would be aroused.[28]

That Cicognani may have communicated the same sentiments to the U.S. hierarchy cannot be precluded for lack of available written evidence. Nor is it possible to confirm whether or not diocesan editors were apprised by their bishops of Cicognani's message or turned of their own volition to past Papal statements in lieu of more recent public guidance from Rome. Nevertheless, for the diocesan press, at least from outward appearances, direction came from exponents of Catholic opinion in the Holy Land itself.

Brother Anthony Bruya, an American Franciscan in Jerusalem, was the correspondent for the National Catholic News Service.[29] He was responsible for most of the dispatches from Palestine printed in the American diocesan press. Bruya's mind on the Palestine question was made up far in advance of 1947. During the war, in a series of letters on the "Effects of the Present War on Palestine," Bruya proudly recalled his 1922 prediction that the Jews would never establish an autonomous state. He had then asserted that "equality in protection, in holding office, and the recognition of Hebrew, together with English and Arabic," would be the sum total of Zionist accomplishments. Now, as a consequence of the White Paper, Bruya sanguinely wrote that his words were being fulfilled.[30] When changes were bruited about after the war, Bruya stolidly stood his ground.[31] He was fully supported by Msgr. Abraham Assemani, representative of the Latin patriarch in Jerusalem to the United States. Assemani sounded the tocsin in a widely reprinted article in 1945, when he warned that Christian rights in the Holy Land were being ignored. He urged Christians to demand absolute sovereignty over all the holy places, and the establishment of an Allied Commission to safeguard Christian interests.[32]

When the Anglo-American Committee of Inquiry released its report on April 30, 1946, the apprehensions raised by Assemani reverberated. And Bruya took up the cudgels. "Christian Rights Overlooked," "Christianity Ignored in Verbal Battles over Arab, Jewish Control of Holy Land," were typical headlines for the Bruya dispatches in the diocesan press. Bruya attacked the Anglo-American report and angrily took the committee to task for having placed Christianity after Islam and Judaism when dealing with religious interests in Palestine. Bruya drew up a list of essential Christian rights in the Holy Land, which included the freedom to preach the Gospel and the rights to convert non-Christians, to maintain Christian schools, and to secure all the holy places in Christian hands. In conclusion, he warned that Christian rights in Palestine were not only the concern of the indigenous Palestinian community, but of Christians throughout the world.[33]

The decisive turn for the worse came on November 29, 1947 with the United Nations decision on partition. Sporadic fighting broke out all over the Holy Land, and the news from Palestine reached a fever pitch.[34] Heading the avalanche of reports was the publication of a statement issued by the "Christian Union," a group composed of eleven Christian communities, Catholic and non-Catholic, in Palestine.

> The Christian Union wishes to declare in unequivocal terms that they denounce the partition plan being of strong convictions that this plan involves a violation of the sacredness of the Holy Land, which by its nature and history is indivisible. . . . It is our firm conviction that peace will not be restored . . . unless those bodies who undertake the determination of the future of Palestine remove the causes which have made a battle of the Holy Land. . . .[35]

Following on the heels of this statement came Bruya's continuous and grim dispatches on the deteriorating situation resulting from the persistence of the United Nations in going ahead with partition. Diocesan readers must have shuddered as they read of the closing of Catholic schools, the fleeing of nuns and priests, the murder of innocent

Catholics, and finally the bombings and desecrations of Catholic institutions. "Tragedy, Terror Stalk Holy Land," "Where Christ Walked Now Strife Strides," blared the Palestine correspondent.[36]

Support for Bruya and fellow-Catholics in Palestine was liberally given by the prestigious Catholic Near East Welfare Association (CNEWA) in New York City. Established in 1926 by Pope Pius XI, the organization served (and still serves) as the Pope's official mission and relief agency in the Near and Middle East. In all matters relating to Palestine, CNEWA was the primary spokesman for American Catholics, on both the national and international scenes. The hierarchy invariably turned to CNEWA, as the authoritative voice, whenever a question on the Middle East arose. Leading bishops in the nation formed the board of trustees, and the archbishop of New York served as the president. These trustees, who also held important posts in NCWC, received annual reports from CNEWA's national secretary. As a dispenser of information and guidance, CNEWA's influence was far-reaching.[37] The leading personality of CNEWA at this time was Msgr. Thomas J. McMahon, the national secretary of the organization from 1943 to 1954.[38]

When the Palestine Resolutions of 1944 were debated in Congress, McMahon warned of the dangers which would accrue to the dispersed Christian communities in the Middle East if the West should propose a postwar settlement of Palestine unfavorable to the Arabs. He professed that his sole concern was the welfare of the Christian minorities under Islam, and asserted that in order to ensure their safety, some concessions would have to be made to Arab nationalism.[39] A year later, when the resolutions had been conveniently discarded, McMahon approached the Palestine question from a different tack.

In an article entitled "Threat to the Holy Places," McMahon urged that Christians throughout the world should raise their voices in a united demand that the "homeland of Jesus be kept sacred and inviolable." He was most emphatic that the Christian factor be kept uppermost in any postwar settlement of Palestine. While Islam could not "expel Jesus from His homeland," McMahon feared that a Jewish state would do just that. Neither the incorporation of Palestine into an Arab federation of states nor its incorporation into a Jewish commonwealth with separate international enclaves for the holy places would be adequate for safeguarding the Holy Land. Quoting Bruya that the "whole land is one Christian sanctuary centering around the Holy Sepulchre of Christ," McMahon advocated internationalization of the entire country. *Sign,* which carried this article, prefaced it with an illustration reminiscent of the medieval ecclesia-synagoga imagery. On the upper right was a depiction of pilgrims celebrating the Way of the Cross, and on the lower left was the "Wailing Wall," where "Jews lament faded glory of Israel."[40]

When UNSCOP held hearings on alternative solutions to the settlement of Palestine, CNEWA's request to appear at the hearings as the representative of Palestinian Christians was publicized in the press.[41] In a letter to the United Nations, McMahon stressed:

> We are completely indifferent to the form of the regime which your esteemed Committee may recommend, provided that the interests of Christendom, Catholic, Protestant and Orthodox, will be weighed and safeguarded in your final recommendations. Primarily, all our sanctuaries should be respected, not only with cold juridicism but with local reverence.[42]

Amplifying this latter point in an article published at the same time, McMahon emotionally pleaded that the settlement should not be "allowed to exile Jesus."[43] Custody of the Holy Land in a spirit of "local reverence" was within the capability only of Christians.

While the views of CNEWA and Bruya pervaded the Catholic press, the opinions of those Catholics who took a publicly pro-Zionist stand, such as Claire Huchet Bishop, Francis E. McMahon, and Bartley C. Crum, did not find a forum in the same press.[44] There is a surprising dearth of statements even from the few members of the Catholic clergy who participated in the Zionist-sponsored Christian Council on Palestine,[45] later the American Christian Palestine Committee. Even Father George Barry Ford, who loyally attended every meeting of the committee, made no public statements. The prominent French theologian Jacques Maritain, well known for his public condemnation of anti-Semitism, was on the membership list of the Christian Council. However, when writing in the national Catholic press, he ambiguously stated, "... it appears that the solution of the Hebrew state in Palestine, inevitably, will be the next solution attempted by the angel of an ever-sorrowful and frustrated history."[46]

The zealousness of a majority of the Latin American countries in furthering the cause of a Jewish state was an interesting aspect of the United Nations debates. But readers of the Catholic press were uninformed of the enthusiastic support of these Catholic representatives.[47]

A stroke of good fortune for those Christians who objected to Zionism was the establishment of the American Council for Judaism in 1943.[48] This organization maintained that since the Jewish people were solely a religious association, any nationalist ambition was in contradiction to, and incompatible with, Judaism. The denial of nationhood fitted in nicely with prevalent Catholic conceptions. Moreover, the convenience of presenting anti-Zionist opinion in the words of an American Jewish organization was of inestimable psychological value for a press wary of the onus of anti-Semitism. In this manner, a journalist for *Catholic World* could fortify himself in a barrage against Zionism: "It is with reluctance and trepidation that a denial of Jewish aspiration can be expressed. But many Jews themselves are opposed to the movement on the ground of its probable harm to Judaism."[49] *America*, which had reservations on open immigration to Palestine, could note that "the American Council for Judaism, hardly to be considered inimical to Jewish interest," also supported alternatives to Palestine immigration.[50] Whether in sincerity or in shrewdness, the Council was deferred to as the more representative and bona fide organization among American Jews in contrast to the Zionists.[51]

The third factor which loomed in the background of the Palestine question was Catholic uneasiness over Soviet intentions in the Middle East. Catholics mistrusted postwar Russian expansion, and their fears were frequently expressed in the press.[52] *America*, which had been closely watching Russian maneuvers ever since the close of the war, published an ominous article on "Soviet Shadows in the Arab East" at the beginning of 1946. In continuing comments and articles, *America* dwelt on the fear of Russian exploitation of Arab nationalism and Arab unrest.[53] To preempt the Russians, the West would have to make concessions to Arab aspirations. It was this reasoning which motivated the editors to condone British pro-Arab policy in 1946, despite protestations of sympathy for the Jews. Two years later the same editors, overriding Arab objections, supported enforcement of partition. Their reasoning remained consistent. Enforcement was necessary in order to prevent a chaotic situation which "would provide an opportunity too strong for the Soviets to resist."[54]

A new dimension entered when the Soviet delegate to the United Nations, Simon Tzarapkin, endorsed partition on October 13, 1947 and declared that the Jewish people had a right to a state of their own.[55] For Catholics, this unexpected move revived the specter of the Jew as Communist agent. Russia's vote was interpreted as an indication of her expectations that the Jewish state would become the key to unlock the entire Middle East. With little regard for facts, one Catholic writer imaginatively wrote:

> There is apparently still more behind the Russian stand. Moscow has many agents in the Jewish Stern Gang in Palestine, reported to be largely Communistic. She [Russia] is also supporting the emigration, from the countries that she controls in Eastern Europe, of thousands of Jews who are Communists or Communist sympathizers. It is said that she has distributed arms among them preparatory to their move to Palestine. They are to form the nucleus of a Communist movement in the new state.[56]

Political suspicions commingled with religious bias to heighten Catholic opposition to the establishment of the state.

The half-year between November 29, when the United Nations General Assembly voted for partition, and May 15, when the mandate was scheduled to end, was a period of tension and anxiety for all concerned with Palestine. As plans for a Jewish state reached the final stages, a mood of near-hysteria gripped many Catholic papers. The diocesan press shook with reports of confusion and bloody disorder in the Holy Land. Warnings of impending disaster mixed with proposals for a "Crusade" to defend the holy places.[57] In the national press, the shrillest cries came from *Catholic World* and *Sign*. *Catholic World* was apprehensive of a full-scale war. Ever since the appearance of the idea of a Jewish state in United Nations discussions, the paper had warned against it. Harking back to the alleged Jewish responsibility for drawing the United States into World War II, *Catholic World*'s commentator on the Middle East charged:

> No one will doubt that a powerful force behind America's entrance into the war was compassion for the persecuted Jews of Germany. . . . the American government was under the pressure of a powerful Jewish lobby. . . . they sharpened the talons of the American Eagle to fly him against the European cormorant that gorged the Star of David. . . . She has rescued the Jews from the Nazis only to find that she will have to save them again. . . . Is the Star of David to become another star in the American flag?[58]

In March 1948, the same writer marshaled a whole array of arguments besides the threat of war. The partition plan was one-sidedly considerate of Jewish interests; a Jewish state would spearhead a Communist takeover; oil fields essential to America's defense would be cut off; and finally, American boys would be dragged into the inevitable war. The futility and injustice of a Jewish state in Palestine echoed in his words; "The fact remains that even in Biblical times the Jews had only a tenuous hold on Palestine. . . . More significant still, they made a final exit in A.D. 70."[59]

Sign tenaciously clung to hopes of a settlement which would not "exile Jesus." The editor, Fr. Ralph Gorman, C.P., denounced partition as a tragic mistake, and in his editorial of April 1948, he pressed for a United Nations trusteeship which would consider Christian interests.[60]

Commonweal and *America* conceded to partition, but grudgingly. *Commonweal* openly brooded over the outcome. Its managing editor, C. G. Paulding, congratulated the Zionists on their victory, but made it clear to his readers that the minuscule state was by no means a solution to the Jewish "problem."[61] Suspicion and foreboding seethed underneath an exterior of genuine friendship. Paulding's frequent tirades against the Jewish terrorists, justifiable as they may have been, went far beyond condemnation. His objectivity is suspect in his exclusive denunciation of Jewish "murderers," while ignoring Arab provocations and terrorism. On May 2, 1948, he wrote:

> It is not a step . . . toward anything save a future of misery when a certain number of Jewish fanatics forget all the Jews throughout the world and pretend to create, in Palestine, by extreme violence, something they would call a nation, but which would be nothing but a self-administered ghetto. In Palestine they are not opening a new world to the Jews, they are closing to the Jews the world toward which we are working. . . .[62]

Though Paulding was friendly to the Jews and untiring in his condemnations of all forms of discrimination against them, the nationalist passion of Zionism irritated him. Zionism victorious clashed with his Christian vision of the Jews as a religious people dispersed throughout the nations.[63]

America did not bare its feelings on the implications of Zionism, though its editors spoke uncomfortably of a Zionism "bedeviled by Jewish nationalism."[64] On the solution of Palestine, however, *America* displayed a hard realism. Though a United Nations trusteeship was most preferable, the partition plan was considerably better than turning Palestine into an exclusively Jewish or Arab state. The fly in the ointment, giving non-Christians sovereignty over the Holy Land, was somehow anesthetized by the compromise plan of amputated states, which gave neither group all it had hoped for, and, most importantly, reserved Jerusalem and the holy places for the "rightful" owners.

> Fortunately, the UNSCOP report, and the solution adopted by the General Assembly, take into full consideration the religious aspect of the Palestine problem. This is due in part at least to the efforts of Catholics concerned with the problem.
>   The Holy Land will remain such, even if the United Nations have to oversee the protection of religious shrines and rights themselves. No constitution can be written for either of the proposed States which would jeopardize religious freedom or the sacred character of the Holy Land. Christians, who felt themselves left on the outside in a controversy concerning the land sanctified by Christ, can rejoice at this aspect of the U.N. solution.[65]

On April 24, 1948, *America* adopted a suggestion of one of its former editors, Fr. John O'Rourke, S.J., who was then director of the Pontifical Institute of Jerusalem. The paper designated May 15 as *dies* *fatalis.*⁶⁶ Optimism was overcast by forebodings and tremors, and even the veiled hope that the Jewish state would not materialize failed to prepare Catholics for May 15. The establishment of the State of Israel created a new reality which amounts to far more than just another chapter in Jewish history. As an event in Catholic-Jewish relations, its profound significance is still emerging.

V
New Realities: Israel in the Holy Land

A German nun, living in Jerusalem when the State of Israel was proclaimed, recently recalled: "I well remember our firm conviction that it would never come into being."[1] James O'Gara, an American Catholic journalist, echoed the same sentiments in an autobiographical essay in which he observed, "There are those who spread the myth that the Jews were condemned to wander through the world until the end of time—a myth so strong that many Christians feared that the establishment of the State of Israel contradicted the Sacred Scriptures."[2] The incredulity and consternation felt by Catholics, laymen and religious alike, was confirmed in a scholarly article by Fr. Edward Flannery. Indeed, shock was the most pervasive immediate reaction of Catholics to the Jewish state, and this shock was rooted in a theological assumption that the dispersion of the Jews was a divine punishment of perpetual duration.[3]

The impact of the new reality was neither tempered nor allayed by official statements of the Church. At this time, a full account of Vatican diplomacy vis-à-vis the new state is still not available, and one can only conjecture the reactions of leading Vatican circles on the basis of what was officially said and what remained unsaid. Nevertheless, it seems that the Vatican, too, was in a quandary. On the one hand, it did not cherish the idea of Palestine being engulfed again in the Moslem world, and on the other hand, it could not be happy with Jewish dominion over the Holy Land. Misgivings toward the former were rooted in a history of strife; discomfiture with the latter was enmeshed in theological sensitivities. At the same time, the Vatican could not easily disregard the repentant mood of the Christian world following the Holocaust, and oppose a Jewish state. Perforce, its policy veered toward a noncommittal silence. As late as two weeks before the proclamation of the state, a papal encyclical touching on the events then transpiring in Palestine made no mention of the two proposed states in the area. The Pope only expressed his "keen anxiety" for the safety of the holy places, and alluded with masterful vagueness to a just solution to the Palestinian strife.[4] In the later allocutions and encyclicals, the political entity of Israel was deliberately and consistently ignored. When the Pope wished to refer to the territory of Israel, he used the terms *Holy Land* or *Palestine*.[5] Nonrecognition surely did not indicate a positive attitude toward the state, but neither were there *official* statements of outright condemnation.

Taking its cue from the Vatican, the American hierarchy refrained from comment on the establishment of Israel. The diocesan press, likewise, reflected a pervasive hesitation and ambivalence. Most of the papers simply ignored the existence of Israel, with its connotations for Christendom, and narrowed their attention, as the Pope had done, solely to the fighting in Jerusalem and the danger to the holy places. The notable exceptions were those papers which had been openly hostile to Zionism in the pre-state period. The Brooklyn *Tablet,* for example, published a bitter attack on the state. Its editor denounced Israel for being a wholly secular, modern, and materialistic state which would respect neither God, nor Jesus, nor the "mementos of Christ." Concluding his censure of "modern Israel," Scanlon recommended that "Christians meanwhile, must pray that God deliver the Holy Land from the blind and the wicked who know not God."[6] *Sign*'s editor waited, but after the Bernadotte truce in June 1948, sanguine confidence in the ephemerality of Israel dwindled. The July issue of *Sign* carried abrasive criticism in its news comments, in a signed editorial by Ralph Gorman, and in an article by Kermit Roosevelt, then the executive director of the pro-Arab Committee for Justice and Peace in the Holy Land.[7] Gorman deplored the mistake of the United States in permitting a Jewish state to arise in Palestine, and the news editorial decried the lavish and complimentary coverage the "self-proclaimed" state was receiving in the press and on the radio. The paper chided Christians for hesitating to criticize Israel for fear of being labeled anti-Semites.[8] Also in July, the editor of *Catholic World* spoke up. Fr. Gillis lashed out against President Truman's "unholy haste" in recognizing the Jewish state in Palestine and condemned the "special pleading" which had brought about its establishment.[9]

It should be noted that following the President's recognition of Israel, the National Catholic News Service in Washington prepared a carefully worded statement which took cognizance of the fact without official comment. The release quoted, however, Senator Arthur Vandenberg's explanation of the President's action as a "logical and proper step," and readers were further informed that the new state's declaration promised to ensure religious equality and the safeguarding of the shrines.[10] Several days later, the NC-NS received bulletins from its Vatican bureau. These releases, quoting liberally from the *Osservatore Romano* and the Catholic Action daily, *Quotidiano*, denounced the fighting in the Holy Land as sacrilegious and blasphemous. While the *Osservatore* blamed Christians for "spiritually abandoning" the Holy Land, the *Quotidiano* urged the Church to take immediate action.[11] As the weeks went by, the reports streaming into the diocesan press reinforced the anxieties of the Vatican release, rather than the guarded assurances of the Washington release.

Resort to theological arguments in response to Israel was generally rare in the press. The associate editor of the *Catholic Worker* opened his May 1948 editorial with a subtle reminder that a Jewish state belongs to the "Old Dispensation," but developed the theme that the Dispensation of Jesus called for an end to "all national States as desirable entities."[12] Far more pointed was the opinion expressed in the monthly of the Catholic Central-Verein. The *Social Justice Review* turned to a Jewish convert to Catholicism for an assessment of the new state. In his article, David Goldstein emphatically denounced the validity of any theological claim to Palestine on the part of the Jews: "There was a time when such a Palestine claim was warranted; that was during the days when the Jewish religion was God's one and only religion. . . . That was when they were given the land for the purpose of carrying out Israel's divine mission. That mission they have no more."[13] Even the few papers which took cognizance of the state in more positive tones did so with ambivalent feelings. The papers, singled out in the previous chapter as not unfriendly to Jewish aspirations in the pre-state period, now assumed the stance of interrogators, some with barely veiled suspicions.

Typical of this distrust were the questions raised by an editorial in *Commonweal* on May 28. Entitled "In Exitu, Israel" as if it were a legal brief, the editor pummelled the new state with questions. Would Israel be able to curb its extremists? What would be its relationship to Russia? What were its expectations regarding boundaries? Explicit criticism of Israel, however, was confined to a Christian demurrer on the name of the state.

> As Catholics, Israel's arrogation of a universal name for so local an habitation must distress us. It is a good example of what Prof. Toynbee has called an archaizing tendency. Israel, for every Christian, is the whole redeemed world, and all peoples, since the Incarnation, are equally chosen in fulfillment of the prophecies to be heirs to the glory. Despite our sympathy for Israeli and Jew, we must not forget that to think of the Law and the Prophets as historically given only to their physical descendants, is a minimizing and a belittling of the greatest fact in history.[14]

America's first editorial on Israel began with yet another rehearsal of Arab versus Jewish claims to Palestine, but concluded,

> The recognition extended by seven governments to the new state is recognition of a fact: that the Jews have staked their claim and do not intend to abandon it. . . . The extermination or subjugation of Israel would not sit well with world opinion. And that again is a fact which should be recognized.[15]

Nonetheless, apprehensions for the safety of the holy places and the security of Christian missions in Arab lands lent a quavering tone to *America*'s support.

To sum up Catholic press reactions to the State of Israel, one may say that there are few discordant notes in what seemed to be an orchestrated response. The majority of the papers prudently adopted a "wait and see" attitude. Only those papers with well-known anti-Zionist biases were outspoken in opposition to the state, while the papers reputedly sympathetic to Zionism were less than enthusiastic. As the months wore on, reports from Catholic functionaries and observers in the Holy Land began filing into the press, and neutrality gave way.

By the first week of June 1948, Catholics in Jerusalem had lodged a number of protests against Israel. The first was in the form of a manifesto of the "Christian Union of Palestine." Drafted at the office of the Latin Patriarchate and signed by Catholic and non-Catholic clergy, the manifesto charged that three priests had been killed and fourteen Christian institutions destroyed or damaged "since the Jews began the attack." Moreover, the union claimed that the "largest part of the shells falling on the Holy Sepulchre and on churches, convents and Christian institutions are of Jewish origin." The same statement praised the Arabs for their reverence of the holy places and absolved them of all guilt in the war damages.[16] Despite the blatant misrepresentation of facts,[17] the manifesto received serious attention in the Catholic press.[18] Simultaneously, another statement of protest, signed only by the Catholic priests in Jerusalem, was sent to the Vatican and the United Nations. Over the signatures of Msgr. Michael Assaf, vicar general of the Greek Catholic patriarchate, Vicar James Ghergossian of the Armenian Catholic patriarchate, and Msgr. Alberto Gori, the Franciscan custos, the letter vigorously objected to Israeli military operations. Included in the protest was the sinister allegation that the Jewish purpose in attacking Jerusalem was "to plunder it as they had done in Haifa, Tiberias and Jaffa." Again, the Arabs were pardoned. "If they [the Arabs] have occupied a certain convent it was only to defend the Holy City against Jewish attackers who tried to penetrate and spread death and confusion. . . . if the Arabs shelled Notre Dame de France and the Convent of the Reparatrice Sisters . . . it was to return fire."[19]

Meanwhile, the Franciscans were agitating for the formation of an international militia to guard the shrines. As tensions mounted, over 1,000 applications were received daily by the Franciscan Delegazione di Terrasanta in Rome.[20] Although the plans for a militia dissipated, news from the Holy Land continued to sound ominous. Bro. Anthony Bruya, the NC-NS correspondent, kept the diocesan papers informed from Arab Jerusalem. Hardly a communique failed to report damages and desecrations.[21]

Alarm reached a peak in August 1948. Msgr. Antonio Vergani, vicar of the Latin Patriarchate for the Galilee, warned that the Jews may "start a continual expropriation of ecclesiastical properties which may have not small repercussions in the Christian world."[22] Msgr. Thomas McMahon promptly drafted a letter to the United Nations which quoted the Vergani accusations and referred, as well, to other reports from the Holy Land of maltreatment of Catholics and desecrations of the holy places. McMahon urged the United Nations to begin an immediate investigation and closed his letter on an admonitory note. "It is our considered opinion that if these overt acts continue or are explained by ascribing them constantly to irresponsible forces, then the entire Christian world is justified in its apprehension over the disregard of Christian spiritual and material interests in the newborn state of Israel."[23] The Israeli minister for religious affairs, Rabbi J. L. Fishman (Maimon), categorically denied the allegations that Israel intended to expropriate Church property. He ordered an immediate investigation of other alleged abuses and damages, and pledged severe punishment for all offenders. The Israeli army had already instituted drastic steps to enforce the security of Church property.[24]

To counteract possible anti-Jewish sentiments arising from these desecration charges, the American Jewish Committee, too, stepped into action. Its Community Service Division distributed a report, released by the Israeli Mission in Washington, which refuted exaggerated and unfounded accounts of vandalism. The same report included testimonials given by Catholic clergy and laymen in Israel praising the government's exemplary behavior toward Christians. Attached to the report was a memorandum of the Community Service Division urging that the information be made available to Catholic papers in local communities. Indeed, the report was sent to every diocesan weekly and national Catholic periodical.[25]

Even Vergani and McMahon eventually issued statements testifying that the Israeli troops treated Christians fairly, and that the Israeli government genuinely desired to repair the damages and maintain "proper" relations with the religious institutions.[26] Nevertheless, accusations discrediting Israel continued to appear in the press.[27] Hardly any attempt was made to balance the criticism of the Israelis with parallel criticism of Arab aggression or of continuing Arab threats and terrorism. Inevitably, a distorted, one-sided image of the new state was formed—that of Israel as the brute aggressor and Arabs and Christians as the innocent victims.[28]

In the early years following the establishment of Israel, American Catholic opinion crystallized around two specific issues: internationalization of Jerusalem, and the Arab refugee problem. Despite popular impressions to the contrary, internationalization was not originally a Vatican proposal. The idea of international territory in the Holy Land was first proposed by secular governments with rival interests in the Middle East. Soon after the outbreak of World War I, Sir Mark Sykes, a British orientalist, and Charles George-Picot, a former French consul in Beirut, prepared a draft agreement for the postwar disposition of the Ottoman Empire. Their proposed map provided that Palestine, west of the Jordan between Haifa and Gaza, be established as an "international administration." In the course of the war, this plan was superseded by other secret agreements, and the recommendation of an internationalized area did not reappear until 1937, when it was again suggested by a secular government.[29]

In conversations with the Vatican prior to the Balfour Declaration, the Zionist representative, Nahum Sokolow, suggested extraterritorialization of the holy places. Pope Benedict XV intimated that he would be satisfied if a charter would be drawn up assuring the protection of the holy sites, and he ungrudgingly gave his approval to a Jewish homeland in Palestine. Internationalization of the *city* of Jerusalem was not raised by the Pope.[30] Later when Benedict XV became apprehensive over the consequences of the Balfour pledge on the Holy Land, he was most explicit in his concern for Christian custody of the holy places. In his allocution of March 12, 1919, the Pope stated:

> But there is one matter on which We are most specially anxious and that is the fate of the Holy Places, on account of the special dignity and importance for which they are so venerated by every Christian. Who can ever tell the full story of all the efforts of Our Predecessors to free them from the dominion of infidels, the heroic deeds and the blood shed by the Christians of the West through the centuries? And now that, amid the rejoicing of all good men, they have finally returned into the hands of the Christians, Our anxiety is most keen as to the decisions which the Peace Congress at Paris is soon to take concerning them. For surely it would be a terrible grief for Us and for all the Christian faithful if infidels were placed in a privileged and prominent position; much more if those most holy sanctuaries of the Christian religion were given to the charge of non-Christians. . . .[31]

When the mandate was awarded to Great Britain in July 1922, the mandatory was directed to appoint a special commission "to study, define and determine the rights and claims relating to different religious communities in Palestine." The League left the details of the commission's structure and the nomination of its members to the mandatory, but made the final decision subject to the approval of the council.[32] Vatican objections to the British proposal are revealing of the Vatican's conception of its position in the Holy Land.

The British plan provided for three subcommissions, one Christian, one Moslem, and one Jewish. The chairman of the entire commission was to be an American Protestant, and if a disagreement could not be resolved in any subcommission, it would be referred to the American chairman for decision. The Vatican strongly opposed the plan for fear that (1) the Catholic members of the Christian subcommission would be outnumbered by other Christians not in communion with Rome, (2) the Christians would be overwhelmed by the Moslem-Jewish majority, and (3) the Protestant chairman would be endowed with an undue power of decision. The Vatican's preferred plan would have provided for a Catholic majority.[33] Since the council repeatedly failed to agree on the structure of the commission, the British authorities in Palestine assumed full responsibility in connection with the holy places and resigned themselves to a strict maintenance of the status quo.[34] The Vatican, anxiously guarding its inherited privileges in the holy places, offered no strenuous objections.

Special treatment for Jerusalem and Bethlehem was not again considered until a British Royal Commission recommended the partition of Palestine into sovereign Arab and Jewish states. As the Peel Commission explained, in its report of 1937, "The partition of Palestine is subject to the overriding necessity of keeping the sanctity of Jerusalem and Bethlehem inviolate. . . ." It was, therefore, recommended that these two cities and their environs, as well as a corridor to the sea, remain under permanent mandatory administration. The commission also added, "We think it would accord with Christian sentiment in the world at large if Nazareth and the Sea of Galilee (Lake Tiberias) were also covered by this Mandate."[35]

When the partition scheme was abandoned by a subsequent Royal Commission and supplanted by an arrangement for an eventual Palestinian state, constituting an Arab majority, the recommendation of a permanent mandate for Jerusalem-Bethlehem was not retained. Only the guarantees for the safety of the holy places and freedom of access were included.[36] It was not until the United Nations resurrected the proposal of separate Jewish and Arab states that the question of Jerusalem surfaced again.

The majority plan of the United Nations Special Committee on Palestine (UNSCOP) divided the country into three units: an Arab state, a Jewish state, and the city of Jerusalem. The latter territory was to be placed, after a transitional period, under an international trusteeship system.[37] It is interesting to note that during the UNSCOP hearings, held from June to July 1947, the representative of the custos of the Holy Land, Bro. Bonaventure Simon, refrained from endorsing an international regime for Jerusalem. He addressed his concern solely to the holy places and implied a preference for a Western Commission, designed along the lines of a "protector" system, similar in role to that of France during the Ottoman period.[38] In the modification of the majority plan by the Ad Hoc Committee on Palestine, the city of Jerusalem was designated a *corpus separatum*, with a statute to be detailed and approved by the Trusteeship Council. The governor, who would be neither Arab nor Jew, was to be appointed by, and responsible to, the Trusteeship Council.[39] This latter scheme of territorial internationalization, incorporated in the majority plan, was adopted by the General Assembly on November 29, 1947. No official approval came from Rome. Yet it seems that the Vatican preferred the majority plan, which included the internationalization of Jerusalem, and in discreet diplomatic activity let that preference be known.[40]

The announcement of the United Nations decision on partition inflamed the Arab world and set off a new wave of explosive violence in Palestine. Jerusalem was attacked on January 3, 1948. On May 1, on the eve of a rumored truce for the walled city, the Pope issued an encyclical, *Auspicia Quaedam,* in which he spoke of his "keen anxiety" for the safety of the holy places. After extolling Palestine as the land which should be "most dear to every cultured person" because of its association with the life and martyrdom of Jesus, he asked the following: "We desire, therefore, Venerable Brethren, that supplications be poured forth to the Most Holy Virgin for this request: that the situation in Palestine may at long last be settled justly and thereby concord and peace be also happily established."[41] The ambiguous phrase "settled justly" is nowhere explicated, and the Pope's words contain no clearly stated advocacy for the internationalization of Jerusalem. The uneasy truce of May 2 fell apart on May 15, when full-scale war broke out in the Holy Land. By June 2, when another truce was being arranged for Jerusalem, the Arabs still held an advantageous military position in the city. Just a few days earlier (May 29), the Jewish Quarter had succumbed.[42] During the night of June 1, the Pope received word of the Israeli acceptance of a cease-fire, and the next day he addressed the College of Cardinals on "la guerra in Palestina." Again the Pope made no specific mention of internationalization for the war-ravaged city, although he intimated that the Christian world would not "look on with indifference or with barren indignation while the Holy Land . . . is still being trodden by troops at war and subject to air bombardments."[43] Concerning the holy places, the Pope displayed increasing anxiety, precipitated perhaps by the May 31 manifesto of the "Christian Union" and the letter from the Catholic priests in Jerusalem detailing the damage to churches and institutions. "We do not believe that it [the Christian world] could allow the devastation of the Holy Places to become complete, the great "Sepulchre of Christ" to become destroyed. May it be God's will that the peril of this horrendous scourge be finally dispelled."[44] Several days before this allocution, the United Nations mediator, Count Folke Bernadotte, in a conversation with French Foreign Minister Bidault, revealed his plan for incorporating Jerusalem in the Arab state. Even after June 28, when Bernadotte's recommendation was officially delivered to the United Nations, the Pope made no plea for internationalization.[45] It was not until October 1948 that the Vatican openly and specifically espoused the United Nations plan. By then, there was good reason to fear that the temporary division of the city, with Israel in control of West Jerusalem, would harden into a permanent arrangement. In the encyclical *In Multiplicibus,* Pius XII stated,

> We are confident that these supplications and hopes, indicative of the value which such a large number of people attribute to the Holy Places, will deepen the conviction in the high assemblies in which the problem of peace is being discussed that it would be expedient, as a better guarantee for the safety of the sanctuaries under the present circumstances, to give an international character to Jerusalem and its vicinity. . . .
> It is also necessary to assure with international guarantees both the right of free access to the Holy Places scattered throughout Palestine and the freedom of religion and the respect for customs and religious traditions.[46]

Several months later, the Pope found it necessary to issue yet another encyclical on internationalization. Since the United Nations had failed to implement its proposal on Jerusalem, the Palestine Conciliation Commission was authorized by the General Assembly to draw up a new plan which would take into account the changed circumstances in the city since the hostilities of May 1948. The commission, therefore, was entertaining suggestions which would provide maximum local autonomy for Jordan and Israel. On April 7, 1949, the Israeli government informed the commission that it would be willing to concede to a functional internationalization (i.e., international control of the holy places), though it remained adamant on the point of territorial internationalization.[47] One week later, Pius XII issued the encyclical *Redemptoris Nostri,* which restated Vatican demands for full territorial internationalization, and furthermore, exhorted Roman Catholics to pressure their respective governments to support this plan. The intensity and urgency of the papal appeal is extraordinary.

> We have already insisted in Our Encyclical letter "In Multiplicibus," that the time has come when Jerusalem and its vicinity . . . should be accorded and legally guaranteed an "international" status, which in the present circumstances seems to offer the best and most satisfactory protection for these sacred monuments.
> We cannot help repeating here the same declaration. . . . Let them, wherever they are living, use every legitimate means to persuade the rulers of nations, and those whose duty it is to settle this important question, to accord to Jerusalem and its surroundings a juridical status. . . .
> Encourage the faithful committed to your charge to be ever more concerned about the conditions in Palestine and have them make their lawful requests known, positively and unequivocally, to the rulers of nations.[48]

U.S. Catholics responded. The American hierarchy drew up a statement on April 27 which reiterated the plea of Pius XII. Cardinal Cushing spoke out forcefully on the issue at a mass rally in Boston's Fenway Park. The entire Catholic press, both diocesan and national, carried the papal pronouncement, and some appended editorials and articles reemphasizing the Vatican view.[49] With Cardinal Spellman in command, diplomatic activity centered in New York City.[50]

Among Cardinal Spellman's monsignori, the most influential exponent of internationalization was the executive secretary of the Catholic Near East Welfare Association, Msgr. Thomas McMahon. During a visit to Israel in the winter of 1948–49, McMahon gave the impression of having other duties than the official charitable mission on which he came.[51] In fact, the Israeli Ministry for Religious Affairs had opened negotiations with him prior to his visit, and a member of the ministry referred to him as an "unofficial representative of the Holy See on political matters." Confirming this impression, Pius XII told James G. McDonald that he hoped McMahon would be able to work out a settlement with the Israeli government.[52] Indeed, McMahon may have been responsible for more than just implementing papal directives; he may have been instrumental in formulating the Catholic position on internationalization and in securing Vatican backing for his views.

McMahon's position on internationalization rested on concepts which went beyond the rubrics of freedom of access and safety of the holy places. He insisted on the need for the full restoration and growth of the Christian population in Jerusalem in order to save the shrines from becoming mere "museum pieces." Jerusalem must develop into a vital center of Christianity. Only territorial internationalization would provide the atmosphere for the growth of a Christian population large enough to support such a center. Anything less than full territorial internationalization would compromise the Christian stake in the Holy Land, as McMahon understood it.[53]

In September 1949 the Conciliation Commission forwarded to the secretary-general its draft for Jerusalem. According to the commission's plan, Jerusalem would be divided into two zones, an Arab zone administered by Jordan, and a Jewish zone administered by Israel. The protection of the holy places would be the responsibility of the United Nations commissioner, and a system of international courts would deal with questions involving the holy places. The plan was neither fully territorial nor fully functional in its approach to internationalization. On the first day of the United Nations debate, the Australian representative introduced a draft resolution to reaffirm the territorial internationalization provisions of the 1947 partition plan. The Vatican radio commended the Australian resolution, and all Catholic action was channeled in its support.[54] Perhaps the most heralded effort was made by Cardinal Spellman, who was later credited with garnering crucial Latin American votes in support of the Australian resolution.[55] In the final vote, on December 9, 1949, the General Assembly rejected the Conciliation Commission's plan for Jerusalem and reaffirmed full territorial internationalization. The Vatican hailed the vote, but the implementation of the decision was again thwarted by Jordanian and Israeli opposition. By the spring of 1950, the resolution was paralyzed by a stalemate in the General Assembly.[56]

Official Catholic persistence in calling for the implementation of territorial internationalization continued unabated. In the United States, the campaign was waged by the Jesuit weekly *America* and by the articulate spokesman for the CNEWA, Msgr. McMahon, who asserted that "Come what may through the politics of *fait accompli* and the ineptitude of the U.N., the Church and churchmen have by no means abdicated their just right to demand their stake in the Holy Land of Jesus Christ."[57] *America*'s editors were ever on the alert to call attention to the unrequited claim of Christianity. Time and again the paper urged the United Nations to implement its decision, even advising that sanctions be imposed to force compliance. Editorials reminded Truman of his campaign pledge to support internationalization, and both Christians and Jews were criticized for praising Israel as long as it did not abide by the United Nations order.[58] One editorial even went so far as to draw a macabre analogy: ". . . the World Jewish Congress insisted that the graves of Nazi concentration-camp victims should not be entrusted exclusively to Germans—so, too, shrines of Christians cannot be entrusted exclusively to Jews and Arabs."[59] Apprehensions lessened somewhat as the Israeli government took effective action to eliminate causes of complaint. Access to Christian shrines in Israeli territory was open, incidents of desecration were rare, and the Israeli government was paying reparations for the damages.[60] Though the official Catholic stand on internationalization remained unchanged,[61] the crusading spirit in the press ebbed. Critical reactions to Israel now turned largely on the second issue, the Arab refugees.

The Arab refugee problem can hardly be described objectively. Its history is enmeshed in polemic, news reports are charged with emotion, and most evaluations tend to disintegrate into political-moral debates. However, in order to place the Catholic response in a reasonable perspective, it is important to briefly review the "facts" and the range of their interpretation.

On the origin of the problem Arabs and Jews differ. The Arab view claims that the Jews drove out the Palestinian Arab by use of force, terror, and intimidation. The Arabs point to the Deir Yassin incident as a confirmation of Israeli guilt and responsibility.[62] The Israeli counterclaim maintains that though the Jews wished to govern their United Nations–approved state in peaceful coexistence with the Arabs, the neighboring Arab countries invaded Israeli territory from all sides. Arab nationalist leaders encouraged, and even ordered, native Arabs to leave their homes to make room for the invading armies, while assuring the fleeing Arabs a speedy return to a wholly Arab country.[63]

A dispassionate study of the problem reveals that the leaders of the Jewish state neither planned nor anticipated the Arab exodus. Much of the mass flight was voluntary, although sociological and psychological factors inhering in the 1948 situation contributed enormously to a contagious flight psychosis. Not the least of these factors was the collapse of Arab morale, the absence of native Arab leadership, and the hysteria which fed on increasing Israeli military victories. Based on the precedents of Arab warfare, the Palestinian Arabs could expect nothing less than massacres if the Jews were victorious, and an isolated incident gave credence to such fears.[64]

The United Nations struggled with the refugee problem for many years. The numerous commissions and plans attest to the complexity of the problem.[65] The first solution attempted was repatriation. Of interest is the initial Arab reaction to this proposal. Until 1949 the Arabs were opposed to repatriation, reasoning that it implied a recognition of the state and a reminder of their inability to dislodge the Israelis. In contrast, the Israeli government had no fixed position concerning the problem.[66] The tables were reversed after the signing of the armistice treaties in the spring of 1949. Now the Arabs demanded repatriation, while the Israelis moved toward categorical rejection.[67] The United Nations then turned to schemes of resettlement of refugees in Arab states, where their absorption would not only be economically feasible, but also beneficial to the host countries. These programs met with steadfast opposition from the Arab states. Even small-scale work-relief programs failed for lack of cooperation.[68] Unsolved, the problem remains a festering sore in the Middle East.

The Catholic Church took an early interest in the refugees. It prided itself on having preceded the United Nations in care and relief activities.[69] In the United States, the New York–based CNEWA played a very prominent role in this charitable work. In August 1948, Archbishop Arthur Hughes, papal internuncio to Egypt, appealed for large-scale relief funds for the refugees. He sent one telegram to the Vatican and the other to Cardinal Spellman. In less than a month, Spellman dispatched $50,000 from CNEWA and another $25,000 from the War Relief Services of the NCWC.[70] Shipments of food, clothing, and other supplies followed. At the Bishops Conference in November 1948, McMahon was authorized to go to the Holy Land as special representative of the American hierarchy, in order to investigate the needs of the Arab refugees and to disburse $75,000 of Emergency Relief funds. By January 1949, the diocesan press was printing appeals by McMahon to "adopt holy towns like Nazareth." McMahon returned in March, as the papers said, "Weeping at What He Saw." His report stimulated a Bishops Emergency Drive, which made a nationwide appeal for funds on March 27, at the Laetare Sunday Mass.[71]

Whether by design or inadvertently, the Catholic press presented the refugee problem largely from the Arab perspective. Phrases such as "driven out," "forced to flee," "brutally uprooted," left no doubt that the guilt lay solely with the Jews.[72] Reports detailed the misery and deplorable living conditions of the refugees, but failed to note the reluctance of the Arab states to make any provisions for their kinsmen. It was the human-interest angle, the emotional tug of the story, that seized the attention of the press, while the political background of offers and counter-offers went unheeded. More telling than the contents of the stories were the analogies employed. In some papers the Israelis were likened to the Nazis, in others to Titus and a string of tyrants; and in still others the Arab "expulsion" was paralleled hypothetically to "shipping off all U.S. Negroes to Portugal."[73] A typical conclusion was that of the syndicated weekly, *Our Sunday Visitor:* "Israel is a state that should not exist. How can it have God's blessing, how can it flourish when it is founded on the robbery of the 900,000 innocent people?"[74] Opposition to Jewish nationalism could now be legitimately couched in moralistic terms, and there was, indeed, a high correlation between earlier denunciations of Zionism and present moral indignation.

Only a small percentage of the refugees were Catholic, yet Catholics plunged wholeheartedly into relief efforts. Over 2,000 priests and nuns ministered to their needs in refugee camps.[75] Without questioning the humanitarian impulse which inspired these efforts, for Christian missionaries have always been involved in humanitarian causes in all parts of the world, one may ask if there were other motivating factors. McMahon's own words are suggestive. "For the Catholic effort in this humanitarian endeavor illustrates the fact that the Palestine problem is not bipartite but tripartite. There is a Christian stake in the Holy

Land."[76] It did the Church no harm to give visibility to its claim of historical and contemporary interest in Palestine.

Of at least equal importance was the concern of the Vatican for the safety of Catholic minorities in the Middle East. The precariousness of the position of these minorities was heightened during crises or periods of intense nationalism, when Arab was frequently equated with Moslem.[77] Moreover, Christian communities were afraid of being identified with the Western countries which supported Israel. For fear of reprisals, many Christians sought to outdo the Moslems in support of the Arab cause.[78] The solicitude of the Vatican for the Arab refugees, regardless of religion, could serve effectively to demonstrate Catholic solidarity with the Arab cause. In June 1949, Pius XII set up the Pontifical Mission for Palestine to consolidate and strengthen worldwide Catholic relief efforts in the Middle East. McMahon was appointed president of the mission, and in his report of November 1951, he announced that the Pontifical Mission had already expended ten million dollars in aid for the Palestinian refugees.[79] The magnanimity of the Church was both commendable and expedient.

To question the legitimacy and justness of a Jewish state may also have appeared as a necessity, a theological necessity. Theologians were faced with the obvious dilemma of how to fit the unexpectedly renascent Israel into Christian doctrine and eschatology.[80] And on the practical level, there were difficulties in preserving the atmosphere of a pilgrim's Holy Land in the technologically progressive and secular Jewish state.

As theologians tried to come to grips with Israel, reinterpretations evolved. At the outset, though, a conservatively traditional assessment dominated Catholic thinking. This approach assigned no positive role to modern Israel. It looked upon the state as a secular aberration, potentially inimical to Christianity. Jewish control over the Holy Land could not be lasting, for the land was promised to the "spiritual sons of Abraham," the *verus Israel,* which is the Christian Church.[81] Invoking Romans 9:6, "They are not all Israelites who are sprung from Israel," Msgr. Matthew Smith, editor of the *Register,* explained, "Therefore the present Zionist state can have nothing spiritual to contribute to the world, and on Biblical grounds it has not [sic] right to the

Holy Land. If God has given any group a mandate to occupy the country, it is the Christians. . . ."⁸² Speculations on the eschatological significance of the Jewish state were not lacking. *Pilot* adjured its readers to view the events and the war in the Holy Land "as something vastly different" from similar political events elsewhere, and mused upon the likelihood of its bringing about the Second Coming.⁸³ In line with a popular belief that the state was inherently evil, some even subscribed to the view that it would beget the Antichrist.

> There is an old legend, accepted by many Christian Fathers, that the Antichrist will be of Jewish descent and from the tribe of Dan, that he will be circumcised, will rebuild Jerusalem and the Temple, in which he will set himself up as God. Likewise, he will begin his seduction among the Jews, who will accept him as the Messiah.⁸⁴

Rev. Edward A. Cerny, in a presidential address to the Catholic Biblical Society, also spoke of the "messianic" implications of the new state. "Perhaps it is too early to say," he admitted, "but we cannot help taking notice. The question is already being put to us by our pupils." Cerny observed that there were two possible explanations for Israel's functioning again, "at least temporarily," as a nation. Either it was Divine Providence to bring back Israel to her ancient homeland as a "preliminary to that conversion and to her ultimate incorporation into the Church where she is destined to play a glorious part before the end," or it is that "*an* Antichrist, if not *the* Antichrist expected before the end, is already operating in Israel."⁸⁵

The first possibility found echoes in other voices. *Catholic Word* printed a sermon contending that the political renascence would usher in a new era of conversion. Articles reiterating this expectation appeared in influential American Catholic journals with large clerical readership.⁸⁶ An in-depth theological development was assayed by a French Dominican theologian, Yves Congar.⁸⁷ In his view, modern Israel was a stage in the fulfillment of the final promise. Political restoration was necessary in order to bring into the Holy Land a representative cross-section of the entire Jewish people, who would ultimately find, in the disappointing realities of return, the way to Jesus. The "realities" which would jar Judaism from its complacency would be the disparity between statehood and the messianic vision of the prophets, the difficulty of adapting the "laws of Moses" to a modern state, and the complications that would arise with the rebuilding of the Temple. All of these problems would force the Jews into "a blind alley of grace," that is, Jews would recognize Christianity as the only solution. The new state, then, had a "positive" mission, although the generosity of Congar and the theologians who espoused the same idea sprung from their expectations of Jewish conversion.[88] It was not until after Vatican II, when ecumenical-minded theologians began to recognize the validity of post-Christian Judaism, that an appreciation of the Jewish state, apart from missiological connotations, could emerge.

Preservation of the Christian *image* of the Holy Land was the practical problem which troubled Catholics. Not fundamental theologically, it nevertheless exerted a considerable psychological force. For Christians, the importance of the land lies primarily in its religious memories. It is the birthplace of Jesus, the land of his ministry, and the place of his martyrdom. The excitement of the land is not in its present, but in its past. Although some churches have invested heavily in establishing religious and eleemosynary institutions, the Holy Land is still primarily a place of shrines, and all Christian efforts on its behalf have been to safeguard these sacred places and to provide access to them for pilgrims. The pilgrim who comes to venerate these sites, consecrated through their association with the life of Jesus and his apostles, wants to find them in their first-century setting. He wants to be able to experience the land of the Bible and the Gospels.

Not so the Jews. While they, too, have numerous biblical and post-biblical recollections which endow the land with a sacredness, the land, in and of itself, is venerated as the home of the Jewish nation. The land is part of an ongoing and pulsating national life. The ties of the people are to its climate, to its soil, and to its growth. The country, which served a glorious past, lives very much in the present, with great expectations for the future. Therefore, technological development enhances the land for the Jews, while for the Christians, development is an intrusion which disfigures its essence. The pilgrim wants to recapture the presence of Christ's time, not a modern, bustling country! Understandably, pilgrim sympathies tend to be with the Arabs who (unwittingly) preserved that life, rather than with the Jews who (unwittingly) disturbed that image.[89] Pilgrim literature reverberates with the longing for a pilgrim's Palestine. Happy is the visitor who can write, "The Holy Land, for the most part, has changed little since the time of Christ. . . . shepherds still roam the fields, oxen still pull the plows, the fisherman's nets can still be seen drying on the shores . . . . the colorful garb of the natives provide genuine biblical atmosphere."[90]

The decade that followed the establishment of Israel brought with it an alleviation of some of the antagonisms felt toward the new state. In part, this was due to Israel's own efforts. In larger part, it was due to events outside Israel. A not insignificant factor in creating the change in perspective was the political upheaval in neighboring countries in the Middle East. The relative security of Christian institutional and personal life in Israel, vis-à-vis the growing insecurity of Catholics in Arab countries subject to leftist coups, bears close watching in the next chapter of Catholic-Israeli relations.

VI

Reassessments: The Factors of Communism and Ecumenism

Looking at the political configuration of the postwar world, American Catholics found the expansion of Soviet power alarming. For Catholics, the Communist ideology was no mere political philosophy, but a veritable Antichrist movement, dedicated to the destruction of Christianity. From its very inception, communism had declared itself hostile to religion in general, and to institutionalized religion in particular. Since this hostility manifested itself both in theory and in practice, Communist persecution of the Church had been of grave concern to Catholics ever since the success of the Bolshevik revolution.[1]

After World War II these apprehensions intensified as Communist governments were established in Europe and the Far East. Hungary, Romania, Czechoslovakia, Poland, and the Baltic States, all with large Catholic populations, were drawn into the Russian orbit. France and Italy harbored huge blocs of Communist voters. The Italian Communist party, aided by Marxist left-wing socialists, became the largest Communist party in the West. Catholicism in Europe saw itself besieged. It was gripped by the fear of the enemy at the gate.

For American Catholics, too, the climate of the Cold War had turned hot by the 1950s. The Korean conflict actively involved U.S.

military forces. On the home front, Senator Joseph R. McCarthy's "investigations" exposed Communist infiltration within the government itself. Scores of pamphlets and books, written by Catholics, warned of the imminent dangers of communism. The utmost vigilance was necessary to prevent the spread of this menace to all parts of the globe. Catholic assessments of international affairs were thus colored by the conflict between the West and the Soviet Bloc.[2]

Even before the end of the Second World War, Russian designs in the Middle East were evident. In 1945 Stalin demanded joint management of the Turkish Straits and encouraged the dismemberment of Iran.[3] Though these early Soviet advances were repulsed, the threat of future forays was pervasive. For Catholics, then, the friends in the Middle East were those nations which could be counted upon to resist the inroads of communism. Based on the conservative premise that secularism and liberalism were the natural incubators of communism and religion its natural enemy, the Moslem countries were expected to provide a natural bulwark against the forces of irreligion. The formation of an Islamic-Christian front was suggested, on the assumption that both, as natural enemies of communism, could work together to stem the tide.[4]

There was, however, one breach in the Middle East, and that was Israel. Epithets of "atheist," "socialist," and "communist" were long associated with the Jewish settlers in Palestine. Soviet support of the partition scheme in the United Nations and the precipitate recognition of Israel by the USSR seemed to confirm these charges. If any doubt of a Communist foothold in Israel remained, it was dispelled by the arrival from Moscow of a new archimandrite for the Russian Orthodox Church in the Holy Land. Until then the Russian Orthodox clergy in Jerusalem had been implacably hostile to the Communist government in Russia. Archimandrite Leonid came to Israel in November 1948, right on the heels of the establishment of the state—or so it seemed. Leonid's intimacy with the Soviet minister to Israel, Ivanovich Yershov, and his frequent appearances at official Israeli functions, led many to believe that he was a tool of Soviet policy. Even more incriminating was the passage of a Knesset bill in 1949, which gave the USSR full control over all Russian mission property in the state. In contrast to her Arab neighbors, Israel appeared to be, at best, a porous barrier to communism. At worst, she was a breeding ground of dangerous left-wing developments.[5]

The Czech-Egyptian arms deal of 1955 jolted these assumptions. For the next four years, confidence in an Arab bastion against communism suffered a series of disappointments, while Israel became firmly attached to the Western cause. Actually it was only after Stalin's death in 1953 that the Soviet Union began to woo the Arabs. The first steps in that direction were taken in the United Nations Security Council in 1954, when Soviet diplomacy began to champion the Arab cause and to posture as protector of the Arabs. With the consummation of the Czech arms deal with Egypt in 1955, Soviet prestige in the Middle East received a tremendous boost. The following year Syria and Yemen, as well as Moslem (but non-Arab) Afghanistan, added their names to the growing list of the USSR's military clients in the area. Later that year, during the Suez crisis, the USSR openly sided with Egypt against Britain and France. From that point on Soviet-Arab friendship became even more intimate, and trade agreements, loans, and technical assistance further enlarged the Soviet presence in the Arab world. In 1958, when a radical military coup overthrew the Western-oriented monarchy in Iraq, a development which was seen as a direct threat to Lebanon and Jordan, the Western powers finally reacted. The United States landed marines in Lebanon, while Britain flew troops into Jordan. Yet these Western counteractions were short-lived. They failed to stem the Soviet penetration of the Middle East.[6]

At the same time revolutionary coups and uprisings punctuated the internal situation of the Arab states. This tumultuous decade did not leave the Catholic minorities in the Arab countries undisturbed. Catholics in the Middle East were well aware of the handicaps attached to any Western allegiance. Even though most of the Catholics in these minority communities were Arabs, the stigma of Western imperialism was easily attached to them because of their religious ties to Rome, and further accentuated by the presence of clergy, missionaries, and teachers from Western countries. Anti-Western feelings were intensified after 1948, when Arab opinion blamed the West for the establishment of Israel. It was therefore considered a wise policy, even for foreign Catholics residing in the Middle East, to become "de-westernized" by full integration into the national life of Arab countries. Pius XII, in his missionary encyclical of June 1951 (*Evangelii praecones*), supported the necessity for such a policy when he exhorted the foreign missionary to seek the advantage of his adopted country and tender it exclusive patriotism.[7] Father G. C. Anawati, who reputedly maintained excellent relations with the Naguib and Nasser governments in Egypt, conceded in his study of Catholic communities in the Middle East that in certain Arab countries, Egypt among them, Catholics suffered from the social and economic upheavals. However, Anawati blamed those Catholics who were frightened by the trend of revolution for being "too much westernized," and therefore unduly upset by reforms which seemed too totalitarian and too socialist for their tastes.[8] In the aftermath of the 1956 Anglo-French Suez intervention, Catholic communities were rocked by waves of anti-Western agitation. Though legislative restrictions and discriminatory acts occurred only sporadically, a growing uneasiness and uncertainty developed over the future of the Catholic communities in Arab lands.[9]

Christian life in Israel, however, was less bleak than expected. Although the mass exodus of Arabs in 1948 depleted the Christian population considerably, the Catholic Churches emerged as the most substantial group.[10] The Roman Catholic Church maintained over 100 churches, schools, hospices, and eleemosynary institutions in Israel.[11] Contrary to early premonitions of hardship or even persecution in a Jewish land, Christians found the Israeli government sensitive and, more often than not, responsive to their day-to-day needs.

The Israeli Ministry of Religious Affairs set up a special Department for Christian Communities, whose first task was to extend effective aid and protection to the Christian population, its sanctuaries and religious life. The most serious complaints facing the new state in 1948 were in regard to damage to Christian churches and institutions resulting from the war, and the occupation of ecclesiastical properties by the military. Even before the question of reparations was settled, of its own accord the government carried out repairs and renovations in over twenty churches and institutions. By November 1955 all outstanding claims of the Roman Catholic Church in Israel were settled. Restitution of ecclesiastical property was also carried out with relative dispatch, twenty of the thirty buildings having been restored to their owners within a year after hostilities ended. The remainder of the buildings, for which rents were paid by the Israeli government, were returned as soon as security permitted.[12]

Insofar as the legal status of the Christian communities was concerned, the new state retained the *millet* system of the Ottoman and mandate periods. Under this system, recognized religious communities enjoyed internal autonomy and the right to adjudicate on matters of personal status. Attention to the specific needs of the churches and their adherents was expressed by the government in a number of ways. Travel restrictions, an onerous but necessary security measure, were lifted for priests and religious personnel, and entry permits for priests from Arab countries (particularly from Jordan) were issued to hundreds of ecclesiastics. Holy places were not only safeguarded by the government, but the custodians also received assistance in keeping the shrines in proper repair. In all government schools in which there were Christian pupils, catechists to provide religious training were appointed by the churches concerned and paid by the government. Though Saturday was ordained as the official day of rest in Israel, Christians were specifically authorized to observe Sunday and all Church holidays as their days of rest. The Israeli radio station, Kol Yisrael, broadcast Christian religious services on major holidays, and every Sunday afternoon provided a program of church music and sermons.[13]

Of course, one must be careful not to infer from the optimistic picture drawn by the Israeli government's Department for Christian Communities that an idyllic situation existed for Christians in Israel. Far from it. Complaints were indeed heard and openly voiced. These ranged from problems of a civic nature arising from the uncertain position of Christian Arabs in Israeli society, to specific church issues, such as Christian missionary efforts.[14] Nevertheless, the situation as it evolved was far better than anticipated in 1948, and by 1955 it offered more possibilities for the future.

While the shadows of communism were moving away from the Jewish state, they fell ever more ominously on neighboring Arab countries. And while the future of Christianity in Israel seemed to grow brighter, the prospects in Arab countries, particularly those undergoing revolutionary upheavals, grew dimmer. To what extent, then, did this changing scene influence American Catholic attitudes toward Israel?

In the period from 1955 to 1958 an interesting pattern of responses emerged. The press had been generally unsympathetic or critical of Israel in the preceding decade. Now another viewpoint was emerging. The uniformity of American Catholic opinion was split, and though the two viewpoints were not always in juxtaposition, they were divergent.

It would be incorrect to label the new attitude "pro-Israel"; it was, rather, a tolerance of Israel which stemmed from an increasingly negative reaction to political developments in certain Arab countries. Some papers, however, exhibited within this framework of response more positive support of Israel. Salient among these papers was the syndicated diocesan weekly, the *Register*, which was the official publication for thirty-two dioceses.[15]

Accusations against Israel had appeared frequently in the *Register* during the first few years of the state. Msgr. Matthew Smith, the editor, once even speculated on a possible connection between the Antichrist and the restored Jewish polity.[16] A change in opinion was first noticeable in 1955. In an editorial written by the managing editor, Paul H. Hallett, Islamic nationalism was censured as "one of the most disheartening things that have occurred in this stormy twentieth century." Among the objectionable actions of Islam, Hallett counted the provocations of the Arab League "against the tiny State of Israel." He also criticized Egyptian pressure on the Sudanese to withdraw subsidies from Christian schools and the spread of Egyptian propaganda fomenting hatred against the West.[17] Immediately following the Suez War of 1956, Hallett rose to the defense of Israel. Although he conceded that "technically" Israel was the aggressor in the conflict, Nasser and his "Moslem confederates" were equally to blame. Furthermore, he warned that Christendom, as well as Jewry, would suffer extinction in the Middle East if the Arab League reigned supreme. "Among all her neighbors in the Middle East, Israel is by far the nearest to a free society. . . . Nothing in the Arab world can match Israel for literacy, health standards, stability, living standards. . . ."[18]

Two weeks later, Hallett again praised Israel for her courageous fight for survival against the Arabs, "who have never ceased their depredations." In a resounding affirmation of Israel's right to existence, the *Register* declared, "Although territorially minute, Israel has the potential to become a major bulwark of Western civilization in the struggle we are now waging with the Communist empire."[19]

In contrast, the only other syndicated diocesan weekly, *Our Sunday Visitor*, remained firm in its anti-Israel stand. When the paper published a particularly virulent editorial against Israel in March 1956, however, a deluge of protesting mail induced the paper to print "Another View," which was a full-page encomium on the accomplishments of the State of Israel. Several months later, when the Suez War broke out, *Our Sunday Visitor* significantly refrained from editorializing on the conflict.[20]

While not converting to a pro-Israel view as did the *Register*, the journal of the Catholic Central-Verein, *Social Justice Review*, also contended that the combination of Islam, communism, and nationalism constituted the greatest threat to the Middle East. A noted Catholic commentator on the international scene, Richard Pattee, was quoted as saying:

> For some time after I had been in the Middle East I thought that perhaps there was some basis for the hope that Moslems and Christians, both believers in God, might find a common ground, not in dogma, but in action against the adversary of both who believes in no God at all and in no human dignity. Three months in Africa have convinced me of the contrary: that Islam is a powerful and dangerous foe as it was centuries ago. . . .[21]

Ave Maria was also very uneasy over the advances of communism in the Middle East, but its editor, John Reedy, did not feel that this concern need imply any support for Israel. In fact, Reedy took pains to point out that anti-Zionism was not anti-Semitism and, as such, was not reprehensible. One could think that "the establishment of an Israeli State in Palestine in the particular circumstances of our day was unwise and even unjust."[22] Reedy was jolted, though, by the events of July 1958, when the Iraqi monarchy toppled and there was talk of "international communism" sweeping across the Middle East. In his August editorial, Reedy looked more benignly upon Israel, and even summoned the Arabs to recognize the state. "In the morass of problems that make up the Middle East situation, the stubborn refusal of the Arab nations to admit that Israel does exist as a world recognized state presents the most exasperating difficulty."[23]

For other Catholic papers, however, analysis of the new political realities only reinforced their negative feelings about Israel. According to their view, if Arab governments were drifting toward leftist or radical leadership, it was the duty of the West to accelerate and expand its efforts to win back Arab friendship. It was taken for granted that U.S.-Arab relations had deteriorated on the issue of Israel. Therefore, improved relations would require a reversal of U.S. policy toward the Jewish state. All troubles in the Middle East were traced to the West's frustration of Arab nationalist aims in Palestine. And Christianity, which was identified with the West, also shared in the blame. "The great symbol of Christian arrogance in Moslem eyes was the imposition of the Jews in the Moslem world, and that, for which Americans and British are both responsible, remains the fundamental obstacle to any reconciliation."[24] Most papers, however, stopped short of demanding the extinction of Israel as the ultimate solution.

A more extreme view was taken by the journal of the religious order of Passionist Fathers, the *Sign*. The outspoken hostility of its editor, Father Ralph Gorman, C.P., was noted in the preceding chapters. He remained implacably and vehemently opposed to Israel throughout his long period of editorship, which lasted until 1967.[25] In Gorman's writings, personal biases and theological convictions mixed explosively on the topic of Israel. Gorman attributed his sensitivity to Palestinian problems to the fond memories of his student years (1925–28) spent in the Dominican Ecole Biblique in Jerusalem. In a sentimental editorial of 1957, he recalled these personal experiences of his first encounter with Palestine. What a contrast were those wonderful years of study in Jerusalem, when he "scarcely met a Jew," to the distressing conditions he found on his return in 1953, when the entire country "has been taken over by the invaders."[26] The conservative theology, with which Gorman identified himself, could hardly make him feel kindly toward the Jews. He never tired of insisting that the Gospel condemnation of the guilt of the Jews for the crucifixion of Jesus was an historic truth not to be minimized. He made no secret of his concern that Pope John XXIII and Vatican II's deliberations might lead to a "watering down of essential beliefs."[27]

Precisely timing editorials on the iniquities of the State of Israel during the Easter season, *Sign* waged both a political and a theological attack against that state. On one hand, Gorman argued that the Holy

Land belonged rightfully *only* to Christians, who were the spiritual heirs of Abraham, and so the heirs of the promise. On the other hand, readers were warned that the entire Middle East would fall into Soviet hands, unless "we help the Arab occupants to do what they please." His unreserved support of the Arab stand on Israel led to a blurring of judgment in reference to Arab internal politics. Despite his opposition to communism, he condoned and occasionally defended the leftist tendencies in certain Arab states until irate readers took him to task.[28]

Sign urged the "de-Zionization" of Israel, which in practical terms would mean the destruction of the Jewish state, and its restructuring along the political and ethnic lines of Lebanon. When Gorman spoke of territorial concessions needed, he pressed for "substantial" concessions which would drastically reduce the state.[29] Not surprisingly, Gorman's invective and deep-seated animosity aroused charges of anti-Semitic motivation. Gorman denied these charges, and even confided that he was "nauseated" by the mail he received from outright anti-Semites "who nudge up cozily as if we were one of them." Nevertheless, Gorman made extensive use thereafter of Jewish anti-Zionist material, primarily from the American Council for Judaism.[30]

While the position which *Sign* took during the fifties could have been foreseen a decade earlier, the stance adopted by *America* came somewhat as a surprise. Throughout our discussion of American Catholic attitudes toward Jews, Zionism, and Israel, we generally found that *America* and *Commonweal* were the two periodicals which consistently maintained a nonhostile attitude. At best they were friendly. At worst they were skeptical. In the 1950s, *America* and *Commonweal* parted ways.

Commonweal moved closer to a position of sympathetic tolerance, and even appreciation, of Israel. It is likely that this warmth was encouraged, as in some other Catholic papers, by disappointments over the leftist trend in Arab politics. Russian incursions in the Middle East were recognized by *Commonweal* as a major threat in the area, but the paper was explicit in advocating that counteraction should not involve any repudiation of Israel. Increases in technical and economic assistance to the Arab countries was the solution offered in *Commonweal* editorials.[31] In their support in early 1956 of Israeli requests for U.S. arms to counter Russian assistance to Egypt, they demonstrated their concern for the security of Israel. *Commonweal* regarded these requests as necessary and reasonable.[32]

During the Suez crisis, *Commonweal* provided a comprehensive coverage of events, which was notably well informed and evenhanded. This is not to say that *Commonweal* was not critical of Israel, for the paper frequently was. But, unlike so many other Catholic papers, *Commonweal* did not maintain an ostrichlike attitude in reference to Arab culpability. One editorial was sharply critical of the onesidedness of the United States condemnation of Israel following the Suez War.

> Our action implies that the Suez crisis involves but one act of aggression to be righted. It appears to ignore Nasser's uncooperative attitude and his provocative military build-up with the help of Russian arms, the barring of the canal to Israeli ships and the arming of Syria by the Soviets—the ill-conceived plans of several Arab states for an eventual all-out attack on Israel.[33]

Commonweal stood firm in its avowal that Israel had an inalienable right to existence. It defended Israel in her insistence that this right should be protected by strong guarantees. After the Suez War, the editors sided with Israel in demanding that such guarantees precede her withdrawal from Gaza. They also urged the United States to support Israel even at the risk of losing the goodwill of the Arab nations. That Israel was not to be sacrificed on the altar of Arab friendship was made crystal clear.[34]

When John Cogley, editor of *Commonweal,* addressed the annual conference of the American Friends of the Middle East in January 1954, his call for Arab recognition of Israel caused no little surprise and consternation in his audience.[35] "I think [we] should bury the past as much as possible and begin with the present situation as it actually exists. . . . Israel is here to stay, and the sooner the Arabs accept that fact, the better for everybody. . . ."[36] Later, in a *Commonweal* article, Cogley argued that the refugee situation continued to increase anti-Israel feelings because the Arab nations were "stubborn" and "willful" on the question of resettlement.[37]

America, too, moved away from its 1948 neutrality, but in quite the opposite direction from *Commonweal*. This change can be attributed to the opinion of one of the associate editors, Vincent S. Kearney, who had spent three years in Egypt before joining the staff of *America*. Before discussing Kearney's views it should be noted that the execution of *America*'s editorial policy differed from most of the other periodicals under discussion. Its editorials were actually the product of its editorial board. Once a week the editor-in-chief met with his associate editors to decide upon subjects for editorial and news comment. Responsibility for a particular editorial was given to the editor in whose specialization the topic lay. For example, labor issues would generally be assigned to Paul Masse and race relations to John LaFarge. Kearney handled the Middle East because of his period of study there. After the editorials had been composed the editors reconvened for board approval. Though there may have been differences of opinion among the editors, the editorials generally remained unchanged—unless there was overwhelming opposition. As we shall see, there may not have been unanimity among the editors on Kearney's views, despite his monopoly of opinion.[38]

Kearney began to take a hard line on Israel in 1951, when he reported anti-Western propaganda in Arab countries. He pinpointed the blame for this development on U.S. support of the partition scheme in 1947, whose consequences "remain to plague the Western world." With the threat of Russian exploitation of the Arab-Israeli conflict, Kearney advocated that the United States "take a second look" and "see that our security interests lie . . . with nations which made up [the] traditional Middle East." He further warned that "the West cannot afford to have 325 million Arabs shift their allegiance to the Soviet Union." Holding aloft the banner of expediency and Realpolitik, Kearney proceeded to urge the withdrawal of aid to Israel and to promote a U.S. commitment of unqualified support for the Arab countries. Only such a complete reversal of policy could, in his opinion, restore Arab confidence in the West and save the Middle East.[39]

The extent of Kearney's feelings toward Israel became evident in a report on his visit to Egypt, Lebanon, and Iran in the spring of 1954. His friends in these countries felt that the only solution to the conflict-ridden Middle East was to liquidate Israel. Kearney concurred. Kearney suggested, however, that this be accomplished without bloodshed by means of economic strangulation. If American aid, private and government-sponsored, were removed, Kearney believed, Israel would disintegrate and thus the problem of the Middle East would be solved.[40] In another article, Kearney wrote contemptuously of the insignificance of Israel as compared to the oil-rich and heavily populated Arab lands. In "plain, blunt language," he advised the United States to concern itself only with the Arabs.[41]

The militant rhetoric of the Arab states was brushed aside with the explanation that Israel, after all, had emerged from the 1948 war with all her territorial desires satisfied, and so she could pose as an exponent of peace. The Arabs, however, were left with their territorial needs unmet. Thus, Kearney ignored Arab terrorism and raids on Israeli territory, but pounced on Israeli reprisals as evidence of that state's depredation of her neighbors.[42]

As mentioned earlier, Kearney's one-dimensional approach to Israel and the Middle East probably did not have the unanimous approval of *America*'s staff. After a particularly scathing attack on Israel, a letter criticizing Kearney was published by the editors, not in the correspondence column, but in a featured column in order to give it more prominence and to permit fuller discussion. Occasionally news comments, conciliatory in tone, tried to restore a balanced picture. An unsigned editorial, following the Suez War and written in a style unlike Kearney's, affirmed Israel's right to a secure existence and defended her refusal to withdraw from Gaza without firm guarantees. A few weeks later, however, a Kearney-style editorial recanted *America*'s defense of Israel's position. With typical pugnacity, the editorial blamed Israel for maintaining a continued state of belligerence by her occupation of Gaza. Kearney's arguments were also occasionally countered, though subtly, by Wilfred Parsons in his regular column "Washington Front." Parsons drew attention to the Arab provocations of Israel, and to the instability and unreliability of the Arab governments. Nevertheless, Kearney's opinion dominated the paper, and as one reader of *America* noted, Kearney's "interpretative reporting" was essential for Catholics because the news in the daily press was so slanted.[43]

In examining press reactions to Israel and the Middle East, emphasis has been placed on shifting political alignments as a factor in the change or reinforcement of attitudes. However, the fifties also saw the emergence of another important factor which was pivotal in creating a change of attitude. The seeds of ecumenical thought began to sprout on American soil, although ecumenism, as a movement, did not burst into full flower until the 1960s, when it was nurtured by the spirit of the Second Vatican Council.[44] Even in its budding stages, however, ecumenism promoted a more sensitive handling of the Israeli problem, and its influence was felt in the American Catholic press before Vatican II.

The most striking example of the force of ecumenical thinking in regard to the formation of attitudes on Israel is found in *Catholic World*. Under the editorship of James Gillis, C.S.P., the journal was notoriously antagonistic to Zionism. One of the last editorials which Gillis penned in 1948 bitterly censured President Truman for his "unholy haste" in recognizing Israel.[45] When Gillis retired in September 1948, he was succeeded by John B. Sheerin, C.S.P. A change of approach was evident in the lead article of Sheerin's first issue. "Jews and Christians Get Together" keynoted the new direction of the journal.[46] Sheerin wrote no editorials on Israel for the first several years, as if he deliberately wished to avoid an explosive issue in Jewish-Christian relations. Other than one article on the Arab refugee problem, published early in 1949, the paper steered clear of articles criticizing the new state.[47] Quite the reverse, a sermon by Eugenio Zolli, published in the summer of 1949, actually acclaimed the political renascence of Israel.[48] Though the thrust of the sermon was clearly conversionary, its enthusiasm for the new state was a departure from the earlier *Catholic World* perspective. In the following years, Sheerin directed the attention of the Paulist paper to an opening of dialogue with the Jews. The emphasis on continuing dialogue finally propelled Sheerin to commit himself openly and positively in support of Israel.[49]

Though Sheerin was by no means alone in reacting to the Jewish state from an ecumenical perspective, *Catholic World* may be considered the periodical which spearheaded such an approach. The direct correlation of a positive stand on Israel and the success of dialogue with Jews became clear to the Catholic world in 1967, and Sheerin was one of the first to say so in print.[50]

The relationship of anti-Israel attitudes and anti-Semitism was early recognized by *Commonweal*. When tensions ran high on the Middle East situation in the spring of 1956, *Commonweal* warned that discussions on the conflict must be conducted on such a level as not to arouse anti-Semitic passions. The paper urged Catholics to be sensitive to Jewish feelings when discussing Israel, and not to use terms which would "play into the hands of anti-Semites."[51]

Perhaps even more important than the press was the emergence of personalities on the American Catholic scene who took public positions in support of Israel. In the late forties and early fifties very few Catholics were prominent as outspoken friends of Israel. The pro-Zionist American Christian Palestine Committee (ACPC)[52] could count less than a handful of active Catholics on its membership lists. The only Roman Catholic priest who attended meetings and participated in conferences and seminars was Father George Barry Ford of the Corpus Christi Church in New York City. However, Father Ford's involvement was more on a personal rather than a public level, and no speeches or statements outside of the committee indicated the extent of his commitment to Zionism and Israel.[53]

Unlike their Protestant counterparts,[54] the outspoken Catholics on the ACPC were laymen. Foremost among them were Thomas Sugrue and Claire Huchet Bishop. Following a visit to Israel, Sugrue published a stirring report on the new state in 1950,[55] and at the same time joined the Speakers' Bureau of the ACPC. Unfortunately, Sugrue's work was cut short due to the tragic and painful illness which took his life in 1953.[56]

Claire Huchet Bishop participated in the ACPC since its inception, and continued to be active in Christians Concerned for Israel (American Christian Association for Israel). Though she has been vocal on behalf of the state, the main thrust of her concern is Christian-Jewish relations. Mrs. Bishop feels that past Christian persecution of Jews can be atoned for by Christians today only through wholehearted acceptance of Israel. In her view, as expressed in various articles and speeches, Zionism and the creation of Israel represent a direct Jewish response to the persecutions of the past; therefore "It is we [Christians] who have an obligation to serve Israel, because we are inescapably involved in its development, which clearly grows out of twenty centuries of Christian inhumanity."[57]

The influence of these Catholics on their own co-religionists was limited. They were, however, the pioneers and the forerunners of the later protagonists who emerged from the ranks of the clergy. Msgr.

John M. Oesterreicher and Father Edward H. Flannery, in particular, brought about a favorable hearing on Israel within the American Catholic community, through their own personal involvement and through their publications.

In October 1953, Msgr. Oesterreicher opened the Institute of Judaeo-Christian Studies at Seton Hall University. In his inaugural address, Msgr. Oesterreicher pointed out that the establishment of Israel was one of the factors which made Judaeo-Christian studies particularly relevant today.[58] The yearbook of the Institute, the *Bridge* (in 1970, *Brothers in Hope*), which was devoted to the investigation of topics relating to Jewish-Christian relations, included in its scope the State of Israel.[59] The institute's interest in the state resulted from the recognition that Israel, in a political sense, is an integral element in Jewish-Christian relations. It should be noted, however, that for many years Oesterreicher spoke with a tone of cautious reserve on the politics of Israel, and like Sheerin, it was not until 1967 that he became unequivocal in his defense of the state.

Illustrative of Oesterreicher's outspoken commitment after 1967 was his moving plea for "Justice for Jerusalem," which was printed on the Op-Ed page of the *New York Times*.[60] Despite the known position of the Vatican on internationalization, Oesterreicher, hinting that the Pope was no longer adamant on the issue, championed the cause of Israeli sovereignty over Jerusalem. Though Oesterreicher has repudiated the "mission" motif in his genuine acceptance of Israel, he still attaches to it eschatological significance.

> Christians who have not yet understood the signs of the time, and thus the meaning of Israel's rejuvenation, will have to reconcile themselves to the fact that Jerusalem is a Jewish city, in origin, destiny and significance.[61]

> A Christian theologian must, it seems to me, see in the new State . . . a significant event. The living reality of the State will, for the most part, evoke his respect and admiration. More than that, if he understands what has happened and still happens there, he will become a champion of the State's independence and integrity.[62]

Father Edward H. Flannery worked for many years in close association with Msgr. Oesterreicher. His interest in Jewish affairs came about as a result of his penetrating research on the history of their persecution through the ages.[63] From "the anguish of the Jews" of the past he developed a genuine interest in the concerns of contemporary Jewry. Over the years, he has grown in an understanding and a positive appreciation of Israel. Moreover, he has shown an unusual willingness to come to terms with Israel on Jewish grounds. In the estimate of A. Roy Eckardt, the Protestant theologian, Flannery stands "in the forefront of Christian moral and theological support for Israel."[64] Fr. Flannery served as the executive secretary of the American Bishops Secretariat for Catholic-Jewish Relations and as a member of the Vatican Secretariat for Promoting Christian Unity.

The fact that both Oesterreicher and Flannery head official Catholic institutions should not be underestimated in assessing the effectiveness of their work for Israel. Although their respective institutions, the institute and the secretariat, were not established with the intention of promoting support for Israel, their sincere efforts to understand the Jews and Judaism inevitably fostered an understanding of Israel. The authority, the public forum, and the financial support which such institutions provide helped to propagate their pro-Israel views among the American Catholic public.

It was not until the sixties that a major shift in Catholic opinion took place. It was marked by a change from isolated individual commitments to Israel to more widespread involvement. Pope John XXIII can be credited with having lifted the curtain which separated Catholics from Jews, and it is in his spirit of *aggiornamento* that progress continues. Although there is still no official statement from the Vatican or the American hierarchy as a body in recognition and support of Israel,[65] theological reassessments and ecumenical thinking have paved the way for many Catholics to regard the state with respect and sympathy.

VII
Theological Reinterpretations and the State of Israel

In the wake of the Holocaust and the establishment of the State of Israel, a movement toward theological reinterpretation of the role of the Jews was initiated. Some of the new views were formulated during the Second Vatican Council. That one is entitled to speak of a shift in theology in the scheme on the Jews was reluctantly conceded by Cardinal Bea, head of the Secretariat for Promoting Christian Unity. Bea directed the drafting of the various texts which finally resulted in the conciliar statement on the Jews incorporated in *Nostra Aetate*. Though he tried to deemphasize any innovative theological breakthrough, Bea admitted:

> For Catholics, one of the chief difficulties will be the task of correctly integrating the teaching of the Declaration with what they have already been more or less explicitly taught. For them, both the general principles of the Declarations and their application as presented therein will be somewhat new.[1]

What have Roman Catholics been "more or less explicitly" taught? The popular theology which permeated the catechisms, sermons, and ecclesiastical literature until recent times has already been surveyed in the introductory chapter.[2] Among Christians a general consensus existed on the role of the Jewish people *until* the coming of Christ. As for Catholics, this view did not essentially change even with Vatican II. The form and manner of description have varied, revealing the personal sympathies or prejudices of individual authors, but from Abraham to the prophets, each event and revelation was depicted in terms of a *Praeparatio Evangelica*. Each phase of biblical history symbolically prefigured the culminating phase and was significant only in its preparation for the final revelation of Jesus, in whom Jew and Gentile were said to converge.[3]

When the Jews rejected Jesus, the question arose: What status do the Jewish people or the religion of Judaism have thereafter? What is their status in relation to God, and consequently in relation to the Church?

Traditional Christian thinking can be summarized as follows: The Jewish people, by denying the divinity and message of Jesus, failed to bring their own mission to fruition. Furthermore, as a result of their collective guilt in the killing of Jesus, the Jews became a reprobate and accursed people. Rejected by God, they could no longer be the Chosen People. The "Israel according to the flesh" was superseded by the "Israel according to the spirit." Not only did the Christians replace the Jews as "verus Israel," as the true offspring of Abraham in reference to the promises and salvation, but according to Augustine, the Old Testament, too, belongs more to the Christian who fulfills it in spirit. Consequently, the Jewish people could justly be regarded as religiously and morally bankrupt.[4]

Some of the tenets of this popular theology were challenged during the deliberations of the Ecumenical Council, held in the Vatican from 1962 to 1965. A statement on the Jews, within the framework of a schema on ecumenism, was prepared by the Secretariat for Promoting Christian Unity. Yet it was not placed on the agenda during the first session. Instead it was distributed to the Council Fathers during the second session in November 1963. Subsequently, the text was revised and detached from the original schema. As part of a separate "Declaration on the Relationship of the Church to Non-Christian Religions," it was discussed at the third session of the council in September 1964.[5]

A theology of the Jews was grappled with even before the "declaration" was debated, and certain formulations were incorporated in the schema on the "Dogmatic Constitution on the Church."

Already from the beginning of the world the foreshadowing of the Church took place. It was prepared in a remarkable way throughout the history of the people of Israel and by means of the Old Covenant.

. . . He [God] therefore chose the race of Israel as a people unto Himself. With it He set up a covenant. Step by step He taught and prepared this people, making known in its history both Himself and the decree of His will making it holy unto Himself. All these things, however, were done by way of preparation and as a figure of that new and perfect covenant, which was to be ratified in Christ, and of that fuller revelation which was to be given through the word of God Himself made flesh.

Christ instituted this new covenant, the new testament, this is to say, in His Blood (cf. I Cor. XI, 25), calling together a people made up of Jew and gentile, making them one, not according to the flesh but in the spirit. This was to be the new People of God. For those who believe in Christ, who are reborn not from a perishable but an imperishable seed, through the word of the living God (cf. I Peter I, 23), not from the flesh but from water and the Holy Spirit (cf. John III, 5–6), are finally established as "a chosen race, a royal priesthood, a holy nation, a purchased people . . . who in times past were not a people, but are now the people of God" (I Peter II, 9–10).[6]

Clearly this is a reaffirmation of the traditional view of the Jewish role as the *Praeparatio Evangelica*. And what of postbiblical Jewry? The last paragraph certainly implies that the Jewish mission as "people of God" has been appropriated by the sons of the New Covenant. Nonetheless, the Council Fathers concluded with yet another paragraph which foreshadows the more positive theological direction guiding the later declaration.

Finally, those who have not yet received the Gospel are related in various ways to the people of God. In the first place we must recall the people to whom the testament and the promises were given and from whom Christ was born according to the flesh (cf. Rom. IX, 4–5). On account of their fathers this people remains most dear to God, for God does not repent of the gifts He makes nor of the calls He issues (cf. Rom, XI, 28–29).[7]

It is emphasized that God does not repent His gifts or even the election of the Jews, for the Jewish people remain "most dear to God." There is also the implication that because of their patrimony, the Jews still have a somewhat elevated position among the peoples who do not recognize Jesus. These theses were later given a central position in the statement on the Jews in *Nostra Aetate*.

Four versions of the text were drafted during the council meetings. The final draft, however, clearly showed the traces of a conservative retreat.[8] On one hand, the final version recapitulated the thesis of *Praeparatio Evangelica*. It refrained from a clear statement absolving the Jews from the charges of deicide and reaffirmed that "Jerusalem did not recognize the time of her visitation, nor did the Jews in large number accept the Gospel." At the same time, the statement explicitly noted that "Jewish authorities and those who followed their lead pressed for the death of Christ" and that the "Church is the new people of God." On the other hand, the declaration accentuated the Jewish origins of Jesus and the early Church. It repudiated anti-Semitism, and it highlighted an attitude of confraternity by giving prominence to Paul's teaching on the continuous election of the Jews. The new spirit is seen in the alternate lines of the declaration. For example:

> The Church keeps ever in mind the words of the Apostle about his kinsmen: "Theirs is the sonship and the glory and the covenant and the law and the worship and the promises; theirs are the fathers and from them is the Christ according to the flesh" (Romans 9:4–5), the Son of the Virgin Mary. She also recalls that the Apostles, the Church's mainstay and pillars, as well as most of the early disciples who proclaimed the Gospel of Christ to the world, sprang from the Jewish people. . . .
>
> God holds the Jews most dear for the sake of their Fathers; He does not repent of the gifts He makes or of the calls He issues . . .
>
> . . . still, what happened in His Passion cannot be charged against all the Jews, without distinction, then alive, nor against the Jews of today. . . .
>
> . . . Jews should not be represented as rejected by God or accursed. . . .[9]

The declaration as it stands is not an outright negation or a radical modification of the traditional theology. Each of the new points was vaguely phrased. This was done deliberately in order to accommodate conservative and politically sensitive members of the council. As it finally emerged, the statement on the Jews could be read either to one's satisfaction or to one's despair. But for those who were ready to implement its positive directions the statement provided leeway for a major breakthrough in the theology of the Jews. Since much was left unsaid in the final formulation, it is important to take note of the interventions of the American bishops during the debates. They indicate how strongly the American hierarchy felt on the question of the relation of the Church to the Jews and how far they were willing to go in the implementation of the declaration.

When the second draft of the schema on the Jews was officially distributed to the Council Fathers on September 21, 1964, sections of the original draft had undergone considerable rephrasing and weakening. The revised text dropped the abjuration against implicating the Jews of the past, collectively, in the crucifixion, and omitted the exhortation against using "deicide" in reference to the Jewish people. It also did not specifically condemn anti-Semitism, and added the hope of the Church for the conversion of the Jews.[10] The dissatisfaction of the American bishops with the weakened version was made abundantly clear when they caucused at the Pontifical North American College and pledged themselves to work for a more positive and stronger statement on the Jews.[11]

Richard Cardinal Cushing of Boston was the first among the American hierarchy to speak when the debate on the schema opened in the council. In his intervention of September 28, 1964, Cardinal Cushing urged the Council Fathers:

> First: We must make our statement about the Jews more positive, less timid, more charitable. . . . Therefore, in this declaration, in clear and evident words we must deny that the Jews are guilty of the death of our Savior. . . . All of us have seen the evil fruit of this kind of false reasoning. In this august assembly, in this solemn moment, we must cry out. There is no Christian rationale—neither

theological nor historical—for any inequity, hatred or persecution of our Jewish brothers.[12]

Cardinal Cushing further entered a "mea culpa" sorely missing in the council's handling of the Church's relations to the Jews.

> Thirdly, and finally, I ask, Venerable Brothers, whether we ought not to confess humbly before the world that Christians too frequently have not shown themselves as true Christians, as faithful to Christ, in their relations with their Jewish brothers? . . . There is no need to enumerate the crimes committed in our own time. If not many Christian voices were lifted in recent years against the great injustices, yet let our voices humbly cry out now![13]

Albert Cardinal Meyer of Chicago followed Cardinal Cushing's speech with a masterful line-by-line critique of the disputed sections of the revised text.[14] Joseph Cardinal Ritter of St. Louis, in his intervention, bluntly repudiated the negative thinking of the past. In forceful language he reasserted the theologically progressive position of the original schema.

> We Christians, for many centuries now, have been guilty of error and injustice against the Jews. We, as many others, have been assuming that God has abandoned this people. Christians, even in Church documents, have been accusing the Jewish people of the passion and death of Christ. In prayers they have been called "the perfidious people," "the deicide people," who "upon themselves have once called the blood of the Savior." The opportunity now presents itself today that we, gathered in an ecumenical Council reject and repair such errors and injustices.
>
> The declaration should speak more fully and explicitly about the religious patrimony which the Jewish people and the Christian people once and even today share. The promises made to Abraham by God, which do not fail nor are able to fail faith, pertain now to the Jews. Divine love itself is extended in a special way to Jews and Christians, and because of this there ought to grow between us and them the sharpest unity of love and esteem. And so, this spirit of love, which was found in the original schema, should also shine forth even more in this declaration. Our debt and witness before the

Jews, which in this scheme are acknowledged hesitantly and somewhat forebodingly, should be proclaimed with great joy.[15]

The American delegates presented five oral and five written interventions on the schema on the Jews. The favorable revisions in the third draft may have been due to the pressure they exerted. Disappointment was keen, then, when the final draft again made concessions to conservative opinion. Bishop Stephen A. Leven of San Antonio, Texas, made a last-ditch effort to restore the force of the earlier text, but it was too late in the conciliar process for the attempt to be successful.[16] The declaration was passed on October 15, 1965, and on the very same afternoon Bishop Francis P. Leipzig of Baker, Oregon, assumed the chairmanship of a Subcommission on Catholic-Jewish Relations (later Secretariat for Catholic-Jewish Relations) created by the American bishops. While Bishop Leipzig noted that there were "imperfections" in the text of the declaration, he committed himself and the members of his subcommission to carry out the *intent* of the schema and its overall spirit of "kinship, reverence and determination."[17]

The intent of *Nostra Aetate* was energetically carried out in the extensive and multifaceted activities of the secretariat. Guidelines for Catholic-Jewish relations were drawn up, a newsletter was published, position papers were written, and textbook inspection was promoted. To advance an understanding of Judaism among Catholics, training institutes were set up for Catholic teachers, and conferences, lecture series, seminars, and workshops were convened, many with the joint sponsorship of Jewish organizations.[18]

What still remained vague in the declaration, and even in its "intent," was the role of Jewry and Judaism in postbiblical times. If anything, the declaration minimized the value of postbiblical Jewry by stressing that the Jews are "most dear for the sake of their Fathers," so implying that there was little of objective value and contribution in the later periods. Yet it was the contemporary Jewish experience, specifically the establishment of the State of Israel, which challenged traditional thinking on the role of the Jews in Catholic theology and eschatology. As has been noted, one of the more popular eschatological interpretations of the establishment of the state was Yves Congar's theory that it "was a strategem of divine providence to drive Israel into a blind alley of grace," or, in other words, a plan to expedite the conversion of the Jews.[19] Until recently this was the extent of Catholic religious appreciation of Israel.

The declaration was silent about the existence of the State of Israel. This was one subject scrupulously avoided in the Church statements and vociferously denied as being relevant to council deliberations. As Cardinal Bea emphasized and reiterated in his speeches before the Council Fathers, "There is no national or political question here. In particular, there is no question of recognition of the State of Israel. . . ."[20] The dialogues, stimulated and encouraged by the declaration, did not at first place Israel on the agenda either. Nevertheless, it was the dialogical trend which eventually led to a recognition that the State of Israel could not be avoided. Dialogue, in itself, did not make Christians aware of the almost mystical link of Israel to Judaism, for it was not within the Catholic experience to link religion with country of origin. It was the trauma of the Six-Day War, when the mere silence of Catholics threatened the disruption of all further dialogue, that moved Catholics to realize the vital position of contemporary Israel in the religious consciousness of the Jews.[21] If Catholics were to continue a dialogue with Jews, they would have to understand this aspect and integrate it in their understanding of Jews and Judaism. Consequently, Israel, as a topic of study, began to appear on the agendas of dialogical workshops and lecture series.[22] Attention to its importance was paid in a quasi-official document which appeared in December 1969 in the form of a working paper drawn up by the American branch of the Secretariat for Promoting Christian Unity.

The document, drafted under the supervision of Lawrence Cardinal Shehan of Baltimore, began by expressing the need for an updated theology on the Jewish people.

> Cognizance is increasingly being given in the Church of the actual place of the Jewish people in the history of salvation and of its permanent election. This fact points towards a theological renewal and toward a new Christian reflection on the Jewish people.
>
> The history of Judaism does not end with the destruction of Jerusalem, but continues to develop in a rich and spiritual tradition.[23]

THEOLOGICAL REINTERPRETATIONS 115

The document then went on to define, somewhat gropingly, the position of the State of Israel in the religious experience of the Jews.

> Fidelity to the covenant was linked to the gift of a land, which in the Jewish soul has endured as the object of an aspiration that Christians should strive to understand. In the wake of long generations of painful exile, all too often aggravated by persecutions and moral pressures, for which Christians ask pardon of their Jewish brothers, Jews have indicated in a thousand ways their attachment to the land promised to their ancestors from the days of Abraham's calling. It could seem that Christians, whatever the difficulties they may experience, must attempt to understand and respect the religious significance of this link between the people and the land. The existence of the state of Israel should not be separated from this perspective; which does not in itself imply any judgment on historical occurrences or on decisions of a purely political order.[24]

Though this working document was withdrawn by the Vatican, its proposals found their way into the thinking of American Catholics. When Father Flannery presented a report of the Secretariat for Catholic-Jewish Relations to the National Conference of Catholic Bishops in November 1970, he noted that the Catholic dialogist was learning more of the "intense bond uniting Jews to Israel," to the mutual benefit of Catholic-Jewish relations. He also underscored the need for a genuine Catholic understanding of Israel as a vital factor in the success or failure of dialogue.[25] The basic points of the Shehan paper were also repeated in an October 1971 statement issued by the sixth synod of the archdiocese of Cincinnati. The document urged Catholics to attempt to understand "the depth of concern that most Jews feel for the state of Israel."[26] It is important to stress that these Catholic exhortations in no way implied that Catholics should commit themselves to the political support of Israel. Rather they called for an *understanding* and an *appreciation* of the significance of Israel to Jews and Judaism.[27] To put this understanding in a theological framework was the task undertaken by Msgr. Oesterreicher. In a review of *Nostra Aetate* five years after its promulgation, Msgr. Oesterreicher had this to say:

> The Council said nothing about the one reality crucial to Jewish existence today: The State of Israel. . . . To me the State of Israel is the visible expression of the God-willed permanence of the Jewish people. As is Judaism, so is the State of Israel, a banner of God's fidelity. Jewish history began with the promise of the Land. Or, more precisely, the promise of the land antedates the existence of the people. . . . The Christian must not ignore that the foundations of the State are thus even deeper than an act of the world community and a decision of the settlers of the Land.[28]

In Oesterreicher's words there is an echo of the Pauline theme of irrevocable promise enunciated in the declaration. While concern for the continuation of dialogue spurred Catholics into a recognition of the meaning of Israel to the Jews, the emphasis placed by the Second Vatican Council on Romans 9:4–5 and 11:28–30 alleviated somewhat the uneasiness Catholics may have felt over what seemed a rebuke to traditional thinking in the attainment by the Jews of political supremacy in the Holy Land. The glory and the promise were, after all, substantiated by the events.

Progressive theological steps continued to be made, encouraged both by ecumenical thinking and by historical realities. A glimpse of this progress can be found in a paper delivered by Father Cornelius Rijk director of the Vatican Office of Catholic-Jewish Relations at a Seton Hall University conference in October 1970.[29] Because of his position, one may expect him to echo the most advanced theological thinking on the topic which could receive the official imprimatur.

Rijk's paper drew attention to the fact that certain documents and guidelines subsequent to Vatican II emphasized, in particular, the permanence of religious values in Judaism. He added the following remarks:

> If, as has already been observed, according to Christian theology, the world religions are a way of salvation for the nations, the Jewish religion is so even more. . . .
> Thus, Judaism is considered as it is in itself an answer to the permanent presence of the Lord, is without any doubt, a legitimate world religion, with great values for the whole world. . . .
> The continuity of the permanent validity of Judaism is fundamentally based on God's fidelity to the world and to his people.[30]

The above observations, though they demonstrate an evolution in thinking, are at least grounded in the discussions of the Second Vatican Council. Rijk's final observation, however, may indicate an entirely new trend in the theology concerning the Jews.

> I think the text of Matthew 5:17: "I did not come to abolish the Law and the Prophets, but to fulfil them," should be taken seriously. Not only in this sense that Jesus according to our Christian faith in fact fulfilled the covenant with God in an exceptional and surprising way, but also in the sense that he really did not abolish it. I mean by this, that where his people, or the majority of his people did not accept him as the fulfillment, the Word of God, the promises and the gifts of God, the covenant relationship with God were not taken away from them, were not abolished, but continued to build up the covenant relationship between God and the Jewish people, in view of the final fulfillment of all the prophecies in the final establishment of the kingdom of God all over the world, in the whole of mankind.[31]

Rijk's contention here marks a revolutionary breakthrough in Catholic thinking. It appears from his statement that there are two equally valid roads to salvation; either to live by the Law, as was given to and developed by Judaism, or through faith in Jesus to fulfill the same covenant in an "exceptional and surprising way." Rijk further comments that "as long as the final kingdom of God has not been established on earth, God acts in an explicit way through *Israel and* the Church [emphasis added]. Israel still receives the gifts of God, because 'the gifts and the call of God are irrevocable.' " Following this line of thought through to its ultimate conclusion, Rijk contends that the coming of Jesus caused a split within the covenant people, so that there are actually two peoples of God, "moving side by side towards the final and glorious coming of the Messiah."[32]

Advancing in the same direction, though espousing a theology not yet encountered in official circles, was the position taken by Prof. Charlotte Klein, a Roman Catholic theologian teaching at Frankfurt University. In a paper read at the same Seton Hall conference of 1970, Dr. Klein went beyond Fr. Rijk.[33] Her approach was radical in that it attempted to assess the significance of the State of Israel by taking into account a Jewish self-understanding of its role and relationship to the

Holy Land. At the same time, she flatly rejected the exegetical and theological perspectives which permit Christians to determine the role of the state in the divine scheme.

Dr. Klein's thesis can be summarized as follows: In all promises and covenants between God and the Jewish people, the land of Israel as the place of their fulfillment is central. If one is prepared to accept, in the spirit of *Nostra Aetate,* that the election of the Jews and the promises to them have not been abrogated, then it follows that the bond which links the Jews to the land has to be accepted as equally still in force. Those covenants which are of paramount importance to the Jews—the covenant of the Torah and the covenant of the land—remain eternally valid. In words similar to Rijk's, Klein advances the proposition that for "those who had encountered Jesus as the Christ, much of the former dispensation has come to an end. Yet those who did not recognize Jesus, and according to Romans 11 this is not culpable blindness but part of the scheme of God . . . for them the covenant (of the Torah), which in many biblical passages is termed 'eternal,' is by no means abrogated." Here a doctrine of two equally valid covenants, one for Christians and one for Jews, is strongly hinted at.[34]

A fuller exposition of this doctrine is presented by an avant-garde Catholic theologian in the pages of the *Journal of Ecumenical Studies.* In her article, Dr. Monika Hellwig readily admitted that "for many Christian scholars it has been axiomatic that there are two covenants, the Old Covenant (of anticipation) and the New Covenant (of realization) which abrogated the Old or former."[35] Dr. Hellwig, however, built up a strong case for a reconsideration of the traditional view of an outdated covenant. Positing her argument on the text of Scripture alone, she called attention to the fact that there were a number of covenants mentioned in the Scriptures where "new" simply indicated an affirmation of the previous covenant. "The question arises whether in continuity with the Christian tradition, it might more reasonably be said that Christians claim participation along with Israel . . . in a covenant made by God with all men. . . . That Israel is the first-born of the covenant and irrevocably remains so, is an ineluctable fact of history. . . ."[36] Dr. Hellwig acknowledged that the consequences of a doctrine of "simultaneous and complementary participation in the same covenant" would require a rethinking of certain key concepts in

Catholicism. Two beliefs, in particular, present themselves as major obstacles. "Jesus is recognized by the Christians as divine and the inner reality of God is understood as triune, while the Jew rejects both claims as blasphemous." However, in Hellwig's view, these concepts lend themselves to reinterpretation in light of present-day theological discussion on the nature of religious language.[37]

In accordance with these premises, Hellwig advocated that Catholics should "learn from God revealing himself in Israel's experience today with exactly the same reverence accorded to the testimony of God revealing himself in that experience recorded in the Bible. . . ."[38] The novelty in Hellwig's approach is not only the validation of contemporary Judaism as an authentic religious revelation on equal footing with Christianity, but the attempt to interpret Christianity as a valid and positive religious experience from the perspective of Judaism.

It is hard to pinpoint the immediate factors which prompted this movement of theological reinterpretation. If anything, the movement emerged in a pattern of chain reaction. The consequences of a Church-tolerated anti-Semitism shocked the Church into a reexamination and reformulation of its attitudes concerning the Jews. As the Holocaust was responsible for the *Nostra Aetate* of the Second Vatican Council, so the Second Vatican Council was responsible for the candid dialogues which characterized Catholic-Jewish relations in the following years. And the dialogues, in their turn, promoted a deeper understanding of Judaism and the *present* experiences of the Jewish people, which ultimately led to further theological reinterpretations to integrate this new understanding.

The process of history revealed to Jews and non-Jews alike that Israel is integrally linked with Judaism. A response to one must naturally affect the response to the other. And if the State of Israel can be said to have opened a new phase in Jewish history, it is also true that it has initiated a new phase in the Christian response to Judaism and Jewish history, at least among certain circles in American Catholicism. After fifty years, and much blood and sweat, there are Catholics who are beginning to echo the sentiments of Pope Benedict XV to the Zionist delegate, "Yes, yes, I believe that we shall be good neighbors."[39]

KEY TO ABBREVIATIONS

AAS Acta Apostolicae Sedis
ACJ American Council for Judaism
ACPC American Christian Palestine Committee
ACQR American Catholic Quarterly Review
AJComm. American Jewish Committee
AJCongress American Jewish Congress
AJHQ American Jewish Historical Quarterly
Ave M Ave Maria
AZEC American Zionist Emergency Committee
Cath Action Catholic Action
Cath Bib Q Catholic Biblical Quarterly
Cath Dgst Catholic Digest
Cath Mind Catholic Mind
Cath Worker Catholic Worker
CHR Catholic Historical Review
CMW Commonweal
CNEWA Catholic Near East Welfare Association
CNI Christian News from Israel
CW Catholic World
E Ch Q Eastern Churches Quarterly
JES Journal of Ecumenical Studies
JSS Jewish Social Studies
MC Michigan Catholic
NC-NS National Catholic News Service
NCWC National Catholic Welfare Conference
NW New World
NYT New York Times
OSV Our Sunday Visitor
PAJHS Proceedings of the American Jewish Historical Society
RNS Religious News Service
SJR Social Justice Review

Notes

CHAPTER 1

1. *The Diaries of Theodor Herzl*, ed. and trans. Marvin Lowenthal (New York: Dial Press, 1956), pp. 428–29.

2. The full text of the working document, which was later withdrawn by the Church, appeared in the *Catholic Review*, the diocesan weekly of Baltimore, on December 12, 1969, pp. 1.

3. Several articles have been published on limited aspects of Vatican relations to Zionism/Israel, e.g., Y. Minerbi, "The Vatican and Zionism," *Molad* 27 (May–June 1971): 139–49, but this study does not go beyond 1924; Edward B. Glick, "The Vatican, Latin America and Jerusalem," *International Organization* 11 (Spring 1957): 213–19, but this study is restricted to Vatican influence on certain Latin American votes in the U.N. on the subject of internationalization. Two recent doctoral dissertations, however, treat Protestant opinion more extensively. Judith N. Elizur, "The Image of Israel in Protestant Eyes" (Ph.D. diss. Harvard University, 1972), is based on the Geneva records of the World Council of Churches, from 1946 to 1969. Hertzel Fishman, "American Protestantism and the State of Israel, 1937–1967" (Ph.D. diss., New York University, 1971), treats mainline American Protestant opinion.

4. Using the term *American Catholics* to refer exclusively to those living in the United States is an arrogance. However, for the sake of literary ease—and with apologies to our neighbors in South America—I will retain this usage for the duration of the study.

5. For example, Apostolic Delegate archives in Washington, D.C.; National Catholic Welfare Conference archives, also in Washington; Catholic Near East Welfare

Association archives in New York City (to which I had only limited access); personal papers of leading members of the hierarchy in various Church archives.

6. Unfortunately there is no Frank Luther Mott for the Catholic press. Apollinaris W. Baumgartner, *Catholic Journalism: A Study of Its Development in the United States, 1789–1930* (New York: Columbia University Press, 1931), is the only book-length study. While it is helpful until 1930, its focus is primarily chronological history. Baumgartner rarely attempts to assess the quality or contributions of the various periodicals and newspapers he cites. One of the best monographs on the subject is John G. Deedy, "The Catholic Press," in *The Religious Press in America*, ed. M. E. Marty (New York: Holt, Rinehart & Winston, 1963). Other articles which provide valuable insights into the Catholic press of the twentieth century include Albert J. Nevins, "A Profile on the Catholic Press in the United States," in *Twentieth Century Catholicism*, vol. 3, ed. Lancelot Sheppard (New York: Hawthorn Books, 1966), and John B. Sheerin, "Developments of the Catholic Magazine in the History of American Journalism," *U.S. Catholic Historical Society—Historical Records and Studies* 41 (New York, 1953). Also, Jerome Breunig, "Present Position of the Catholic Press," *America* 92 (February 19, 1955): 532–34.

7. "The local Catholic weekly newspaper usually chronicled the local news . . . and, in editorial opinion, expressed the views of the local ordinary . . . and when in doubt the editors usually said nothing on controversial items." Thomas T. McAvoy, *A History of the Catholic Church in the United States* (Notre Dame and London: University of Notre Dame Press, 1969), pp. 582–83. In surveys of the Catholic press, the prevalence of this assumption is recognized. Nevins, op. cit., p. 48, and B. L. Barnes, "Catholic Press in the United States—20th Century Newspapers," *New Catholic Encyclopedia* (1967), vol. 3, p. 324. Both of the latter authors, however, enter caveats against a blanket acceptance of such a correlation. Two points of caution must be stressed here. Firstly, it would be incorrect to assume that the Catholic press is monolithic. This study, itself, will demonstrate the range of diversity of opinion. Secondly, freedom of editorial opinion in the American Catholic press has always existed, although the degree of freedom varies from diocese to diocese.

8. Deedy, op. cit., p. 95; *RNS*, May 16, 1957.

9. See the discussion in Baumgartner, op. cit., pp. 23–26. The importance of the press to the Church was epitomized in the words of Pius X, who said: "In vain you will build churches, preach missions, found schools; all your good works, all your efforts, will be destroyed if you cannot at the same time, wield the defensive and offensive weapons of a press, Catholic, loyal, sincere." Quoted in *1954 National Catholic Almanac*, ed. Felician A. Foy (Paterson, N.J.: St. Anthony's Guild), p. 514.

10. Quoted in Baumgartner, op. cit., p. 38.

11. Deedy, op. cit., pp. 68–79. Deedy divides the history of Catholic journalism in the United States into three epochs: (1) "Immigrant phase" (nineteenth century), whose hallmark was an ethnic press, largely apologetic and defensive. It was also characterized by a spate of intramural controversies. (2) "Post-immigrant phase" (1900–1945)—at which time the press was largely Church controlled and operated. Its hallmark was docility. (3) "Modern period" (1945–1962)—characterized by the bur-

geoning of lay journalism and the infusion of lay talent in already existing papers. In this period, according to Deedy, the papers began to respond with liveliness and alertness to problems of the world outside the parish.

12. Warren G. Bovee, "The Professional Needs of the Catholic Press," *SJR*, 49 (February 1957): 330–33. *Religious* designates a member or members of a religious order.

13. Both editors' remarks were made in addresses to the Catholic Press Association Conference of 1958. The remarks are quoted in *RNS*, May 22, 1958 and May 23, 1958. See also the concurring opinion expressed by the lay editor of the *Tablet*, Patrick Scanlon, in his appraisal of *Pilot* policy, *CMW*, 12 (May 21, 1930): 76–78.

14. Msgr. Francis J. Lally to the author, August 3, 1972. See also Thomas J. Stritch, "Communications and the Church," in *Contemporary Catholicism in the United States*, ed. Philip Gleason (Notre Dame and London: University of Notre Dame Press, 1969), pp. 333–35. Stritch, however, cites the example of the *Delmarva Dialog*, diocesan weekly of Wilmington, Delaware, whose editor, John O'Connor, was forced out of his post in 1967 after a long struggle with the bishop, who opposed his liberal views. The bishop never interfered with O'Connor's editorial independence—but he did fire him.

15. *CMW*, 1 (November 12, 1924): 5. The paper was not exempt from hierarchial criticism, nor even rebukes of the Catholic press. When *CMW* criticized the hierarchy for their handling of the 1961 campaign for federal aid to parochial schools, for example, the *Catholic Messenger* of Davenport, Iowa, labeled *CMW* "a Pontius Pilate." Deedy, op. cit., pp. 97–98. The lay *National Catholic Reporter* also met with ecclesiastical reprimands for its independent views, and was even asked by the bishop of Kansas City (where the paper is published) to remove the word *Catholic* from its name. Stritch, op. cit., p. 334.

A troubling question for the Catholic press, whether religious or lay, is the extent to which a Catholic paper may go in offering guidance on matters not directly affecting doctrine. Submissiveness to the hierarchy in doctrinal matters is generally conceded, but a certain amount of tension continues to exist on the degree of subservience in temporal matters. Deedy, op. cit., pp. 99–103.

16. Ibid., p. 103.

17. The statistics are given in Barnes, op. cit.

18. The latter qualification was not always easily obtainable. Catholic papers, until recently, were parochial in their interests. Even the *Pilot*, from which I drew considerable information nevertheless, characterized its news coverage as "1900, Irish; 1920, Catholic; 1940, Catholic; 1960, ecumenical." Quoted in Barnes, op. cit., p. 323.

19. Many diocesan papers have not been preserved on microfilm. The American Catholic Historical Society archives in Philadelphia houses a fairly large selection of early Catholic newspapers, but the series are frequently incomplete. Microfilm collections of newspapers are found in Marquette University in Wisconsin, which in 1958 undertook to establish a permanent archive for the American Catholic press, and in Catholic University of America in Washington, D.C.

20. See the June issues of the *Catholic Journalist* (1945–), published monthly by

the Catholic Press Association. Records of the awards are kept in the New York office files of the Catholic Press Association.

21. Dale Francis, "The Press and Communications," in *The American Apostolate*, ed. Leo Richard Ward, C.S.C. (Westminster, Md.: Newman Press, 1952), pp. 283–84.

22. I have given the popular designations of the religious orders. The official designations for the periodical affiliations are, in consecutive order, as follows: Society of Jesus; Congregation of the Holy Cross; Society of Missionary Priests of St. Paul the Apostle; Congregation of the Passion; and Order of Friars Minor. With the exception of the *Crusader's Almanac*, these periodicals were widely read by people outside their specific orders. Thus, the influence of these periodicals on the general Catholic audience may have been considerable.

23. L. E. Hart, "Knights of Columbus," in *New Catholic Encyclopedia* (1967), 7:215–17; *1970 Catholic Almanac*, ed. Felician A. Foy (Paterson, N.J.: St. Anthony's Guild), pp. 59, 654.

24. In the first issues of 1908–1909, the title was *Central Blatt*, and the journal was published wholly in German. The next year an English section was added and the title became *Central Blatt and Social Justice Review*. In the following years the English section gradually expanded and the German section dwindled. Finally, in 1940 the journal dropped *Central Blatt* from its title and discontinued the German section.

25. M. L. Brophy, "Catholic Central Union," *New Catholic Encyclopedia*, (1967), 3:264–66.

26. It suspended publication in 1953.

27. The Catholic Association for International Peace was established in 1926 under the auspices of the NCWC. The organization was dissolved in May 1969 and replaced by the Division of World Justice and Peace organized within the structure of the U.S. Catholic Conference. *1970 Catholic Almanac*, p. 167.

28. Baumgartner, op. cit., p. 87.

29. Sheerin, op. cit., p. 11.

30. Benson Y. Landis, *The Roman Catholic Church in the United States* (New York: E. P. Dutton, 1966), p. 69.

31. Sheerin, op. cit., p. 10.

32. For example, Catholic University; Woodstock; St. Charles and St. Meinrad Seminaries.

33. *America*, 75 (April 6, 1946): 3. The journal was staffed largely by the editors of *America*.

34. Sheerin, op. cit., The journal began publication in 1945, succeeding the *Acolyte*.

35. *Review of Politics*, 1 (October 1939): 369.

36. For a fuller list of the periodicals and newspapers used, consult the bibliography.

37. McAvoy, op. cit., p. 4. The most comprehensive and up-to-date history of the Catholic Church in the United States is that written by McAvoy. For a briefer survey, see John Tracy Ellis, *American Catholicism*, 2d ed. rev. (Chicago: University of

Chicago Press, 1969). Also, Theodore Maynard, *The Catholic Church and the American Idea* (New York: Appleton-Century-Crofts, 1953).

38. Ellis, op. cit., p. 133.

39. F. D. Cohalan, "The Organization of the Church in the United States," in *The Catholic Church, U.S.A.,* ed. Louis J. Putz (Chicago: Fides Publishers Assoc., 1956), pp. 65–67.

40. Ibid., pp. 68–73.

41. Originally, National Catholic Welfare Council. In 1922, after a brief period of repression, it was revived under the name of National Catholic Welfare Conference. McAvoy, op. cit., p. 403. The NCWC is unique in Catholic intranational ecclesiastical structures. It has been cited by the Vatican as a model which hierarchies of other countries might well follow. Ellis, op. cit., p. 143. For a history and description of the scope of the NCWC, see William F. Montavon, "The National Catholic Welfare Conference," in *The American Apostolate,* ed. Leo R. Ward (Maryland: Newman Press, 1952), and McAvoy, op. cit., pp. 363–69, 375–83, 403–406. The general organization and operations of the NCWC were transferred in January 1967 to the U.S. Catholic Conference (USCC). In 1966, the National Conference of Catholic Bishops was established as a strictly ecclesiastical body with defined juridical authority over the Church in this country. *1970 Catholic Almanac,* pp. 168–69.

42. The pronouncements were made in the name of the hierarchy after being submitted for approval to the assembled prelates in their annual meetings held in November, and, as dryly noted by F. D. Cohalan, "after the civil elections in deference to Protestant prejudice." Cohalan, op. cit., p. 74.

43. Montavon, op. cit.

44. For an excellent sociological study of Catholics and Jews in American society, see Will Herberg, *Protestant-Catholic-Jew* (Garden City, N.Y.: Doubleday, 1955).

45. See the detailed study of Richard Robbins, "American Jews and American Catholics: Two Types of Social Change," *Sociological Analysis,* 26 (Spring 1965): 1–18. Robbins compares the two populations in terms of immigration and ethnicity, social class and mobility, institutional separatism, and problems of minority-group status.

46. Marc H. Tanenbaum in *Jewish-Christian Dialogues* (Washington: National Council of Catholic Men and National Council of Catholic Women, 1966), p. 3.

47. The indispensable scholarly study on the formation of early Christian attitudes is James Parkes, *The Conflict of the Church and the Synagogue* (New York: Meridian Books, 1961), originally published in 1934 by Soncino Press. A Scottish Catholic, Malcolm Hay, published a penetrating survey of the development of negative attitudes throughout the Middle Ages down to the present in *Foot of Pride: The Pressure of Christendom on the People of Israel for 1900 Years* (Boston: Beacon Press, 1950), republished in 1960 as *Europe and the Jews.* The persistence of these attitudes in contemporary American society is attested in Charles Y. Glock and Rodney Stark, *Christian Beliefs and Anti-Semitism* (New York: Harper & Row, 1966). See also the incisive indictment of Jules Isaac, *The Teaching of Contempt: Christian Roots of Anti-Semitism,* trans. Helen Weaver (New York: Holt, Rinehart & Winston, 1964).

48. Augustin Cardinal Bea, S.J., *The Church and the Jewish People,* trans. Philip Loretz, S.J. (London: Geoffrey Chapman, 1966), p. 18.

49. On the historical sequence of the Synoptic Gospels, see Morton Scott Enslin, *Christian Beginnings* (New York and London: Harper & Bros., 1938), pp. 374 ff., and Parkes, op. cit., pp. 42 f. I am using the traditional order accepted in the Catholic version of the New Testament. Likewise, quotations from the New Testament will follow the Douay-Rheims text reprinted in *The Holy Bible* (Baltimore: John Murphey Co., 1914) and published with the approbation of James Cardinal Gibbons. Since 1952, several revised American Catholic translations have appeared. The most recent and authoritative is *The New American Bible,* trans. by members of the Catholic Biblical Association of America and sponsored by the Bishops Committee of the Confraternity of Christian Doctrine (New York: P. J. Kenedy, 1970).

50. Matt. 3:7. In the Baltimore edition, a note explains the Pharisees and Sadducees as "two sects among the Jews, of which the former were for the most part notorious hypocrites; the latter a kind of freethinkers in matters of religion."

51. For a scholarly assessment of the Pharisees, see R. Travers Herford, *The Pharisees* (Boston: Beacon Press, 1962). For a theological analysis of the conflicts between Pharisaic Judaism and early Christianity, see Martin Buber, *Two Types of Faith: The Interpenetration of Judaism and Christianity,* trans. Norman Goldhawk (New York: Harper & Row, 1961).

52. Parkes, op. cit., p. 37.

53. Matt. 23:2-3.

54. Matt. 23:28.

55. Gregory Baum, O.S.A., *The Jews and the Gospel* (Westminster: Newman Press, 1961), pp. 98 f. So, too, Dominic M. Crossan, O.S.M., "Anti-Semitism and the Gospel," *Theological Studies,* 26 (June 1965): 193-99.

56. Baum, op. cit., pp. 131 and 8.

57. The evasive handling of Jesus' origins is particularly evident in the catechism. See *The Catholic Catechism,* drawn up by Peter Cardinal Gasparri and trans. by Rev. Hugh Pope, O.P. (New York: P. J. Kenedy, 1932), pp. 244-46. When the life, preaching, and martyrdom of Jesus are treated, neither the term *Hebrew* (which is the appellation used for the Jewish people in the pre-Christian period) nor the term *Jew* is used to describe Jesus, his family, or his apostles. The term *Jew* is first introduced to describe those who reject Christ, e.g., "Shortly afterwards [after the crucifixion] Jerusalem with its Temple was destroyed, and the Jews scattered to all parts of the earth." Ibid., p. 246.

58. Phil. 3:2, 8.

59. Rom. 11:11-26.

60. 1 Thess. 2:14-16. See the discussion in chap. 7 on the renewal of Paul's positive teaching.

61. Notably in the writings of Tertullian, Cyprian, and Origen and in the sermons of Chrysostom and Cyril. Nor should one minimize the influence of Jerome and Augustine, who were responsible for giving these attitudes theological respectability. Parkes, op. cit., pp. 126, 157-59, 163-66. Isaac, op. cit., pp. 44 f. For selections and

commentary, see Karl H. Rengstorf and Siegfried von Kortzfleisch, eds., *Kirche und Synagoge: Handbuch zur Geschichte von Christen und Juden* (Stuttgart: Ernst Klett, 1968), 1:85–97, and A. Lukyn Williams, *Adversus Judaeos: A Bird's-Eye View of Christian Apologiae until the Renaissance* (Cambridge: Cambridge University Press, 1935), pp. 50, 53–55, 57–59, 90, 132–35.

62. Parkes, op. cit., p. 158.

63. Hay, op. cit., p. 82. The quotations of Chrysostom are taken from Williams, op. cit., pp. 132–35. For the persistence of the demonic image in medieval times, see Joshua Trachtenberg, *The Devil and the Jews* (New Haven: Yale University Press, 1943).

64. Parkes, op. cit., pp. 96–106. For examples of typology in the arts, see Joseph Reider, "Jews in Medieval Art," in *Essays on Antisemitism,* ed. Koppel Pinson (New York: Conference on Jewish Relations, 1942), pp. 45–56.

65. Parkes, op. cit., p. 106.

66. Ibid., pp. 125–50.

67. Isaac, op. cit., p. 109.

68. This belief persisted in Christian thinking down to the twentieth century. Glock and Stark, op. cit., pp. 53–54, published statistical evidence of the prevalence of this belief among American Christians. Examples of its inculcation in the religious texts of Catholic high schools in the U.S. are given in the study of Sister M. Rose Albert Thering, "The Self-Concept Potential in Religious Texts" (Ph.D. diss., St. Louis University, 1961). Since the 1960s, however, Catholic publishing houses have undertaken an overhauling and rewriting of religious texts used in parochial schools.

69. Salo W. Baron, *The Social and Religious History of the Jews,* 2d ed. rev. (Philadelphia: Jewish Publication Society, 1958), 1:105 f., 164–71.

70. Gedalia Alon, *A History of the Jews in Palestine during the Mishnaic and Talmudic Epochs,* 2 vols. (Tel Aviv: Hakibbutz Hameuchad, 1954). (Hebrew)

71. An alternate termination of Israel's history is 135 C.E., the date which Martin Noth used and explained as "the ghastly epilogue of Israel's history." *History of Israel,* 2d ed. (New York: Harper & Row, 1960), p. 454. For a survey of the treatment of the postbiblical phase of Jewish history by Western historians, see Gavin I. Langmuir, "Majority History and Post-Biblical Jews," *Journal of the History of Ideas,* 27 (September 1966): 343–66.

72. *Civiltà Cattolica,* 10 (May 1, 1897): 258–70. Quoted in Charlotte Klein, "The Theological Dimensions of the State of Israel," mimeographed (Paper read to a joint seminar of the Institute of Judaeo-Christian Studies and the American Jewish Committee, October 28, 1970).

CHAPTER II

1. For a comprehensive history of the document, see Leonard Stein, *The Balfour Declaration* (London: Vallentine-Mitchell, 1961).

2. Nahum Sokolow, *History of Zionism* (London: Longmans & Green, 1919), 2:84–97. Sokolow provides extensive excerpts (all favorable) from the English papers.

However, for a more sober estimate of press responses in England and on the continent, see Stein, op. cit., pp. 560 ff. Collections of statements and press opinion on the Balfour Declaration and Zionism appear in a pamphlet published by the Zionist Organization, *Great Britain, Palestine and the Jews: A Survey of Christian Opinion* (London, 1918). For American reactions, see Charles Goldblatt, "American Attitudes to the Balfour Declaration, 1917–1922" (master's essay, Columbia University, 1963). Reform Jewry, which was openly antagonistic to the Zionist movement, refrained from publicly denouncing the Balfour Declaration. See Naomi R. Wiener, "The Reaction of Reform Judaism in America to Political Zionism, 1897–1922," *PAJHS*, 40 (July 1951): 361–94.

3. For a detailed account of the Vatican episode, see Florian Sokolow, "Nahum Sokolow and Pope Benedict XV," *Zion* 1, nos. 5–6 (January–February 1950): 48–52; also Sokolow, op. cit., pp. 53 f.

4. Goldblatt, op. cit., pp. 12–17.

5. Ibid., p. 13. The citation is from the *Columbus Dispatch*, April 28, 1917. Similar statements are found in the *Boston Transcript*, May 3, 1917; *Washington Herald*, May 11, 1917; *St. Paul* (Minn.) *News*, May 11, 1917; *Pittsburgh Gazette Times*, May 3, 1917; and *New York Herald*, April 14, 1917.

6. Rihani lived most of his life in the United States, where he achieved a reputation in Arab scholarship. W. F. Albright ranked Rihani alongside George Antonious as one of a small coterie of Arab intellectuals who were influential in propagating a secular Arab nationalism. Esco Foundation for Palestine, *Palestine: A Study of Jewish, Arab and British Policies* (New Haven: Yale University Press, 1947), p. 552.

7. *Bookman*, 46 (September 1917): 7–14.

8. George Antonious, *The Arab Awakening* (Philadelphia: J. B. Lippincott Co., 1939).

9. Based on conversations with Fr. John B. Sheerin, present editor of *Catholic World*, and Fr. Edward Flannery, former editor of the *Providence Visitor*. Cf. M. S. Connaughton, *The Editorial Opinion of the Catholic Telegraph of Cincinnati on Contemporary Affairs and Politics, 1871–1921* (Washington, 1943). The author contends, however, that the *Catholic Telegraph*, as well as a few other Catholic weeklies, did display a lively interest in national and international affairs.

10. Gibbon's letter was dated November 10, 1918 and was published on November 24, 1918. On several occasions Gibbons showed himself to be sympathetic to Jewish concerns. See W. Rosenau, "Cardinal Gibbons and His Attitude toward Jewish Problems," *PAJHS*, 31 (1928): 219–24.

The vigorous protest of Msgr. Barlassina, which followed the cardinal's statement on Palestine, may have been one of the factors which led to a revision of the Vatican position in March 1919. See Y. Minerbi, "The Vatican and Zionism," *Moled*, 27 (May–June 1971): 146.

11. For example, the editorials in *Tablet*, December 15, 1917; *NW*, December 14, 1917.

12. *America*, 18 (December 22, 1917): 258 ff.; see also, *CW*, 106 (January 1918): 557; *Ave M*, n.s. 5 (December 22, 1917): 787. Typical of such expectations was a *NYT* report of January 21, 1918. Mgr. Arthur S. Barnes, Catholic rector of Oxford

University, was quoted as saying that England would declare Pope Benedict XV the Protector of all the holy places in Palestine.

13. *Ecclesiastical Review,* 58 (March 1918): 242; *Extension,* March 1918; April 1919 (front and back covers).

14. St. Malachy was the archbishop of Armagh, Ireland, in the first half of the twelfth century. The "prophecies" attributed to Malachy are generally considered to be a sixteenth-century forgery. *New Catholic Encyclopedia* (New York and St. Louis: McGraw-Hill, 1967), 9:101 f.

15. *Tidings,* November 9, 1917.

16. *Ave M,* n.s. 5 (November 10, 1917): 592 f.; *OSV,* March 31, 1918.

17. *CW,* 71 (September 1900): 857 f.; 108 (December 1918): 415; *Tidings,* May 7, 1920; (London) *Month,* 131 (January 1918): 88.

18. *NW,* December 14, 1917.

19. *Tidings,* April 23, 1920.

20. Similarly, Protestant millenarians applauded the restoration of the Jews to the Holy Land because they understood it to be a preparation for the second advent. For a discussion of millenarian thought in respect of the Holy Land and the Jewish restoration, see Robert T. Handy, "Studies in the Interrelationships between America and the Holy Land," in *Jewish-Christian Relations in Today's World,* ed. James E. Wood, Jr. (Waco, Tex.: Baylor University Press, 1971).

21. *America,* 28 (December 28, 1918): 280 f. It is curious that the Paulist author did not publish in the organ of his own order, *Catholic World,* but in the Jesuit organ. Certain ambiguities of phrase employed by O'Keefe are intriguing, for they provide a wide leeway in interpretation. Read today, with a post-Vatican II frame of reference, one can almost see the ecumenical vision of O'Keefe as a precursor.

22. *ACQR,* 43 (April 1918): 177–204. The blessings cited by the author, Adolf Frenay, are the tenth, eleventh, fourteenth, and seventeenth. Examination of the texts of these blessings hardly supports the harshness of Frenay's view. Even the fifteenth blessing, though outrightly messianic, is not violent. For the English translation of the Amidah, see *Daily Prayer Book,* trans. and annotated by Philip Birnbaum (New York: Hebrew Publishing Co., 1949), pp. 86–90.

23. Stein, op. cit., p. 409.

24. Ibid., pp. 281 f. The anti-Zionism of the Catholic Church in Palestine became more pronounced in the early twenties. See American Consul reports in Frank E. Manuel's *The Realities of American Palestine Relations* (Washington: Public Affairs Press, 1949), p. 293. On the attitude of the Latin Patriarch, Msgr. Barlassina, see Esco, op. cit., p. 544. Also, Chaim Weizmann, *Trial and Error* (New York: Harper & Bros., 1949), p. 284, and Pinchas E. Lapide, *The Last Three Popes and the Jews* (London: Souvenir Press, 1967), p. 270.

25. Barlassina's report is given in Lapide, op. cit. On Cardinal Bourne's impressions, see Ernest Oldmeadow, *Francis Cardinal Bourne* (London: Burns, Oates & Washbourne, 1944), 2:145–48, 166–73. See also Francis Cardinal Bourne, *Occasional Sermons* (London: Sheed & Ward, 1930), pp. 123–28. The Brooklyn *Tablet* (July 16, 1921) observed that Bourne had in his possession a collection of letters from Arabs, Chris-

tians, and British officials to support his allegations.

26. *AAS,* 11 (March 10, 1919): 97–101, particularly p. 100.

27. John Marlowe, *The Seat of Pilate* (London: Cresset Press, 1959), pp. 80, 89. J. C. Hurewitz, *The Struggle for Palestine* (New York: W. W. Norton, 1950), pp. 56f. The agitation of these associations allegedly contributed to the outbreak of violence between the Arabs and Jews in April 1919. Esco, op. cit., pp. 132f.

28. The visitors were the Maronite metropolitan, Joseph Khouri, and the Melchite Maximos Saigh, both having jurisdiction over Tyre and Sidon. *Tablet,* May 8, 1920: *NW,* May 6, 1921. On the Syrian Relief Fund, see *Ave M,* n.s. 12 (January 1, 1921): 23 f.

29. John Tracy Ellis, *The Life of James Cardinal Gibbons* (Milwaukee: Bruce Publishing Co., 1952), 2:282, n. 48. The date of the note was April 15, 1919.

30. *ACQR,* 43 (July 1918): 488–99. *Tidings,* April 16, 1920; April 23, 1920. The French draft for the Palestine mandate at the San Remo Conference in April 1920 attempted to retain for France its prewar rights as Guardian of Latin Catholics and the holy places. Paul L. Hanna, *British Policy in Palestine* (Washington: American Council on Public Affairs, 1941), p. 57.

On the lack of Vatican enthusiasm for a French mandate, see Christopher Sykes, *Two Studies in Virtue* (New York: Alfred A. Knopf, 1953), pp. 200–202.

31. *CHR,* 7 (April 1921): 255. *Ave M,* n.s. 12 (May 21, 1921): 665.

32. Latin text in *AAS,* 13 (June 18, 1921): 281–83. Official English translation is given in *Cath. Mind,* 19 (August 1921): 294–97.

The reference to the "new civil arrangements" may have also indicated the Pope's displeasure at the appointment of a Jewish high commissioner. That Sir Herbert Samuel was well aware of the Pope's apprehensions concerning his appointment is evident in Samuel's autobiography. Viscount Herbert Samuel, *Memoirs* (London: Cresset Press, 1945), p. 145.

33. Quotes are from *Tablet,* July 16, 1921, p. 1.

34. *CW,* 114 (December 1921): 33; *CHR,* 7 (October 1921): 394. An interesting sidelight is the information related by Governor Allen of Kansas to Simon Glazer in regard to a "Syrian Commission, headed by a French-Canadian Catholic priest, touring every state capital in the country, requesting sympathy for the Arabs and protesting the Balfour Declaration." Simon Glazer, *The Palestine Resolution: A Record of Its Origin* (Kansas City: United Synagogue of Kansas City, 1922), p. 100.

35. An Associated Press release from Geneva claimed that "the Vatican was taking a deep interest in the Palestine mandate and was using its influence with the French, Italian and Brazilian delegates" to delay ratification until its objections were met. *NYT,* May 12, 1922. In a memorandum to the League, dated May 15, 1922. Cardinal Gasparri, Vatican secretary of state, protested: "The Holy See is not opposed to Jews in Palestine having civil rights equal to those possessed by other nationals and creeds, but it cannot agree to Jews being given a privileged and preponderating position vis-à-vis other sections of the population." The text of the memorandum is given in the *NYT,* June 16, 1922. To see the Vatican note in the context of the League proceedings, consult Quincy Wright, *Mandates under the League* (Chicago: Chicago Univer-

sity Press, 1930), pp. 56ff., 182. Interesting observations on the diplomatic activity of the Vatican relative to Palestine at that time, are found in Lapide, op. cit., pp. 269–74.

36. For the background of Wilson's letter, see Manuel, op. cit., pp. 175–78. Stephen Wise, *Challenging Years* (New York: G. P. Putnam's Sons, 1949), pp. 194f. The congressional statements were acquired in answers to questionnaires sent by the ZOA. Reuben Fink compiled and edited the responses in *The American War Congress and Zionism* (New York: Zionist Organization of America, 1919).

It is important to note that the State Department took a decidedly different stance than that of the President and Congress. See Selig Adler, "The Palestine Question in the Wilson Era," *JSS*, 10 (October 1948): 303–34. Cf. Manuel, op. cit., pp. 170–204.

37. The initiative for the resolution was taken by a Kansas rabbi, Simon Glazer. His book is a personal account of the groundwork laid for the resolution; Glazer, op. cit.

Henry Cabot Lodge, chairman of the Senate Foreign Relations Committee, introduced the resolution in the Senate on April 12, 1922. A similar resolution had been introduced in the House on April 4 by Rep. Hamilton Fish of New York. For a detailed account of the progress of the resolution in Congress, see Irwin Oder, "American Zionism and the Congressional Resolutions of 1922," *PAJHS*, 45 (September 1955): 35–47.

38. U.S., *Statutes at Large*, vol. 42, pt. 1 (Washington: U.S. Government Printing Office, 1923), p. 1012.

39. *Tidings*, June 9, 1922; *NYT*, July 2, 1922.

40. Hanna, op. cit., pp. 82f.; cf. Richard Meinertzhagen, *Middle East Diary, 1917–1946* (London: Cresset Press, 1959), pp. 118 ff. Meinertzhagen claims that the vote in the House of Lords was, at root, an anti-Semitic vote and reflected a wave of anti-Semitism then prevalent in England. For the Churchill White Paper of 1922, see Esco, op. cit., 1:281–84. When, several days after the publication of the White Paper, a resolution similar to that of the House of Lords was voted down in the Commons, it was attributed to the fact that the reinterpretation of the Churchill paper removed the need for further censure of the mandate.

41. On the Vatican communication, see n. 35.

42. For example, Watts's dispatches in the NC-NS bulletins of June 7, 1922-June 28, 1922, and July 1, 1922.

43. NC-NS bulletin, July 10, 1922.

44. A diocesan paper's responses to controversial issues usually reflect the attitude of the ordinary under whose jurisdiction the paper is published. The *Pilot*'s responses, therefore, should be examined in the light of Cardinal O'Connell's activities and interests. In 1917, O'Connell pioneered in supporting "street missions" for the conversion of Jews and Protestants. On June 24, 1922, he announced, in the *Pilot*, that the month of July had been set aside by Pius XI for prayer for the conversion of the Jews. It is possible, therefore, that his paper sought to avoid antagonizing the Jews. Furthermore, the pro-Zionist congressional resolution was introduced in the Senate by Senator Lodge from Massachusetts. An almost identical resolution passed unanimously in the Massachusetts

General Court earlier, on March 29. O'Connell was an intensely patriotic American and consciously promoted American loyalty in his parish. Even if he strongly differed with the resolution, he may have considered it impolitic to air dissent. For the cardinal's autobiography, see William O'Connell, *Recollections of Seventy Years* (Boston and New York, 1934).

45. The *Tablet*'s harshness towards Zionism may have been an extension of the anti-Jewish attitudes of its editors. Patrick Scanlon, in particular, achieved a degree of notoriety for his enthusiastic support of Father Coughlin less than a decade later. See chap. 3, n. 75.

46. *NW*, June 30, 1922; July 14, 1922. See also editorial, May 14, 1920, which berated two archconservative Catholic papers for their expressions of anti-Semitism. According to the editor, anti-Jewish sentiments were vestiges of the "old world" transplanted in America, but which, he believed, would not flourish here.

47. Notably, *America* and *Catholic World*.

48. On Christian interpretations of Gen. 49:10, see Adolf Poznanski, *Schiloh* (Leipzig, 1904). For relevant medieval legislation, see Jacob R. Marcus, *The Jew in the Medieval World* (New York: Atheneum Press, 1969), pp. 5, 35 f., 139.

49. Stein, op. cit., pp. 282 and 409; Christopher Sykes, *Crossroads to Israel* (Cleveland and New York: World Publishing Co., 1968), p. 11.

50. Quoted in *Literary Digest,* August 19, 1922, p. 36.

CHAPTER III

1. The details of British policy may be followed in the concise scholarship of Paul L. Hanna, *British Policy in Palestine* (Washington: American Council on Public Affairs, 1942). For a more elaborate discussion, see the Esco Foundation study, *Palestine: A Study of Jewish, Arab and British Policies* (New Haven: Yale University Press, 1947), vol. 2, chaps. 9–14. From 1936 onward, the work of J. C. Hurewitz, *The Struggle for Palestine* (New York: W. W. Norton, 1950), is indispensable.

2. A good account of the growth of the Zionist community is given in Israel Cohen, *The Zionist Movement* (London: F. Muller, 1945), pp. 161–76. For a summary of Jewish political development during the mandatory period, see Hurewitz, op. cit., pp. 38–42.

3. See Thomas McAvoy, *A History of the Catholic Church in the United States* (Notre Dame: University of Notre Dame Press, 1969), pp. 344–62. An earlier effort to unite the U.S. hierarchy was made in 1884 at the Third Plenary Council of Baltimore, but the unity was superficial and was soon dissipated by dissensions over nationalism and Americanism. For a detailed account, see John Tracy Ellis, *The Life of James Cardinal Gibbons* (Milwaukee: Bruce Publishing Co., 1952), 2:1–80. On the history of the Central Verein, see John Philip Gleason, "The Central-Verein, 1900–1917: A Chapter in the History of the German-American Catholics" (Ph.D. diss., University of Notre Dame, 1960). On the Knights of Columbus, see Maurice F. Egan and John B. Kennedy, *The Knights of Columbus in Peace and War,* 2 vols. (New Haven: Knights of Columbus, 1920).

4. The name was later changed to National Catholic Welfare Conference.

5. McAvoy, op. cit., pp. 363–87. Also Aaron I. Abell, *American Catholicism and*

Social Action: A Search for Social Justice, 1865–1950 (Garden City, N.Y.: Hanover House, 1960), pp. 188–233.

6. For a summary of the religious changes in Catholic life following World War I, see McAvoy, op. cit., pp. 391–96. The official record of the Eucharistic Congress was compiled by C. F. Donovan in *The Story of the Twenty-Eighth International Eucharistic Congress Held at Chicago, Illinois, United States of America from June 20–24, 1926* (Chicago, 1927).

7. See the analytical studies of these currents of intolerance in John Higham's chapter on "The Tribal Twenties," in *Strangers in the Land* (New Brunswick, N.J.: Rutgers University Press, 1955), pp. 264–99, and specifically, pp. 291 ff., and in Gustavus Myers, *History of Bigotry in the United States,* 2d ed. rev. (New York: Capricorn Books, 1960), pp. 211–26, 258–77. For a survey of earlier anti-Catholic movements, see Ray Billington, *The American Crusade, 1800–1860: A Study of the Origins of American Nativism* (Chicago: Quadrangle Books, 1964). See particularly his chapter on the "Roots of Anti-Catholic Prejudice," pp. 1–32, and his survey of anti-Catholic literature, pp. 345–79.

8. See, for example, *America,* 30 (November 3, 1923): 49; (February 16, 1924): 429; *CW,* 121 (June 1925): 409; 122 (January 1926): 543–45; *OSV,* September 10, 1922, p. 1. In the same spirit, editorials in *CW* warmly greeted the establishment of the Commission to Fight Bigotry, which comprised Protestants, Catholics, and Jews, and the National Conference of Christian and Jews. *CW,* 125 (May 1927): 267; 128 (October 1928): 104.

9. *Ave M,* 13 (April 23, 1921): 538; *Tablet,* May 7, 1921. In 1914 Catholics did propose to initiate action to bar the *Menace* from the mails, but the proposal was scotched by Cardinal Gibbons, who reasoned that meanwhile other unfriendly publications would remain untouched and the action would provoke even greater manifestations of anti-Catholicism. McAvoy, op. cit., p. 361. The furor over the *Dearborn Independent* began with Henry Ford's publication in his paper of the spurious *Protocols of the Elders of Zion.* It was not until 1927, when a Jewish attorney, Aaron Sapiro, brought a libel suit against the paper, that Ford was compelled to repudiate his anti-Semitic propaganda and issue a public apology. For Catholic reactions to Ford's apology, see *America,* 35 (July 23, 1927): 343, and *CW,* 125 (September 1927): 833. Both papers took the occasion to urge anti-Catholic papers to emulate Ford and retract their bigoted statements.

10. For example, *OSV,* December 23, 1917, contrasted the munificence of Jewish contributions to Jewish War Relief with the meager contributions of Catholics to the Knights of Columbus Drive; *CMW,* 7 (October 31, 1928): 647, sponsoring the endowment of a Gaelic Room in the New York Public Library, recalled the generosity of Jacob Schiff in endowing a Jewish Room; Nathan Straus and Julius Rosenwald were eulogized as exemplars of philanthropy in *Sign,* 10 (January 1931): 388 and 11 (February 1932): 389.

11. For example, *America,* 30 (January 26, 1924): 324; *NW,* (June 30, 1922.) Lawrence Frank Pisani, *The Italian in America* (New York: Exposition Press, 1957), p. 191, notes that Italian Catholics used the careers of successful Jewish immigrants as models for their own countrymen.

12. When the Arab riots of 1929 sparked mass demonstrations and protests in the U.S., editors were filled with awe at the immediate responsiveness of the American Jews to the plight of their co-religionists abroad, and urged their readers to learn from the Jews how to protest against persecutions of Catholics in Mexico. *America,* 41 (September 7, 1929): 511; *CMW,* 10 (September 11, 1929): 461; *Tablet* (September 7, 1929): 9; *Pilot,* September 7, 1929, p. 4.

13. *New World* denounced the anti-Semitic statements in the Dubuque *Tribune* and Ohio *Waisenfreund* as "vestiges" of Old World thinking which had no roots in American Catholic thinking. *NW,* May 14, 1920.

14. *America,* 32 (February 14, 1925): 432. This sentiment was incorporated in the cardinal's Easter Sunday sermon following his return from Palestine. Francis Cardinal Bourne, *Occasional Sermons* (London: Sheed & Ward, 1930), pp. 123–28.

15. *CW,* 122 (October 1925): 120.

16. A brief summary of Catholic activity in Palestine during this period is given in Saul Colbi, *Short History of Christianity in the Holy Land* (Jerusalem: Am Hassefer, 1965), p. 53. Also, Fannie Fern Andrews, *The Holy Land under the Mandate* (Cambridge: Houghton Mifflin Co., 1931), 1:158 ff. The *Pilot* of Boston carried a special report on the growth and activities of the Salesian Fathers in Palestine in its issue of July 27, 1929.

17. *Pilot,* June 15, 1929.

18. *CW,* 120 (November 1924): 252–54. The quote was from Reginald Ginn's article in the August 24 issue of the London *Month.*

19. Fr. Barnabas Meistermann, *Guide to the Holy Land,* rev. ed. (London: Burns, Oates & Washbourne, 1923), pp. 59, 69, 71, 82, 87, 442.

20. Ibid., p. v.

21. Chesterton was steeped in the usual stereotype image of the "diaspora" Jews—he maligned them as radicals, Bolshevists, usurers, traitors, aliens, etc. See, for example, his diatribe in *The New Jerusalem* (London: Hodder & Stoughton, 1921), pp. 85 ff.

22. Ibid., pp. 297–300.

23. There are differing opinions on the implication of the mufti in these riots. He was exonerated by the investigating commission, although his share in the responsibility of provocation was not disavowed. Cohen, op cit., p. 196. Cf. Hanna, op. cit. p. 99.

24. Many accounts have been written of these events. A scholarly version is given by Hanna, op. cit., pp. 87–108. The official version is given in the report of the British Commission of Inquiry, *Parliamentary Papers, 1929–30,* Cmd. 3530, pp. 29–66. A highly readable account, full of interesting background detail, is in Christopher Sykes, *Crossroads to Israel* (Cleveland and New York: World Publishing Co., 1968), pp. 126–39.

25. Samuel Halperin, *The Political World of American Zionism* (Detroit: Wayne State University Press, 1961), p. 17.

26. Ibid., pp. 259 f. See also the first-hand accounts of the American response in *New Palestine,* 17 (September 6, 1929): 152–54, 162 f.; Julius Haber, *The Odyssey of an American Zionist* (New York: Twayne Publishers, 1956), pp. 222 f. Official U.S.

reaction is reviewed by Frank Manual, *The Realities of American-Palestine Relations* (Washington: Public Affairs Press, 1949), pp. 303 f.

27. *Commonweal*, in examining the causes of the riots, included as one of the irritants, "Zionist fascisti" (probably a reference to the Revisionists) who staged a demonstration in front of the mufti's house. *CMW*, 10 (September 4, 1929): 342.

28. Ibid. (September 11, 1929): 461.

29. *America*, 41 (September 7, 1929): 511.

30. *CMW*, 10 (September 4, 1929): 342.

31. Diocesan papers had been receiving rumors of Arab molestation of the Latin community in Palestine, e.g., *Pilot*, August 31, 1929. An allusion to these charges was heard in the *Pilot* editorial of September 7, 1929.

32. Ibid.

33. *OSV*, September 22, 1929, p. 1. One of the Christian casualties was a Catholic, Eugene Best.

34. The dispatch was carried in the *Tablet*, August 31, 1929; *Tidings*, September 3, 1929; *NW*, September 13, 1929. Msgr. Barlissina's negative attitudes toward Zionism were remarked upon by Chaim Weizmann in his autobiography, *Trial and Error* (New York: Harper & Bros., 1949), pp. 284 f. Incidentally, the patriarch's obvious annoyance with Zionist "immodesty" in dress was the subject of comment by William F. Albright in Esco, op. cit., 1:544.

35. *NW*, December 27, 1929. The *Tablet* printed similar charges, September 7, 1929, pp. 1, 3.

36. See in particular, the blustering reports in *Tablet*, September 7, 1929, p. 1, and in *NW*, September 13, 1929, p. 4. It is, of course, undeniable that certain forms of socialism and economic communism did exist in the cooperatives and in the collective-farm movements in the Jewish colonies, but some Catholic reports tended to exaggerate these conditions. For a reliable report on the economic and social organization of the Jewish colonies, see Abraham Revusky, *Jews in Palestine* (New York: Bloch Publishing Co., 1945), pp. 121-36, 137-56. Also, Rose N. Stoloff, *Cooperatives and Collectives in Palestine* (New York: League for Labor Palestine, 1935).

37. *NW*, September 13, 1929. According to the official report, *The Palestine Commission on the Disturbances of August, 1929, Evidence*, Colonial no. 48 (London, 1930), 2:1063, Palestinians employed in the civil service during July 1929 numbered 1,176 Christians, 1,111 Moslems, and 714 Jews. Quoted in Hanna, op. cit., p. 185, n. 1.

38. *Tablet*, September 7, 1929, p. 9.

39. The purpose of the British Commission of Inquiry, headed by Sir Walter Shaw, was to determine the immediate causes of the riots. The inquiries were held in Jerusalem from October 25 to December 29, 1929. For an account of the activities and the conclusions of the commission, see Esco, op. cit., 2:615-29; Hanna, op. cit., pp. 97-101.

40. *America*, 42 (February 8, 1930): 419. However some of the decisions of the trial were obliquely questioned. Ibid., February 15, 1930, p. 433.

41. *America*, 43 (April 12, 1930): 3. The commission's report was published on March 31, 1930.

42. *America*, 44 (November 1, 1930): 75. Sir John Hope Simpson was appointed by the British to prepare a report on economic conditions in Palestine, with specific reference to immigration, land settlement, and development. The report was published on October 20, 1930 at the same time that the Passfield Paper was issued. For a summary of both documents, see Esco, op. cit., pp. 635–48.

43. *America*, 42 (December 14, 1929): 235; 45 (August 1, 1931): 402. To understand the significance of the latter comment for LaFarge, it is necessary to recognize LaFarge's fear of the spread of communism, and his suspicion that Jews were largely involved in the movement at that time.

44. Ibid., 42 (December 7, 1930): 213. The reviewer, who is signed as G.G.W., is most likely Gerald G. Walsh, associate editor of *America*.

45. *CMW*, 10 (October 2, 1929): 554–56.

46. One letter, for example, warned that if Jewry were permitted to triumph, the Christian world would find itself, in the words of Herder, the "slave of the despotism of Jewish finance." *CMW*, 11 (December 18, 1929): 18.

47. *CMW*, 11 (January 29, 1930): 360 f.

48. Ibid., p. 361.

49. Ibid., (April 30, 1930): 737–39. Sheean, who testified for the Arabs before the Parliamentary Commission of Inquiry, stated about himself, "I am a non-Zionist. My sympathies with Zionism are non-existent."

Sheean, however, admitted in a letter published in the *Jewish Daily Bulletin* that he had sympathized with the Zionist movement prior to 1929. Meyer Weisgal attributed this switch in sympathies to the ZOA's refusal to grant Sheean $1,500 for an agreed lecture tour. See the revealing exchange of letters between Sheean and Weisgal, replete with Sheean's denial of these charges, in the *Jewish Daily Bulletin*, January 5, 1930, pp. 7 f.

50. *CMW*, 11 (December 25, 1929): 214. The proponent of a bi-national state was Judah L. Magnes, then the chancellor of the Hebrew University in Jerusalem. Controversy was stirred on both sides of the Atlantic by the publication of a pamphlet expounding his views. Judah Magnes, *Like All Nations?* (Jerusalem, 1930).

51. *CMW*, 12 (July 23, 1930): 312. Cf. ibid., 12 (June 11, 1930), 147 f.

52. Ibid., 13 (November 5, 1930): 2 f.

53. Ibid., 13 (February 25, 1931): 450 f.

54 See Edmund A. Moore, *A Catholic Runs for President: The Campaign of 1928* (Gloucester, Mass.: Peter Smith, 1968). According to the Catholic historian Theodore Maynard, the diminution of anti-Catholicism was a direct result of the 1928 election. There was a "recoil of disgust among the decent people of America, perhaps most of all among those who voted against Smith for better reasons than that." *The Catholic Church and the American Idea* (New York: Appleton-Century-Crofts, 1953), p. 105. Cf. McAvoy, op. cit., p. 401, who attributes the fading of bigotry to the common suffering among all groups during the depression.

55. For the early history of the formation of the NCWC, its sudden suppression by Rome in 1922, and its restoration, which quickly followed, see McAvoy, op. cit., pp. 379–83, 403. Also, John Tracy Ellis, *American Catholicism*, 2d ed. rev. (Chicago:

University of Chicago Press, 1969), pp. 141–44. A detailed account of the manifold activities of the NCWC is given in Leo Ward, ed., *The American Apostolate* (Westminster, Md.: Newman Press, 1952), chap. 17, pp. 241–78.

56. The general tenor of the Pastoral letters was that trouble stemmed from a negligence of Christian values. Peace and prosperity would be restored by a renewal of the Christian spirit. Of particular interest, however, are the constructive solutions offered in the Pastoral of 1919, and reiterated in 1933. For the Bishops' Program of Social Reconstruction (February 1919) and the Bishops' Statement on the "Present Crisis" (April 1933), see Raphael M. Huber, O.F.M., ed., *Our Bishops Speak* (Milwaukee: Bruce Publishing Co., 1952), pp. 243–60, 272–300. The reluctance of American Catholics to deal with theological problems, ever since the condemnation of Americanism and Modernism, led many American theologians to concentrate on Catholic programs of economic and social reform. Preeminent among these latter theologians were John A. Ryan and Peter E. Dietz. See McAvoy, op. cit., p. 407, and Andrew M. Greeley, *The Catholic Experience* (Garden City, N.Y.: Doubleday, 1967), pp. 216–34.

57. Pius IX issued the encyclical *Quanta Cura* less than three months after Karl Marx launched the First International. Ellis, op. cit., p. 146.

58. See, for example, the encyclical of Pius XI, *Divini Redemptoris,* in *AAS,* 22 (February 2, 1930): 89 f., and the official statements issued by U.S. bishops during the thirties. Huber, op. cit., pp. 277, 314–18, 310–12.

59. The authoritative Catholic record of persecutions of the Church in Communist countries is Albert Galter's *The Red Book of the Persecuted Church* (Westminster, Md.: Newman Press, 1957). The report and statistics on the USSR are given on pp. 47 f. Cf. Waldemar Gurian, *Bolshevism: Theory and Practice* (New York: Macmillan Co., 1932), pp. 331–52.

60. For a summary of the events, see Frank Tannenbaum, *Mexico: The Struggle for Peace and Bread* (New York: Alfred A. Knopf, 1950), pp. 49–80. For Catholic reactions in the U.S., see George Q. Flynn, *American Catholics and the Roosevelt Presidency, 1932–36* (Lexington: University of Kentucky Press, 1968), pp. 150–94.

61. For a scholarly and objective treatment of this period, see Hugh Thomas, *The Spanish Civil War* (New York: Harper & Bros., 1961). For a Catholic version of these events, see Richard Pattee, *This Is Spain* (Milwaukee: Bruce Publishing Co., 1951). In the introduction of the book, Fr. Joseph Husslein, S.J., wrote:

> [the] author uncovers the factual errors and often, no doubt, the positive falsehoods that abound in the present-day literature on Spain. As for the thoroughly paganized products of the extreme socialist, communist and anarchist combination that has striven to submerge Spain under their godless and destructive rule, there can be nothing but utter contempt.

62. For a well-documented analysis of the Catholic reaction, see George Q. Flynn, op. cit. The two events in the early Roosevelt administration which can be singled out as most alarming to Catholics were the presidential appointment of Josephus Daniels as U.S. ambassador to the Calles regime in Mexico and official recognition of the Soviet Union in November 1933. American volunteers for the Republican army in Spain, the

findings of an American body of Protestant clergy who investigated conditions in Spain, and the congressional debate on aid to the Republicans were all, in the eyes of Catholic observers, evidence of U.S. sympathies with the leftists. See Joseph B. Code, *The Spanish War and Lying Propaganda* (New York: Paulist Press, 1938).

63. Code's pamphlet contains much interesting material on this matter.

64. McAvoy, op. cit., p. 415; Flynn, op. cit., p. 167.

65. *America,* 48 (April 1, 1933): 615. Cf. ibid., 60 (December 3, 1938): 202 f., 218, 243.

66. *Tablet,* November 19, 1938, p. 1; February 25, 1939. Similar remarks abound in *Sign.* For example, 12 (July 1933): 707 f.; 16 (October 1936): 132; 18 (December 1938): 260. *Ave M,* 41 (February 18, 1939): 215 f., was indignant over a proposal in Congress which suggested that the money owed to the U.S. by European nations be set up as a fund to aid Jewish refugees from Nazi persecution. In the editor's opinion it was far more urgent to set up a fund for Catholic refugees, who were both more numerous and more oppressed. Also, ibid., 50 (August 12, 1939): 216.

67. This attitude was expressly advocated by the editor of *Central-Blatt,* 31 (February 1939): 342 f.

68. *Extension,* 33 (October 1938): 18 and (February 1939): 20. The journal is published in Chicago, and is an organ of the Catholic Church Extension Society, dedicated to developing the missionary spirit.

69. *Sign* utilized this reasoning in explaining why the U.S. press was "muzzled" in its reporting on the civil war in Spain. "This indictment offers a solid clue to the reasons why the secular press in general has been unfair to Catholic persecution and most valuable and active with regard to anything that affects the Jews." *Sign,* 18 (March 1939): 495. Also, *Cath Mind,* 32 (October 22, 1934): 381–97; *Sign,* 13 (March 1934): 452 f.: 17 (April 1938): 518 and (July 1938): 710; *America,* 59 (May 7, 1938): 98.

70. *America,* 57 (July 31, 1937): 99.

71. For example, *CMW*'s impartial stand on the Spanish Civil War, which was criticized in the Catholic press. See, for example, the attack on *CMW* in the relatively liberal *Michigan Catholic,* July 7, 1938, p. 1. The latter claimed that *CMW* did not represent Catholic opinion and was in truth a "fringe" publication. *America,* too, took issue with *CMW* on its stand on Spain; 57 (April 10, 1937): 9–11.

72. *CMW,* 11 (January 1, 1930): 239. Also 13 (March 18, 1931): 536.

73. *Cath Worker,* 3 (December 1935): 3.

74. Several excellent treatments of Coughlin have been recently published. See Charles J. Tull's informed study, *Father Coughlin and the New Deal* (Syracuse: Syracuse University Press, 1965); David O'Brien's skillful analysis of Coughlin's thought and influence in *American Catholics and Social Reform* (New York: Oxford University Press, 1968), pp. 150–82; and Andrew Greeley's comparative study of Ryan and Coughlin, in Greeley, op. cit., pp. 216–46. A description of the campaign of Fr. Coughlin and the "Christian Front" organizations he inspired is given in Donald S. Strong, *Organized Anti-Semitism in America: The Rise of Group Prejudice during the Decade, 1930–1940* (Washington: American Council on Public Affairs, 1941). Opposition to Coughlin was most emphatically voiced by *CMW* and *Cath Worker,* while other

papers either contented themselves with mildly critical statements or openly advocated Coughlin's preaching. O'Brien, op. cit., pp. 173–78. The Catholic hierarchy, as a body, did not officially denounce Coughlin, though the administrative board of the NCWC did issue a general statement condemning all forms of bigotry. Huber, op. cit., p. 323. The scarcity of any public and vigorous Catholic opposition probably moved Emanuel Chapman to write an apologia for the Church in his article, "The Catholic Church and Anti-Semitism," *Social Frontier,* 5 (January 1939): 108–11.

75. *Tablet,* February 4, 1939, p. 4. Numerous factors may have contributed to the antipathy felt by Patrick Scanlon, the *Tablet's* editor, toward the Jews. Certainly socio-economic factors played a part. The Irish Catholics in Brooklyn rose slowly on the economic scale, and although they attained lower-middle-class status, many tended to remain at that level. The Jews, who arrived later, quickly attained economic and social positions comparable to the Irish, and the movement continued upward. As a result, tension naturally arose between the two groups. See Richard Robbins, "American Jews and American Catholics: Two Types of Social Change," *Sociological Analysis,* 26 (Spring 1965): 1–18. I would like to suggest yet another factor—Scanlon's self-image as a one-man "Anti-Defamation League" for Catholics, which gave him the opportunity to be a self-righteous and frequent exponent of this antipathy. Working in Brooklyn, an area of concentrated Jewish settlement, Scanlon chose his Jewish neighbors for surveillance. Whenever and wherever he caught an insinuation of a derogatory remark directed against Catholics, he pounced on it. Even a stance of indifference to communism or socialism was sufficient to indict the same as evidence of foresworn hatred of Christianity. See his editorials, "From the Manager's Desk," in the *Tablet,* particularly from 1935 to 1940.

76. For example, *Tablet,* November 19, 1938, p. 1; *OSV,* June 11, 1939; *Sign,* 17 (July 1938): 710; *Ave M,* 40 (May 13, 1939): 600 f.; *Central-Blatt,* 21 (December 1938): 273. Certainly the Jewish blockade of German products and the obvious anxiety displayed by American Jews as reports on the fate of European Jewry grew more ominous lent credibility to some of the suspicions of the press.

77. See Frederick C. Wentz, "The Reaction of the Religious Press in America to the Emergence of Nazism" (Ph.D. diss., Yale University, 1954), pp. 151 f.

78. Selig Adler's *The Isolationist Impulse* (London and New York: Abelard & Schuman, 1957), pp. 239–73, which fully documents the isolationist temper of the thirties, is essential for understanding this decade. See also William Leuchtenberg, *Franklin Delano Roosevelt and the New Deal* (New York, Evanston, and London: Harper & Row, 1963), pp. 215–30. One of the most outspoken isolationists among Catholic editors was James Gillis of *CW.* Beginning with a February 1937 editorial, "Who Wants War?" Gillis barraged his readers with an incessant stream of editorials which purported to ferret out and expose all the conspiracies that were dragging the U.S. into the fray. His influence extended beyond the *CW* audience, for many diocesan papers carried his syndicated column, "Sursum Corda." Gillis took a leading role in the formation and activities of the "America First" Committee. For this aspect of Gillis's career, see James F. Finley, *James Gillis, Paulist* (Garden City, N.Y.: Hanover House, 1958), pp. 158–66.

79. A maximum ceiling of 75,000 Jews would be permitted to enter before 1944,

and thereafter immigration would continue at the pleasure of the Arab majority. The arbitrary figure of 75,000 would freeze the Jewish population at no more than one-third the total population. For details, of this document, see Esco, op. cit., 2: 901–908.

80. The idea of a national legislative council was fostered by Sir Arthur Wauchope, the high commissioner, in the hope of achieving Arab-Jewish unity. Jewish groups rejected the immediate implementation of the plan since numerically they were still a minority group, and as such they deemed it inadvisable to entrust the future of the National Home to a council whereon at least half of the members would be opposed to Zionist aims. The Arabs also criticized the proposal, but did not reject it outrightly. While tentatively approving the council, the Arab majority was dissatisfied with the details of the scheme and with the continued British insistence on the fulfillment of mandate objectives in reference to the Jews. A full account of the history of the council proposal and the responses of both Arabs and Jews is given in Hanna, op. cit., pp. 114–26; Sykes, op. cit., pp. 175–82.

81. The name of the Supreme Arab Committee was later changed to Arab Higher Committee.

82. Hurewitz, op. cit., pp. 69–71; Hanna, op. cit., pp. 122–26; Sykes, op. cit., pp. 18–85. The government hesitated to apply force to repress the disorders so as not to add to Arab discontent. Even after the strike was terminated, Arabs were not disarmed and their leaders were not prosecuted. This restrained policy, however, encouraged the Arabs to think they could defy Britain with impunity, and so left the country in a potentially dangerous situation. For a view sympathetic to the Arab position, see John Marlowe, *The Seat of Pilate* (London: Cresset Press, 1959), pp. 134–59.

83. Hanna, op. cit., pp. 126–31; Esco, op. cit., pp. 836–47.

84. Jewish opinion was divided on the question of partition. See Cohen, op. cit., pp. 221 f. Cf. Weizmann's early satisfaction with the Peel decision, op. cit., pp. 385 ff. Esco discusses the controversy at the Twentieth Zionist Congress in 1937, op. cit., p. 854 f.

85. Quoted in Marlowe, op. cit., p. 150.

86. Sykes, op. cit., p. 215.

87. Hurewitz, op. cit., pp. 86 ff.; Hanna, op. cit., pp. 120 f.

88. Cohen, op. cit., pp. 230 f. However, the decision of the commission had only the force of an advisory opinion. The White Paper was scheduled to come before the League Council in September, but the outbreak of World War II forced the suspension of League activities.

89. For a summary of the Evian Conference, see Mark Wischnitzer, *To Dwell in Safety* (Philadelphia: Jewish Publication Society, 1948), pp. 200–206. Convoked by President Roosevelt, the conference met on July 6–15, 1938, with thirty-two governments participating. With the one exception of the Dominican Republic's generous offer of refuge, Wischnitzer characterizes the mood of the conference as an "atmosphere of evasions and rationalizations." See also Wischnitzer's discussion of England's secret negotiations with the U.S. to remove the issue of Palestine from the table, p. 201.

90. Halperin, op. cit., pp. 20 ff.

91. See *American Public Opinion on British Policy in Palestine* (Washington: American Zionist Bureau, 1939).

92. *NYT,* May 26, 1939, p. 15. See Manuel, op. cit., pp. 307 f., and Joseph B. Schechtman, *The United States and the Jewish State Movement* (New York: Herzl Press, 1966), pp. 19–24, for the attitude of the State Department and Administration.

93. *Central-Blatt,* 31 (January 1939): 284. Wise men should not offer any opinions because "certain interests" have deliberately manipulated the facts in order to stir up public opinion in support of their own benefit. Cf. the admonishment to "wise men" in ibid., 31 (February 1939): 342 f. See also, in 31 (September 1938): 167, the resolution on Palestine adopted by the Catholic Central Verein of America during its annual convention, which urged that a solution to the problems of Palestine be found "in accord with the holy traditions and dignity of Palestine."

94. *CW,* 142 (September 1936): 684–89; 146 (October 1937): 12–18; 147 (February 1939): 553–60. See also n. 78. Similarly, *Pilot,* June 17, 1939, p. 1.

95. *America,* 61 (June 3, 1939): 180. One week later, a less enthusiastic assessment of the White Paper was printed in article form, and it even incorporated suggestions for modification of the harsher measures of the British policy. The author of this more moderate viewpoint was James Coleran, a journalist who had contributed background articles on Palestine in the past. Whether Coleran's article actually reflected a dissenting opinion among *America*'s editors is difficult to judge.

96. Ibid., 55 (May 30, 1936): 172.

97. Many diocesan papers refrained from editorials on the topic, even though they carried news items on Palestine. In a rare instance, *Michigan Catholic,* November 3, 1938, p. 4, spoke editorially, but took neither the Jewish nor the Arab side in the fracas, lashing out only at Britain for having made conflicting promises. Similarly, the *Catholic Worker,* whose attitude toward the Jews was openly sympathetic, did not indulge in editorial commitments on the Palestine imbroglio. However, a poem written by the founder of the paper, Peter Maurin, may reflect *Catholic Worker* opinion. Entitled "Let's Keep the Jews for Christ's Sake," it included the following lines: "They [the Jews] are not a nation / although the Zionists try to build up one / in Palestine . . . / what the Jews are doing / in Palestine / they can do also / in America." *Cath Worker,* 6, (July–August 1939), p. 1.

The denial of nationhood to the Jews is an outgrowth of the traditional belief that the continued existence of the Jews is solely to serve as a "witness people." Again in the words of Maurin: "The presence of the Jews / all over the world / is a reminder to the world / of the coming of Christ." Ibid.

Within this framework, the Jews could not be expected to have a future independent of Christian eschatology. For a fuller discussion on this theological problem, see chap. VII, pp. 107–119.

98. See n. 36. The roots of a socialist Zionism may be traced to the 1898 pamphlet of Nahman Syrkin, published under the pseudonym Ben Elieser, *Die Judenfrage und der sozialistche Judenstaat.* Also, Nahman Syrkin, *Essays on Socialist Zionism* (New

York: Young Poale Zion Alliance of America, 1935). A Marxist emphasis was expounded in the writing of Ber Borochov, *Nationalism and the Class Struggle* (New York, 1935).

99. *CW*, 149 (June 1939): 359 f.; *Cath Mind*, 37 (June 8, 1939): 689 f.; see also *Tablet*, June 17, 1937.

100. *Tablet*, October 22, 1938, p. 8. Similar arguments can be found in *Ave M*, 36 (August 14, 1937): 217; *CW*, 142 (September 1936): 684–91; 146 (October 1937): 12–18. For a full statement of the Arab position as presented to a Catholic paper, see *Tablet*, October 22, 1938, p. 5.

101. *Sign* is published by the Passionists, a religious order which was founded in 1720 and established its first home in the U.S. in 1852. In prayer, penance, and solitude, the Passionist dedicates his being to con-crucifixion in the continuing Passion of Christ, and in redemptive work among the laity. The intense and continual meditation on the scene of the Passion, perhaps, lends to members of this order a greater degree of sensitivity to the question of the Jews and the Holy Land. The journalist who covered Palestine news at this time, and who later became the editor of *Sign*, was Ralph Gorman, C.P., an alumnus of the Dominican Ecole Biblique in Jerusalem.

102. *Sign*, 17 (January 1938): 366; 19 (May 1940): 627.

103. Ibid., 18 (August 1938): 6; also 15 (November 1935): 197; 15 (July 1936): 708; 16 (October 1939): 132.

104. For consistent expressions of opposition to anti-Semitism, see *CMW*, 17 (April 12, 1933): 647–48; 28 (May 27, 1938): 129; 28 (September 16, 1938): 532; 29 (December 30, 1938): 262–64; (April 21, 1939): 706–9.

105. Ibid., 20 (October 26, 1934): 609–11; 24 (June 19, 1935): 201–3; 26 (October 1, 1937): 509 f.

106. As, for example, *America*, 60 (December 24, 1938): 272 f.; 57 (July 31, 1937): 386; *Cath Worker*, 6 (July–August 1939): 1; *Sign*, 18 (August 1938): 6; *Ave M*, 46 (August 1937): 217.

107. *CMW*, 29 (November 4, 1938): 55.

108. Ibid., 28 (October 21, 1938): 658.

109. Ibid., 31 (November 10, 1939): 71 f.

CHAPTER IV

1. The general statements in the introductory pages are fully discussed and documented later in the chapter.

2. Jacob Lestchinsky, "The Destruction of European Jewry," *Congress Weekly*, 9 (September 11, 1942): 6 f.; Marie Syrkin, "German Police Testify," *Jewish Frontier*, 9 (November 1942): 9–11; N. Fry, "Massacre of the Jews," *New Republic*, 107 (December 21, 1942): 816. Mass meetings and protest demonstrations took place in 1942 in many U.S. cities, such as New York, Boston, Chicago, Cleveland, and Los Angeles, among others. AJComm. *Year Book*, 45 (Philadelphia, 1943), p. 192. In 1943, a documented pamphlet detailing the conditions of Jews throughout Nazi Europe was printed under the auspices of the American Jewish Congress. *Hitler's Black Rec-*

ord (New York, March 1943) gave information of Hitler's extermination order, deportations, and concentration camps. A more expanded volume was published several months later under the title, *Hitler's Ten Year War on the Jews*, again under the sponsorship of the AJCongress. This report included statistical appendices.

The two major labor organizations in the U.S., the CIO and the AFL, called the attention of their members to the plight of the persecuted Jews in Europe during their annual conventions in 1943. *CIO Convention Proceedings*, November 1943, and *AFL Proceedings*, October 8, 1943, pp. 358–64.

3. Camille Cianfarra, *The Vatican and the War* (New York: E. P. Dutton, 1944), is an attempt to refute these early insinuations of Vatican collaboration.

4. Prominent among these pronouncements was the encyclical of Pius XI to the German bishops, *Mit brennender Sorge*, March 14, 1937. This and other Church statements were reissued in 1944 in a pamphlet earlier prepared by Rev. Gregory Feige for the Catholic Association for International Peace. *The Church and the Jews* (New York: Paulist Press, 1937). It should be noted that while Pius XII denounced anti-Semitism and all racial intolerance, he never explicitly denounced the Nazi practice of extermination of the Jews. Leon Poliakov, who credited members of the Church for their tireless humanitarian efforts (oftentimes *with* the approval and encouragement of the Vatican), bemoans this lack of explicit pronouncement on the part of the Pope. *Harvest of Hate* (Syracuse: Syracuse University Press, 1954), pp. 295–305. A more severe indictment is found in Saul Friedlander's *Pius XII and the Third Reich: A Documentation* (New York: Alfred A. Knopf, 1966). However, cf. the apologia for Pius XI and Pius XII in Pinchas E. Lapide's *The Last Three Popes and the Jews* (London: Souvenir Press, 1967), pp. 92–265.

That Catholics (clergy, religious, and laity) showed remarkable courage in Europe in rescuing and aiding Jews has been well documented, notably in Philip Friedman's *Their Brothers' Keepers* (New York: Crown Publishing Co., 1957). Official pronouncements and statements of various churches against the policy of anti-Semitism were compiled, during the war, by the National Conference of Christians and Jews in a pamphlet entitled, *Christians Protest Persecutions* (New York, 1943). Since then, spokesmen of various Christian denominations have produced a literature developing the theme.

There is, however, a persuasive body of literature which exposes the debit side of the Church. Gunter Lewy's well-documented indictment of the German hierarchy, *The Catholic Church and Nazi Germany* (New York: McGraw-Hill, 1964), though challenged, remains unanswered. New light may be shed on this controversy as the archives of the Vatican come into print. *Actes et documents du Saint Siege relatifs a la seconde guerre mondiale* (Vatican: Libreria Editrice Vaticana, 1965–69) is edited by Pierre Blet, Angelo Martini, and Burkhardt Schneider. So far, five volumes have been published, covering the period from March 1939 to October 1942.

5. *OSV*, May 7, May 22, June 11, June 25, July 2, and July 9, 1944. Occasionally, when papers attempted to convey the image of Catholic friendship and aid to Jews, some of the examples selected were inaccurate or awkward. For example, the June 11 report in *OSV* of Cardinal Serédi's appeals and interventions on behalf of

Hungarian Jews is misleading. Arthur B. Morse, *While Six Million Died* (New York: Random House, 1968), pp. 350 f., published documents demonstrating that the protest and intervention were made *only* on behalf of baptized Christians of Jewish origin, to "distinguish them from the Jews." Likewise, Jews may find difficulty in seeing Cardinal Innitzer's aid to non-Aryan Catholics in Vienna or the actions of Josef Tiso in Slovakia as bona fide examples of the rescue of European Jewry, as did *America*, 75 (June 22, 1946): 236, and *MC*, March 6, 1947, p. 9.

6. For example, *America*, 71 (July 1, 1944): 350; *CW*, 158 (March 1944): 595; *Ave M*, 62 (October 6, 1945): 211; *OSV*, July 2, and 9, 1944; *Tablet*, July 7, 1945; *NW*, October 12, 1945, p. 1; *MC*, December 6, 1945, p. 1. One of the most widely reported tributes was that of the former rabbi of Rome, Anton Zolli. Zolli, shortly thereafter, converted to Roman Catholicism. For a Jewish, though polemical, assessment of his conversion, see Louis Newman, *A "Chief Rabbi" Becomes a Catholic* (New York: Renascence Press, 1945).

7. *Pilot*, March 3, 1945, p. 1. So, too, a front-page article in the issue of October 20, 1945, which published letters from the German hierarchy, to "show that [the] German Church never yielded."

8. *America*, for example, believed that the Communists were launching an "invidious" campaign to incriminate the Church in anti-Semitism, 71 (May 13, 1944): 159. *Sign*'s editor, Fr. Ralph Gorman, sniffed anti-Catholicism in press attitudes in 1943 and offered the following explanation: "The Spanish Civil War was the tipoff for us Catholics—if we needed any. When the windows of Jewish shops in Berlin were broken by the Nazis, our 'liberals' screamed their protests, held mass meetings, signed petitions and circulated resolutions calling on the civilized world to act. When Spanish Catholics were murdered by the tens of thousands in cold blood, for no other reason than they were Catholics, our 'liberals' were silent." *Sign*, 22 (April 1943): 543. Also, *Tablet*, January 29, 1944 and February 12, 1944, pp. 1, 4; *MC*, March 9, 1944, p. 1, and March 16, 1944, p. 4.

9. *CMW*, 34 (September 26, 1941): 532; 34 (October 10, 1941), 590; 35 (December 26, 1941): 244 f.; 36 (September 25, 1942): 534–37; 38 (June 4, 1943): 181–88; 41 (March 23, 1944): 558–61. *America*, 68 (November 28, 1942): 200; 68 (March 13, 1943): 630; 69 (June 12, 1943): 266; 69 (May 15, 1943): 141. Michael Williams in *CMW* and John LaFarge in *America* were the most outspoken and forthright denouncers of anti-Semitism. *Cath Worker*, too, was notable for its condemnation of anti-Semitism, but the paper expressed its views in tones of "Catholic charity," with strong conversionary nuances, e.g., 9 (November 1942): 1; 10 (September 1943): 2; 11 (January 1944): 8.

10. *CMW*, 37 (December 11, 1942): 202 f.; 38 (June 4, 1943): 181–88; *America*, 67 (September 19, 1942): 654 f. and 658; 67 (August 8, 1942): 480.

11. Statistics of Department of State, presented by Assistant Secretary of State John H. Hildring, in U.S., Congress, Senate, Committee on Foreign Relations, *International Refugee Organization: Hearings on S.J. Res. 77*, 80th Cong., 2d sess., 1947, pp. 30–36. For a documented summary of the postwar DP situation, see Louis W. Holborn, *The International Refugee Organization* (London and New York: Oxford

University Press, 1956), pp. 171–87. Malcolm J. Proudfoot, in his *European Refugees: 1939–52, A Study in Forced Population Movement* (London: Faber and Faber, 1957), notes in his tables of statistics on p. 259 that early estimates of the number of Jewish refugees were inaccurate, because Jews were either reported as "undetermined" or as nationals of their country of origin. Thus, in December 1945, displaced Jews accounted for only 2.5 percent of the total number of DP's, whereas in June 1947 they accounted for 26.1 percent.

12. Catholic press estimates varied. From 55 to 70 percent of the Christian DP's were estimated to be Catholic. *Sign,* 25 (January 1946): 2; 26 (December 1946): 2 and (May 1947): 2; *MC,* April 10, 1947, p. 1, and May 22, 1947, p. 4; *NW,* July 11, 1947, p. 1; *OSV,* April 18, 1948, p. 4.

13. *CW,* 163 (August 1946): 390–92; 164 (March 1947): 489 f.; *Cath Action,* 29 (September 1947): *SJR,* 40 (December 1947): 276; *Extension,* 42 (August 1947): 20, 43 (April 1948): 17; *Sign,* 25 (January 1946): 12–14 and (February 1946): 27–30; *Cath Worker,* 14 (June 1947): 5; *CMW,* 44 (September 1946): 498–502; *America,* 76 (October 19, 1946); 65 f. and (December 1, 1946): 236–38, 76 (February 22, 1947): 564; *Pilot,* May 6, 1947, p. 5; *NW,* July 11, 1947, p. 1; *MC,* April 10, 1947, pp. 1+.

14. Joseph B. Schechtman, *The United States and the Jewish State Movement: The Crucial Decade, 1949–59* (New York: Herzl Press, 1966), pp. 61 f. Frank E. Manuel, *The Realities of American-Palestine Relations* (Washington: Public Affairs Press, 1949), p. 310.

15. Abba Hillel Silver, "A Year's Advance," mimeographed (Political report submitted to the convention of the ZOA, October 15, 1944). Manuel, op. cit., pp. 309, 311 f. For the Zionist climate of opinion among American Jews, see Samuel Halperin, *The Political World of American Zionism* (Detroit: Wayne State University Press, 1961), p. 249; on Zionist political activity at the time, pp. 272–78. For a recent study of the activities of the AZEC, see Doreen Bierbrier, "The American Zionist Emergency Council: An Analysis of a Pressure Group," *AJHQ,* 60 (September 1970): 82–105.

16. *Congressional Record,* December 19, 1945, pp. 12571 f. Hearings were held from February 8 to February 16, 1944, and from the printed testimony it seems that no official representatives of the Catholic Church were heard. U.S., Congress, House, Committee on Foreign Affairs, *Resolutions Relative to the Jewish National Home in Palestine: Hearings on H. Res. 418 and H. Res. 419,* 78th Cong., 2d sess., 1944, pp. 1–388. Congress was ready to pass the pro-Zionist resolutions, only to be thwarted, first in March 1944 by the intervention of the Secretary of War, who claimed that such a resolution "would be prejudicial to the successful prosecution of the war," and again in October by the State Department, which warned that it would be "unwise from the standpoint of the general international situation." Manuel, op. cit., p. 312. Statements of federal, state, and municipal officials favorable to the resolution were collected and published by Reuben Fink, *America and Palestine* (New York: Herald Square Press, 1944).

17. The proposal for allowing 100,000 Jewish survivors to enter Palestine was first raised by Dr. Weizmann and the Jewish Agency in their May and June memoranda to

Churchill. In June 1945, President Truman instructed Earl G. Harrison, American representative on the Intergovernmental Committee on Refugees, to furnish him with a statistical report on the DP's. Upon receipt of the report in late August, President Truman found the calculation of 100,000 Jewish nonrepatriables accurate, and in September, the release of Harrison's report was accompanied by the recommendation of the President for the immediate admission of the 100,000. Christopher Sykes, *Crossroads to Israel* (Cleveland and New York: World Publishing Co., 1968), pp. 277–80. For the terms of reference of the Anglo-American Committee of Inquiry, see Bartley C. Crum, *Behind the Silken Curtain* (New York: Simon & Schuster, 1947), pp. 11 f.

18. *Sign,* 25 (March 1946): 4; 26 (June 1947): 5 f. Gorman accused the Zionists of using the refugees as a tool to force the establishment of a Jewish state. In an earlier editorial, 23 (May 1944): 564, published during the congressional debates on the Palestine resolution, *Sign* opposed the promoting of Palestine as a home for the refugees and suggested, instead, Madagascar or Central Africa, provided the native inhabitants would be amenable. *CW,* 163 (August 1946): 390–92; *America,* 74 (October 13, 1945): 32; 74 (December 1, 1945): 239 f.; 75 (July 6, 1946): 319 f.

19. *CMW,* 44 (May 17, 1946): 109. Also, 47 (December 12, 1947): 219 f.

20. Among these exceptions, for instance, was a letter written by Archbishop Joseph Rummel of New Orleans to Rabbi Emil Leipziger. The letter expressed the hope that the White Paper would be abrogated or suspended to allow European Jewish refugees entry into Palestine. *MC,* February 17, 1944, p. 1. The origin of this letter probably lies in the activities of the American Zionist Emergency Committee, specifically its Committee on Christian Clergy. Under the chairmanship of Rabbi Philip S. Bernstein, rabbis and leading members of the Jewish community were instructed to contact Christian clergy and obtain favorable statements whenever possible. Minutes of Meetings of Executive Committee, AZEC 1943–1949. Minutes of October 5, 1943; August 27, 1945. Box 509, Zionist Archives. Unfortunately, the file of replies from the clergy has not yet been located.

21. A typical example was the development of attitude in *CMW*. The shift from hesitancy to negativism is easily traced in the editorial reaction to Jewish terrorism. *CMW,* 44 (August 2, 1946): 372; 45 (December 13, 1946): 222, (March 21, 1947): 556 f.; 46 (May 7, 1948): 69.

22. Daphne Trevor, in *Under the White Paper* (Jerusalem: Jerusalem Press, 1948), made an exacting study of the events which led to the breaking point. Her description of the British administration in Palestine from 1939 to 1947 includes a detailed discussion on the immigration blockade, arms trials, and arms searches. Her scholarly book is a severe, but documented, indictment of British policy.

23. The history of the underground rescue operations is fully recounted in Yehuda Bauer, *Flight and Rescue: Bricha* (New York: Random House, 1970). On the impact of the Holocaust in galvanizing the Palestinian Jews, see Bauer, *From Diplomacy to Resistance* (Philadelphia: Jewish Publication Society, 1970), pp. 273 ff.

24. The history of Palestinian politics from the end of the war until the liquidation of the mandate is a very hectic one, frequently caught up in a maelstrom of polemic and controversy. I have chosen to follow the definitive study of J. C. Hurewitz, *The Struggle for Palestine* (New York: W. W. Norton, 1950), pp. 212–315, which is dis-

tinguished by its dispassionate objectivity. The British point of view is somewhat defensively presented in Albert M. Hyamson's *Palestine under the Mandate* (London: Methuen, 1950), pp. 147–72. Sykes, op. cit., pp. 264–344 offers a balanced, highly readable summary which also provides a sympathetic rendering of the Arab position. For the Anglo-American Committee, two personal accounts are available, though both tend to favor the Zionist position. Richard Crossman, *Palestine Mission: A Personal Record* (New York and London: Harper & Bros., 1947), and Bartley C. Crum, op. cit. For the activities of UNSCOP, a pro-Zionist but generally accurate account is the personal narrative of the Guatemalan delegate, Jorge-Garcia Granados, *The Birth of Israel* (New York: Alfred A. Knopf, 1949).

25. *AAS*, 60 (May 1, 1948): 171. Pope Pius XII called upon Christians to pray "that the situation in Palestine may at long last be settled justly and thereby concord and peace be also happily established." The encyclical and its implications will be discussed in chap. 5.

26. *MC*, August 8, 1946, p. 5; *OSV*, October 26, 1947; *Pilot*, October 31, 1947; *NW*, October 31, 1947, p. 7. See also, *ECQ*, 7 (January 1948): 348–51. Most of these reports deal with the internuncio to Egypt, Msgr. Arthur Hughes, who was appointed in November 1947. Hughes was formerly apostolic delegate in Palestine.

27. The correspondence is discussed in chap. 2, n. 35.

28. A. G. Cicognani to Myron Taylor, June 22, 1943. *National Archives* 867N.01/6-2443.

29. Bruya was attached to the Commissariat of the Holy Land, located in Washington, D.C. He was the former editor of the Commissariat's quarterly, the *Crusader's Almanac*. In 1939 he was transferred to Terra Sancta College in Jerusalem, where he taught English.

30. *Tidings*, January 2, 1942; January 9, 1942; January 16, 1942. His remarks on the Jewish state are in the January 16 letter.

31. *NC-NS*, March 5, 1945, p. 8, and April 6, 1945, p. 1.

32. Among the many papers reprinting Assemani's article, see *MC*, November 29, 1945; *Pilot*, December 1, 1945, p. 1; *Tablet*, December 1, 1945. Also, *America*, 74 (December 8, 1945): 255. Assemani was a native of Syria who had studied in Jerusalem and served as a missionary in Transjordania. At the time of this writing, he was in Michigan City, Indiana.

33. *Pilot*, June 27, 1947; *NW*, June 27, 1947, p. 6; *OSV*, June 29, 1947, p. 1.

34. Details of these early stages of the Arab-Israeli War are given in Natanel Lorch, *The Edge of the Sword: Israel's War of Independence* (New York: G. P. Putnam's Sons, 1961), pp. 55–84, 87–137.

35. *NW*, March 12, 1948, p. 1; *Tablet*, March 13, 1948, p. 1; *Register*, March 14, 1948.

36. For example, *NW*, March 26, 1948, p. 1; April 2, 1948, p. 6; May 7, 1948, p. 1; *Tablet*, March 13, 1948, pp. 1 f.; March 20, 1948, p. 4; April 10, 1948, p. 1; January 24, 1948, p. 3; May 1, 1948, p. 1; *Register*, March 7, 1948, p. 1; March 14, 1948, p. 2; *MC*, March 25, 1948, p. 1; April 1, 1948, p. 3; April 8, 1948, p. 1; May 6, 1948, p. 2.

37. J. T. Ryan, "Catholic Near East Welfare Association," *New Catholic Ency-*

clopedia, vol. 3 (1967). Much of the early history is contained in *Silver Threads,* a commemorative organizational pamphlet, published in 1951 (Files of CNEWA). The information on the annual reports and the consultative capacity of the organization was related to me in an interview with Msgr. Edward Foster, assistant secretary of CNEWA, on May 23, 1972.

38. Before his appointment in 1943 to the post of national secretary, McMahon taught Church history at St. Joseph's Seminary–Dunwoodie. In his new position, he worked zealously to promote and publicize the activities of the organization. It was under McMahon's administration that page-long ads appeared with regularity in the diocesan press, acquainting readers with the importance of the association while soliciting funds. CNEWA rose in prominence as a result of McMahon's indefatigable output of speeches, articles, and pamphlets. Files of CNEWA.

39. The article appeared in both the diocesan and the national press. *Tablet,* February 26, 1944; *America,* 70 (March 4, 1944): 597–99.

40. *Sign,* 24 (June 1945): 594–96; *MC,* November 23, 1945, p. 1, carried a summary of the article.

41. *Pilot,* May 16, 1947, p. 5; *OSV,* May 25, 1947; *NW,* June 13, 1947. *Cath Mind,* 45 (August 1947): 505–507, expounded on the implications of the CNEWA request to UNSCOP in an article entitled, "The Christian Factor in the Palestine Equation." An added concern was expressed that the Christians in Palestine might be voluntarily or involuntarily transferred to Lebanon. If such an arrangement were made, "the territory would thus cease to be our Holy Land."

42. A copy of the McMahon letter to UNSCOP, June 5, 1947, is in the Zionist Archives, Vertical File, "Christianity and Zionism." Cardinal Spellman of the New York Archdiocese authorized McMahon to represent Christian interests in Palestine at the U.N. and helped McMahon in the preparation of his brief. Robert I. Gannon, S.J., *The Cardinal Spellman Story* (New York: Doubleday, 1962), pp. 354 f.

43. *Sign,* 26 (May 1947): 20. The Christian factor was echoed in a resolution passed at the annual convention of the Central-Verein in August 1947, which called upon the U.N. to find a just solution to the "question of Palestine, the land where our Divine Saviour was born, lived and died for mankind." *SJR,* 40 (September 1947): 176. Also, *Ave M,* 66 (November 22, 1947): 644.

44. For example, an influential book sympathetic to the establishment of the Jewish state was written by a well-known Catholic lawyer, Bartley C. Crum, op. cit. It may very well be that Crum was not interested in publishing in the Catholic press, but it is equally plausible that the Catholic press would hardly consider Crum a responsible Catholic spokesman, since he had served as a legal counsel for anti-Franco underground fighters and wrote for the *Christian Science Monitor.* Another example is Dr. Francis E. McMahon, a prominent Catholic educator and journalist. He was a member of the pro-Zionist American Christian Palestine Committee. In his regular feature in the *New York Post,* "Plainly Speaking" (June 2, 1945), he published a forceful article urging Jewish immigration to Palestine. Occasionally, McMahon wrote for the Catholic press, but not on the topic of Palestine. It may be apropos to note that Dr. McMahon's political viewpoint was outspokenly liberal. He was dismissed from the

faculty of the University of Notre Dame in 1943. At the time, he charged the university with imposing a censorship which violated free speech and academic freedom. *NYT,* November 9, 1943, p. 23; November 21, 1943, p. 24; and December 4, 1943, p. 9. On the manifold activities of Claire H. Bishop, see chap. 6, pp. 104–105.

45. Notably, Msgr. John A. Ryan of NCWC and Fr. George Barry Ford of Corpus Christi Church in New York City. Msgr. Ryan's age, however, restrained him from taking an active part in the council. The Catholic clergy's lack of involvement was corroborated by Rev. Carl Hermann Voss in a personal communication, May 19, 1972. Rev. Voss served on the executive committee of the council. On the restraints which the hierarchy imposed on the "liberal" clergy, see the autobiography of Fr. Ford, *A Degree of Difference* (New York: Straus & Giroux, 1969), pp. 97–103, 107–13. See also my comments on Father Ford, p. 104.

46. *CMW,* 47 (February 27, 1948): 389–92.

47. On Latin American voting patterns, see Edward B. Glick's concise study, *Latin America and the Palestine Problem* (New York: Theodor Herzl Foundation, 1958). The only exception to the general pattern of support for Israel was on the question of the internationalization of Jerusalem. On this issue, Glick maintains that the Vatican was able to exert the decisive influence. Ibid., pp. 142–55. Some of the Catholic papers did follow the U.N. debates, but only reported the views of delegates which corresponded to their own, e.g., *NW,* May 23, 1947, p. 10.

48. The clearest exposition of the ideology and rationale of the American Council for Judaism is found in Elmer Berger's *The Jewish Dilemma* (New York: Devin-Adair Co., 1945). See pp. 243–47 for the history of the birth of the organization, and pp. 245 ff. for the Statement of Principles.

49. *CW,* 162 (February 1946): 396–402.

50. *America,* 74 (December 1, 1945): 239 f.; also 74 (October 13, 1945): 32.

51. For example, ibid. (February 2, 1946): 486 ff.; *CW,* 166 (March 1948): 499. The council actually failed to muster the support of the majority of the Jewish community. Its membership, by its own claims, never exceeded 1,500 persons, or 3 percent of peak Zionist enrollments. Halperin, op. cit., pp. 281–92. Though Halperin correctly evaluated the council as inconsequential in shaping the opinions of American Jewry, he did not sufficiently credit it with influence on other sectors of American opinion. See, for example, *Christian Opinion on Jewish Nationalism and a Jewish State* (Philadelphia: American Council for Judaism, 1944), which is a collection of responses to an editorial published in the council's *Information Bulletin,* April 30, 1944. Also, Schechtman, op. cit., pp. 149, 156–59, on the council's influence on government officials.

52. For example, *Ave M,* 62 (December 29, 1945): 404 and 64 (September 7, 1946): 292; *CW,* 161 (June 1945): 203–209 and (July 1945): 329–35; *Columbia,* 26 (October 1946): 8 and (July 1947), 3 f.; *Sign,* 26 (October 1946): 3 f; *Cath Dgst.,* 20 (June 1946): 69–74; *Cath Mind,* 46 (November 1947): 679 f.

53. *America,* 74 (January 26, 1946): 456–58; 74 (March 9, 1946): 595; 75 (June 29, 1946): 262.

54. Ibid., 76 (August 31, 1946): 515 and 78 (March 6, 1948): 622 f.; cf., however,

ibid. (April 3, 1948): 733 on *America*'s reservations on partition.

55. Avigdor Dagan, *Moscow and Jerusalem* (London, New York, and Toronto: Abelard-Schuman, 1970), pp. 19–27.

56. *CW*, 166 (March 1948): 498 f.

57. Cardinal Griffin, archbishop of Westminster, England, proposed a Crusade, composed of Christians of all denominations, to protect the holy places. *NW*, May 7, 1948, p. 1. Also, *OSV*, January 11, 1948; *Tablet*, January 24, 1948, p. 3; *Pilot*, March 13, 1948, p. 16; *Register*, March 21, 1948, p. 1; *NW*, March 26, 1948, p. 1; *MC*, April 1, 1948, p. 3.

58. John E. Uhler authored the article. His unequivocal stand on isolationism appealed to James Gillis, *CW*'s editor, and Gillis frequently turned to him for comments on the Middle East. *CW*, 165 (June 1947): 248–55.

59. Ibid., 166 (March 1948): 493–501.

60. *Sign*, 27 (April 1948): 4.

61. *CMW*, 45 (October 10, 1947): 613.

62. Ibid., 46 (May 7, 1948): 69.

63. Paulding's liberality modified the harshness of a decree of dispersion in his sincere wish that Jews live contentedly and securely, wherever they be. Ibid. Robert Ludlow, associate editor of *Cath Worker* and also a friend of the Jews, shared with Paulding the same uneasiness concerning Jewish nationalism. In May 1948 issue, p. 1, the lead article on Palestine began with the averment that Jewish nationalism belongs to the "Old Dispensation."

64. *America*, 75 (July 6, 1946): 290 f.

65. Ibid., 78 (December 13, 1947): 286.

66. Ibid., 79 (April 24, 1948): 46 f.

CHAPTER V

1. Charlotte Klein, "Theological Dimensions of the State of Israel: A Christian Perspective," mimeographed (Address to a joint seminar of the Institute of Judaeo-Christian Studies and the American Jewish Committee, October 28, 1970).

2. James O'Gara, "Anti-Semitism: A Catholic View," in *The Star and the Cross: Essays on Jewish-Christian Relations*, ed. Katherine T. Hargrove (Milwaukee: Bruce Publishing Co., 1966), p. 84.

3. Edward Flannery, "Theological Aspects of the State of Israel," *Bridge*, 3 (1958): 304. Flannery cites Augustin Lemann's response to the early rumblings of Zionism as a typical response. Lemann wrote, in *L'avenir de Jerusalem: Espérance et chimères* (Paris, 1901), that "the Temple will never be rebuilt; Jerusalem will never be the capital of a Jewish state; Palestine will never again be the Jewish homeland. . . . There is complete agreement between the Old and New Testaments in treating any attempt to reconstitute a Jewish state in Jerusalem as a chimera. God's plan runs counter to the project of the Zionists." Quoted in Flannery, p. 304. For literature tracing the development of this theological conception, see Fr. S. Munoz Iglesias, "Origen de la creencia vulgar en !as pretendidas profecías sobre la no restauración

politica de Israel," *Estudios Biblicos,* 10 (Madrid, 1951). For similar conceptions among non-Catholic Christians, see H. Berkhof, "Israel as a Theological Problem in the Christian Church," *JES* 6 (Summer 1969): 329–47.

4. *Auspicia Quaedam, AAS,* ser. 2, 15 (May 10, 1948): 171.

5. *Holy Land* is, of course, traditional usage and, indeed, was frequently used. The curious fact is that the Pope did not *always* use *Holy Land* to circumvent the term *Israel,* but did, occasionally, substitute *Palestine.*

6. *Tablet,* May 22, 1948.

7. For a description of the committee and its biases, see Herzl Fishman, "American Protestantism and the State of Israel, 1937–1967" (Ph.D. thesis, New York University, 1971), pp. 174 ff.

8. *Sign,* 27 (July 1948): 2, 4 f., 15 ff.

9. *CW,* 167 (July 1948): 289–90. Cf. the gentle chiding of *Ave M,* 68 (August 7, 1948): 165.

10. NC-NS bulletin, May 17, 1948 (S), p. 4.

11. Ibid., May 24, 1948 (F), p. 1. *Quotidiano* did not specify exactly what action should be taken, but the paper was later involved in promoting a Franciscan militia for the Holy Land.

12. *Cath Worker,* 15 (May 1948): 1. The next issue (July–August 1948) carried a reprint of Peter Maurin's paraphrase of Leon Bloy's "Salvation is of the Jews." Maurin stressed that Jews were a religious, not a national, people, whose future was inextricably tied to Christian eschatology.

13. *SJR,* 41 (June 1948): 75–78. Goldstein wrote a weekly column for the *Pilot* and was a frequent contributor to the diocesan press. His anti-Zionist bias was well known. One of the best examples of his mustering of arguments against a Jewish state is found in an earlier essay written for the Archconfraternity of Prayer and reprinted in the "News and Views" section of the Dubuque, Iowa, Catholic paper, *Witness,* October 3, 1946.

14. *CMW,* 48 (May 28, 1948): 151 f. Surely the name *Israel* must have irritated many Catholics, but I found no editorials as frank as this one on the subject of the name. Some papers substituted *Palestine* or *Holy Land* for *Israel. CMW*'s editorials continued the same skeptical attitude following the truce of June 11. 48 (June 25, 1948): 247 f. and (July 23, 1948): 343 f.

15. *America,* 89 (May 29, 1948): 186.

16. The text of the manifesto is given in the NC-NS bulletin, May 31, 1948 (Th), p. 1.

17. For a reliable account of the war in Jerusalem, see Natanel Lorch, *The Edge of the Sword: Israel's War of Independence, 1947–49* (New York: G. P. Putnam's Sons, 1961), pp. 122–31 and 206–27.

See, also, the military history of the battles written by a non-Zionist, Edgar O'Ballance, *The Arab-Israel War, 1948* (London: Faber & Faber, 1956), pp. 95–110, 160–64.

A United Press report, issued contemporaneously with the manifesto and based on an eyewitness tour of the Old City, asserted that damage to Christian and Moslem sanctuaries was slight, whereas Jewish holy places "are mostly in ruins." *NYT*, June 1, 1948, p. 12.

18. See especially, *MC*, June 3, 1948, p. 2, and *Tablet*, June 5, 1948, p. 1. Even *CMW* disconsolately referred to it and admonished the secular press for relegating the news to a back page. *CMW*, 48 (July 23, 1948): 343 f.

19. The letter was dated May 31, 1948. The full text is unavailable, but excerpts appeared in NC-NS bulletin, June 7, 1948, p. 1. It is a curious fact that Msgr. Gustavo Testa, apostolic delegate for the Palestine, Trans-Jordan, and Cyprus territory, who in May 1948 came to Palestine expressly to supervise the protection of the holy places, was not a signatory to either of these letters.

20. The militia project never got off the ground. From news sources, it seems that the Vatican did not approve such venturesome involvements. *CMW*, 48 (July 2, 1948): 274.

21. NC-NS bulletins, July–October 1948.

22. The charges were made on August 19, and appeared in the syndicated diocesan weekly, *OSV* (together with mention of McMahon's letter to the U.N.), on August 29, 1948, p. 1.

23. McMahon to U.N. Secretary-General Trygve Lie, August 20, 1948. Quoted in full in Constantine Rackauskas, *The Internationalization of Jerusalem* (Washington: CAIP, 1957), p. 78.

24. The statement issued by the Foreign Office on behalf of the Ministry of Religious Affairs was published in the *NYT*, August 24, 1948, p. 11.

25. *Memorandum*, Community Service Division, December 6, 1948. AJComm. Archives, Vertical File: Israel/Holy Places/AJC. One response to the report is found in the *Providence Visitor*, December 22, 1948. The editor noted, "Friends of the new Israeli Government are most anxious to disclaim the government's responsibility for any desecration of Christian monuments and shrines. They have investigated the charges and they can present testimonials. . . . We are inclined to accept the evidence." *Ave Maria* also quoted the Israeli report, but significantly added, "The fact that we give space to the favoring witnesses for the Jews has not by any means led us to erase the affirmations of the two archbishops [Hughes and Hakim]." *Ave M*, 70 (July 1949): 4. For another example of American Jewish Committee involvement, see the *Memorandum* of S. Andhil Fineberg, February 1949. AJComm. Archives, op. cit. In this case, the committee engaged the assistance of the National Conference of Christians and Jews to intercede with the National Catholic Welfare Conference regarding a complaint lodged by the Mother Superior at the Ecco Homo Convent.

The committee's activities on behalf of Israel are fully discussed in Naomi W. Cohen's authoritative history of the organization, *Not Free to Desist* (Philadelphia: Jewish Publication Society, 1972), pp. 309–30. See particularly, p. 319.

26. Vergani's statement was published in *NW*, October 15, 1948, p. 1. McMahon's statement is included in his March 21, 1949 letter to the U.N. (given in Rackauskas, op. cit., p. 79). Cf. Bilby, *New Star in the Near East* (Garden City, N.Y.: Doubleday, 1959), p. 215.

27. For example, the syndicated diocesan weekly, the *Register*, for the period from

November 1948 to August 1949, brought more than a dozen charges against Israel to the attention of its readers. November 21, 1948, p. 1; November 28, 1948, p. 3; December 26, 1948, p. 1; January 9, 1949, p. 1; January 23, 1949, pp. 1, 11; February 6, 1949, p. 6; March 27, 1949, p. 2; June 12, 1949, p. 1; August 7, 1949, pp. 5, 16; August 14, 1949, p. 3. The more serious of these were the accusations of Abp. Arthur Hughes, papal internuncio to Egypt, and of Msgr. Alberto Gori, Franciscan custos, who was elevated to the post of Latin Patriarch of Jerusalem in February 1949. Hughes was quoted in the Catholic press as having said that the Jews made a "deliberate effort" to decimate the Arabs and destroy Christianity in Palestine. Ibid., November 21, 1948, p. 1. Gori complained that the Franciscans in the Holy Land suffered "bitter disillusionment" as a result of open hostility on the part of the government. He also complained that travel restrictions upon Franciscans infringed upon the exercise of their sacred duties. Ibid., June 12, 1949, p. 1. The unfriendliness of certain leading Catholic clergy in Israel toward the government, at that time, was noted by the former U.S. ambassador to Israel, James G. McDonald, *My Mission in Israel, 1948-1951* (New York: Simon & Schuster, 1951), p. 219.

28. Exception must be taken for *America* and *CMW*, which were less guilty of this blind partiality. See, however, the editorial in *CMW*, 49 (January 7, 1949): 317, which is a typical example of slanted criticism.

29. Texts of the Tripartite (Sykes-Picot) Agreement for the partition of the Ottoman Empire (April–October 1916) and the substituted Clemenceau–Lloyd George Agreement (December 1918) are found in J. C. Hurewitz, *Diplomacy in the Near and Middle East: A Documentary Record, 1914-1956* (Princeton, N.J.: D. Van Nostrand Co., 1956), 2:18-25. Also, Esco Foundation for Palestine, *Palestine: A Study of Jewish, Arab and British Policies* (New Haven: Yale University Press, 1947), 1:59-63, particularly the map on p. 62.

30. Florian Sokolow, "Nahum Sokolow and Pope Benedict XV," *Zion*, 1, nos. 5-6, (January–February, 1950): 48-52. However, from accounts of Sokolow's discussion with the papal secretary of state, Cardinal Gasparri, preceding his audience with the Pope, it seems that the Church was considering some form of extraterritorialization, a "reserved zone" which would extend not only to Jerusalem and Bethlehem, but also to Nazareth and its environs, Tiberias, and Jericho. Isaac Minerbi, "The Vatican and Zionism," *Molad*, 27 (May–June 1971): 141 (Hebrew). In his audience with the Pope, Sokolow actually repeated the same promise which Herzl had earlier offered to Pope Pius X in 1904. At that time, Pius countered, "Gerusalemme must not get into the hands of Jews." *The Complete Diaries of Theodor Herzl*, ed. Raphael Patai and trans. Harry Zohn (New York & London: Herzl Press, Thomas Yoseloff, 1960), 4:1601-1605.

31. *AAS*, 11 (March 12, 1919): 100. English trans. in Rackauskas, op. cit., p. 9.

32. Full text of the mandate is given in Hurewitz, op. cit., pp. 106-11; articles 13-15, p. 109.

33. H. Eugene Bovis, *The Jerusalem Question, 1917-1968* (Stanford, Calif.: Hoover Institution Press, 1971), pp. 11-14. The history of the various proposals for special treatment of Jerusalem is discussed, from the Catholic point of view, by Rackauskas,

op. cit. For a dispassionate and comprehensive study of this topic, see Bovis, op. cit.

34. In so doing, the British acted in accordance with article 15 of the mandate, which gave them this authorization. The status quo was established by a decree issued by Sultan Abdul Mejid in 1852 in reference to seven Christian shrines and two Moslem and two Jewish shrines. For a report on the extent and limitations of the decree, particularly as understood by the mandatory, see L. G. A. Cust, *The Status Quo in the Holy Places* (London: H.M. Stationery Office, 1929). Also Paul Mohn, "Jerusalem and the United Nations," *International Conciliation,* no. 464, October 1950, pp. 438 ff. See also the study of Mgr. Bernardin Collin, *Les Lieux Saints* (Paris: Presses Universitaires de France, 1962), which includes not only a full description and history of the holy places, but also a well-reasoned presentation of the Catholic point of view.

35. *Palestine Royal Commission Report* (London: H.M. Stationery Office, 1937), p. 286.

36. Hurewitz, op. cit., p. 223. The full text of the White Paper is given on pp. 219–26.

37. United Nations, *Official Records of the First Special Session of the General Assembly, Resolutions,* A/364.

38. Bonaventure cited the requirements deemed necessary for assuring protection of the holy places in the following order: freedom of access; unhampered conducting of religious services; an enclave for the holy places *in* Jerusalem and the constitution of a commission, composed of Western countries, to whom juridical recourse could be had in cases of interreligious disputes. Bonaventure was questioned closely on what he meant by "enclave," and in his explication he dismissed internationalization of the cities of Jerusalem and Bethlehem as "not in accordance with the Holy Places as such." Bonaventure stressed that Christian holy sites are dispersed throughout Palestine. The Roman Catholic Church had exclusive jurisdiction over forty-five of these places and shared proprietorship with other religious communities in numerous other sites. Ibid., annexes, A/364/Add. 3, pp. 13–19.

39. United Nations, *Official Records of the Second Session of the General Assembly. Ad Hoc Committee on the Palestine Question,* 4th meeting, annexes 19, 19a.

40. See Edward B. Glick, "The Vatican, Latin America and Jerusalem," *International Organization,* 11 (Spring 1957): 213–19. Msgr. Thomas McMahon, in an exchange with Israeli authorities in the summer of 1949, revealed that the Pope had not opposed Jewish statehood in 1947 because he then understood that the Jews would abide by full territorial internationalization. Bovis, op. cit., p. 72. The acquiescence of the Jewish Agency to internationalization has been attributed to the notice that otherwise certain Catholic countries, presumably under Vatican pressure, would be forced to withdraw their support for Jewish statehood. David Horowitz, *State in the Making,* trans. Julian Meltzer (New York: Alfred A. Knopf, 1953), p. 296.

41. *AAS,* ser. 2, 15 (May 10, 1948): 169 f. Eng. trans. in Rackauskas, pp. 68 f.

42. See Lorch, op. cit., pp. 182–88.

43. *AAS,* 15 (June 2, 1948): 252 f.

44. Ibid.

45. Count Folke Bernadotte, *To Jerusalem* (London: Hodder & Stoughton, 1951),

p. 12. Bernadotte later revised his plan for Jerusalem and espoused a scheme of special and separate treatment, as is evident from the posthumous publication of his progress report of September 1948. United Nations, A/648. Cf. Bovis, op. cit., p. 65.

46. *AAS*, 15 (October 26, 1948): 443–46. Eng. trans. in Rackauskas, op. cit., p. 71.

47. The Jewish Agency accepted the plan of internationalization in 1947, and according to informed sources, the majority of the Jewish population was willing to implement the U.N. provision at that time. However, after the savage battles for Jerusalem, and the wholesale destruction of the synagogues in the Old City, few Israelis were still willing to seriously consider internationalization. As Dov Joseph, the military governor of Jerusalem, told a *New York Herald-Tribune* correspondent, "The Christians didn't lift a finger to help us. . . . Do you expect us now to accept United Nations assurances that we will be protected by an international regime?" Bilby, op. cit., p. 202; also Dov Joseph, *The Faithful City* (New York: Simon & Schuster, 1960), pp. 334–36. The Arab League, meanwhile, reversed its position on Jerusalem. Earlier, the League had railed against internationalization as an intrusion on Arab sovereignty, but now that Jerusalem was in the hands of Jordan and Israel, the League clamored for the U.N. plan. Jordan, which had gained control of East Jerusalem, was even more obstinate than Israel in refusing internationalization. King Abdullah flatly refused the scheme of functional internationalization, which the Israeli government was willing to consider. For an analysis of the changing Arab and Israeli stands, see Bovis, op. cit., pp. 60–64, 79 ff., 113–19.

48. *AAS*, ser. 2, 16 (April 15, 1949): 161–64. Eng. trans. in Rackauskas, op. cit., p. 72.

49. Raphael Huber, ed., *Our Bishops Speak, 1919–1951* (Milwaukee: Bruce Publishing Co., 1952), pp. 364 f. The statement was later reissued at the annual Bishops Conference, November 21, 1949 and published in the journal of the National Catholic Welfare Conference, *Cath. Action*, 31 (December 1949): 20. Catholic lay organizations, too, passed supportive resolutions. See, for example, the resolution passed by the Knights of Columbus at their annual convention. *Columbia* (October 1949): 14. Cushing's efforts were praised in *CMW*, 50 (July 1, 1949): 14. For representative editorials commenting on the encyclical, see, in the national press, *America*, 81 (April 30, 1949): 151, and in the diocesan press, *Register*, May 8, 1949, p. 5.

50. See n. 55.

51. McMahon came to Israel as the official representative of the NCWC to investigate the condition of Arab refugees and report on their needs. *Cath Action*, ·30 (December 1948): 2. McMahon left for Israel in December 1948 and returned to the U.S. four months later, after a brief stopover at the Vatican.

52. While in Israel, McMahon met with Dr. Yaakov Herzog, of the Ministry for Religious Affairs, and from Herzog's later comments to James G. McDonald, it appears that McMahon negotiated on matters of interest to the Church apart from the refugee problem. McDonald's audience with Pius XII lent further substance to this impression. McDonald, op. cit., pp. 93 f., 205 f., 190 ff., 206. McMahon published a disclaimer of his diplomatic mission in a pamphlet, *Hills of the Morning* (New York:

CNEWA, n.d. [1954?]), pp. 17 f. However, on the basis of conversations with persons who are familiar with the Herzog and McMahon papers, it appears that McMahon, indeed, was a pivotal figure in American-Israeli-Vatican relations. As yet, I have had no access to the archives to enable me to document this assumption. The pertinent evidence would be found in the CNEWA archives in New York City (where I have limited access), the Spellman papers in the New York archdiocesan archives at St. Joseph's Seminary, Dunwoodie, N.Y., and the Herzog papers, which are now being assembled in Jerusalem.

53. McMahon's thesis was popularized in his numerous speeches and articles for Catholic audiences. He reported on the Palestine issues in the following pamphlets published by CNEWA and contained in their files: *Job and Jacob* (n.d. [1946?]); *Only the Meek* (1949); *The Pope and the Palestine Tragedy* (n.d. [1951?]); *Not by Bread Alone* (n.d. [1952?]); *Hills of the Morning* (n.d. [1954?]). For McMahon, internationalization of Jerusalem was the bare minimum. He was wont to say that the Holy Land, in its *entirety,* is sacred to Christianity, that the whole land bears the "indelible sacred footprints of the Master." *Hills of the Morning,* p. 3. In one of his early pamphlets, he averred that "the entire Holy Land was made sacred by the footsteps of our divine Master. To piece it up, or to make of these shrines a sort of 'Christian enclave' would be the worst gerrymandering." *Job and Jacob,* unpaginated.

McMahon's position was aired at the annual Conferences of Eastern Rites and Liturgies, which he was largely responsible for organizing. At the April 4, 1949 conference, the theme of the meeting was "Rites and Rights in the Homeland of Our Saviour." McMahon's emphasis, in his address, was that Jerusalem *is* the capital of Christianity and, therefore, must be internationalized. CNEWA files.

54. The texts of the commission proposal, the Australian resolution, and the later Netherlands-Sweden proposal for purely functional internationalization are found in United Nations, *Official Records of the Fourth Session of the General Assembly;* Ad Hoc Political Committee, annex, I, A/973; A/AC. 31/L.37. November 12 was designated by the Pope as a day of prayer for the settlement of Palestine in harmony with Christian rights. *America,* 82 (November 26, 1949): 216. On November 17 the American hierarchy reissued their April 27 statement on internationalization. Huber, op. cit. Vatican radio support for the Australian resolution was reported in *NYT,* November 27, 1949, p. 27. See, also, the editorial "Catholic Thinking on the Internationalization of Jerusalem," in *Cath Action,* 31 (November 1949): 3.

55. This was particularly true for Cuba, Haiti, and Bolivia, which had not supported the Australian proposal at the outset, and then changed their votes in the final counting, "in keeping with the wishes of the Catholic countries." Glick, op. cit., p. 216. Glick noted that Spellman directed the papal nuncios in all Latin American capitals to make vigorous representations demanding the Latin American governments take an unflinching stand on *full* territorial internationalization. Others who have noted the same include Pierre Van Paasen, *Jerusalem Calling* (New York: Dial Press, 1950), pp. 214 f.; Hal Lehrman, "The U.N. Tangle over Jerusalem," *Commentary,* 9 (February 1950): 108; and Lillie Shultz, "The Jerusalem Story," *Nation,* 169 (December 17, 1949): 590 f. On Cardinal Spellman's association with the Latin American countries,

see Robert Gannon, *The Cardinal Spellman Story,* (Garden City, N.Y.: Doubleday, 1961), pp. 122–26. On Vatican pressure in the U.N. in reference to the vote on internationalization, see *NYT,* December 13, 1949, p. 1.

56. Bovis, op. cit., pp. 78–91. Bovis gives a concise history of the meanderings of the resolution in U.N. sessions.

57. *Hills of the Morning,* p. 7. See also McMahon's letter to U.N. Secretary-General Dag Hammarskold, September 16, 1953, and his telegram to President Eisenhower, November 4, 1954, in which he protested the U.S. ambassador's presentation of credentials in Jerusalem. Rackauskas, op. cit., pp. 80 f.

58. *America,* 82 (December 31, 1949): 381 and (February 4, 1950): 511; 83 (June 17, 1950): 313 and (September 16, 1950): 619; 74 (November 4, 1950): 124; 86 (December 8, 1951): 275 and (December 15, 1951): 298.

59. Ibid., 83 (June 17, 1950): 313.

60. Israeli Government, *Jerusalem 1948–1951: Three Years of Reconstruction* (Jerusalem, March 1952), pp. 28 f. *Christian News From Israel* published a chronicle of government regulations and transactions relating to the Christian communities. For example, on the restitution of ecclesiastic properties and the repair of churches and religious institutions during 1949–50, see ibid., 1 (August 1949): 2, 8; (September 1949): 3; (December 1949–Jan. 1950): 4; (January–February 1950): 3; (March–April 1950): 5 f. By November 16, 1955 all outstanding claims of the Roman Catholic Church in Israel were settled. Ibid., 6 (December 1955): 21.

61. Robert A. Graham, S.J., authoritative historian of Vatican diplomacy, pointed to Paul VI's recent exhortation on internationalization (June 21, 1971) as evidence that "the pope apparently thought it appropriate to repeat what he thinks about the future status of Jerusalem, because unauthorized reports had been circulated that the Vatican is quite satisfied with the present situation." *Columbia,* 50–51 (August 1917). Despite Graham's gainsaying, knowledgeable observers of the Vatican claim that there has been a softening of the Pope's rigorous stand. Opinions diverging from the Vatican view began to appear in the late sixties and early seventies. Abbot Leo Rudloff, O.S.B. (formerly in the Church of Dormition, Jerusalem) declined to state Vatican opinion on internationalization in a radio interview in 1967, but he added, "Speaking in my personal capacity, I have the impression that the position has actually changed. . . ." Transcript of interview, *Catholic Hour,* December 31, 1967. Msgr. John Oesterreicher, in an essay in the *NYT,* May 26, 1971, p. 43, likewise maintained that the Pope had moved from his former position. Bp. Bernardin Collin, who closely follows Vatican opinion, argued in a 1956 study, *Le Probleme Juridique des Lieux Saints* (Paris, 1956), p. 127, that *only* territorial internationalization would be adequate. However, in a 1971 article, "Essais des Solutions au Probleme des Lieux Saints," *Revue Générale de Droit International Public,* he proposed that a move be made towards "une internationalisation fonctionelle."

For statements of eminent Catholic leaders and theologians supportive of Israeli sovereignty over Jerusalem, see *Christians Support Unified Jerusalem* (Interreligious Affairs Department, American Jewish Committee, October 1971), pp. 15–17, 24–27. In the U.S., the present proponent of unmodified territorial internationalization is Abp.

Joseph T. Ryan of Anchorage, Alaska, formerly the executive secretary of CNEWA and the Pontifical Mission. His statements have been impressively debated by Fr. Edward Flannery, executive secretary for Catholic-Jewish relations, U.S. Catholic Conference. For a summary of the debate, see Judith Banki, "Compendium of Christian Statements and Documents Bearing on Christian-Jewish Relations," mimeographed (Interreligious Affairs Department, American Jewish Committee), pp. 48–50.

62. Fayez Sayegh, *The Palestinian Refugees* (Washington: AMARA Press, 1952), pp. 9–24. Deir Yassin was an Arab village massacred by a Jewish terrorist splinter group on April 9, 1948, before the Israeli military gained control. It was a singular incident in the war.

63. Israeli Government, *The Arab Refugees* (Jerusalem, 1953), pp. 7–14.

64. Don Peretz, *Israel and the Palestinian Arabs* (Washington: Middle East Institute, 1958), pp. 4–8. See also Joseph Schechtman, *The Arab Refugee Problem* (New York: Philosophical Library, 1952), pp. 1–7. Schechtman outlines in detail the three major phases of the flight.

No accurate account of the number of refugees has been made. Relief agency figures are based on ration lists, which have been found to be inflated. Estimates range from less than a half million to over one million. Bernadotte's figures in 1948 totaled less than 4,000. The later estimate of the U.N. Economic Survey Mission for the Middle East, which is generally quoted, totaled 726,000 refugees as of September 1949. See Peretz, op. cit., p. 30, n. 2, for a discussion on the discrepancies in refugee figures.

65. For a summary of U.N. programs and their failures, see ibid., pp. 12–17. Peretz discusses each of these programs in fuller detail in subsequent chapters of his book. Among the many commissions appointed to deal with the problem were the U.N. Relief for Palestine Refugees, Technical Committee on Refugees, Economic Survey Mission for the Middle East, and the Relief and Works Agency.

66. Schechtman, op. cit. In December 1948, the Arab states rejected a U.N. resolution which incorporated the recommendation of repatriation, only to extract the recommendation later, out of the original context of the resolution, and demand its implementation. For early Israeli offers of repatriation, see Peretz, op. cit., pp. 33, 40–50. Israel repatriated 25,000 Arab refugees, and another 8,000 returned under the "family reunion" scheme. Ibid., pp. 49, 55.

67. Israeli opposition was based on fears of harboring a fifth column as long as the insecure political situation, in which no peace treaties were signed, prevailed. These fears were amply supported by Arab rhetoric. Schechtman, op. cit., pp. 24–26.

68. Ibid., pp. 35–41; Peretz, op. cit., pp. 13, 77–94. Schechtman, an authority on worldwide problems of refugees (for example, his *Postwar Population Transfers in Europe, 1945–1955* [Philadelphia: University of Pennsylvania Press, 1962], and *The Refugee in the World* [New York and London: A. S. Barnes, 1963]), maintained that there are no precedents for successful repatriation of populations, whereas resettlement has proven to be a feasible solution. *Arab Refugee Problem*, pp. 31 f. He also maintained that an unofficial exchange of population actually occurred in Israel following the '48 war when Israel absorbed 522,000 Jewish refugees from Moslem countries. *Refugee in the World*, p. 262.

69. *America,* 80 (March 26, 1949): 677.

70. Minutes of the Executive Committee, CNEWA, August 27, 1948. CNEWA archives. Spellman authorized McMahon to send two checks for refugee relief: One of $25,000 to Abp. Testa, apostolic delegate for Palestine, and another of $25,000 to Abp. Hughes. Hughes's telegrams were reported in the *NYT,* August 12, 1948, p. 3. Shipment of the monies was publicized in an NC-NS bulletin, September 13, 1948 (S), 4.

71. Minutes of the Board of Trustees, CNEWA, November 18, 1948. CNEWA archives. Spellman was instrumental in the McMahon appointment and in obtaining papal approval for the mission. McMahon broached the possibility of expansion of CNEWA activities as a result of the refugee tragedy and the bishops voted to set up a special account for "Palestine" in the NCWC War Relief budget. At the annual meetings of the following years, November 17, 1949; November 16, 1950; November 15, 1951; November 13, 1952, progress reports on the relief work were delivered. For press accounts, see *Cath Action,* 30 (December 1948): 2; NC-NS bulletin, January 7, 1949; *Register,* March 27, 1949, p. 2; *America,* 80 (March 26, 1949): 678.

72. These phrases cropped up, for example, in papers as dissimilar as *Cath Mind,* 47 (June 1949): 372; *Columbia,* 35 (October 1955): 4; *Priest,* 11 (December 1955): 982; *SJR,* 41 (February 1949): 350.

73. The most blatant examples are found in *Sign,* 28 (May 1949): 5 f.; 31 (August 1951): 2 and (November 1951): 6; 32 (December 1952): 9–12. Also *Columbia,* 35 (October 1955): 4; *SJR* 48 (November 1955): 276 f.

74. *OSV,* March 25, 1956, p. 2. On the figure cited, see n. 64.

75. Estimates generally run to approximately 150,000 Christian refugees, of which only 55,000 were Catholics. *America,* 80 (March 26, 1949): 677. *Cath Bib Q,* 12 (January 1950): 114, estimated that one out of every ten refugees was Christian, but gave no estimate for the percentage of Catholics. The Pontifical Mission for Palestine Report of 1954 calculated that there were 268 pontifical centers for refugees in the Middle East and 31,000 refugee children enrolled in pontifical schools. Minutes of the Board of Trustees, CNEWA, Nov. 18, 1954, CNEWA archives. Catholic assistance to refugees from 1948 to 1950 climbed to over $6 million out of the total of $10,391,000 in aid given by private agencies. U.S., Congress, House, Committee on Foreign Affairs, *Palestinian Refugees: Hearings on S.J. Res. 153,* 81st Cong., 2d sess., February 16–17, 1950, p. 23.

76. Quoted in *America,* 80 (March 26, 1949): 677.

77. A. H. Hourani, *Minorities in the Arab World* (London: Oxford University Press, 1947), pp. 34–36.

78. *CMW,* 48 (October 8, 1948): 614 f.

79. Minutes of Board of Trustees, CNEWA. November 15, 1951, CNEWA archives. Of this amount, two million was given in cash, and the remainder in goods and services. An extensive report of the agency's founding and the scope of its activities is given in McMahon's pamphlet *The Pope and the Palestine Tragedy,* CNEWA files. See also, *Unitas,* 1 (October–December, 1949), 79 f., and *E Ch Q,* 8 (October 1949): 269–73.

80. See chap. 1 on the image of the Jew, pp. 9–15.

81. *Osservatore Romano,* May 14, 1948, quoted in Pinchas E. Lapide, *The Last Three Popes and the Jews* (London: Souvenir Press, 1967), p. 282. The same belief was echoed in *Sign,* 27 (January 1949): 39 f., in a homiletical piece on the inevitable failure of Zionism.

82. *Register,* March 6, 1949, p. 2.

83. "We cannot but wonder if the problem of Palestine will go on plaguing the world until there is offered with the solution of the Jews and the solution of the Arabs, a solution of the Christians of the world." *Pilot,* August 7, 1948, p. 4.

84. Editorial by Msgr. Matthew Smith in the *Register,* March 27, 1949, pp. 1, 6. In the unfolding of this theory, the Jews will eventually recognize the Antichrist as an imposter and rebel against him. War will ensue, at which time the Jews will convert to Christianity and thus bring about the Second Coming. Vladimir Soloviov, "A Short History of the Antichrist," in *War, Progress and the End of History,* trans. A. Basky (London: University of London Press, 1915), pp. 224–26.

85. The address was printed in *Cath Bib Q,* 12 (April 1950): 119 f.

86. *CS,* 169 (August 1949): 326–29, and 170 (December 1949): 192–97; *Homiletic and Pastoral Review,* 51 (October 1950): 47–49; *American Ecclesiastical Review,* 124 (January 1951): 31–36. In the latter article, Nicholas Rieman, S.J., noted that a "surprising percentage of immigrants to Israel are Christian in sentiment, and at times, in belief."

87. Yves Congar, O.P., "Sens de la restauration (politique) d'Israel au regard de la pensèe Chretienne," Notre Dame de Sion, *Sessions d'Information,* July 1955. Congar's views reached the English-speaking public in the following articles, "The State of Israel in Biblical Perspective," *Blackfriars,* 37 (June 1957): 244–49, and "Modern Israel, Fulfillment of God's Promise?" *Theology Digest,* 9 (Spring 1961): 95 f.

88. For example, Paul Demann, "Signification de l'Etat d'Israel," *Cahiers Sioniens,* 5, no. 1 (March 1951): 32–43; Charles Journet, "The Mysterious Destinies of Israel," *Bridge,* 2 (1956): 77. Fr. Edward Flannery did much to popularize this school of thought in his article, "Theological Aspects of the State of Israel."

89. Frankly stated by an American Catholic visitor to Palestine in 1946, *America,* 74 (January 19, 1946): 428.

90. From a pilgrim's report in *Sign,* 31 (December 1951): 46–49. See also *Cath Dgst,* 26 (December 1961): 110–13, which praised Bethlehem's citizens for striving to retain the biblical image, and Richard Pattee in *Columbia,* 35 (November 1955), who noted the disappointment of Christian pilgrims to find the town of the Bible "modernized."

In Bp. Fulton J. Sheen's account of his own pilgrimage, *This Is the Holy Land* (Garden City, N.Y.: Doubleday, 1962), p. 70 f., he notes: ". . . only in Jordan may one still see the Biblical life of other days preserved by the conservatism of the Canaanite [sic] peasant, who is the Arab." Also, Francis X. Weiser, S.J., *The Holy Land* (Collegeville, Minn.: Liturgical Press, 1965), pp. 52 f., 86, 103, 150 f.

It is important to note that neither Fr. Weiser nor Bp. Sheen intends any disparaging comparisons. They simply rejoiced at the sight of a "Biblical Palestine."

NOTES   161

CHAPTER VI

1. Bp. Fulton J. Sheen, in his popular book, *Communism and the Conscience of the West* (Indianapolis and New York: Bobbs-Merrill Co., 1948), p. 203, identifies the Communist movement with the Antichrist. Msgr. Raymond Etteldorf, *The Catholic Church in the Middle East* (New York: Macmillan Co., 1959), p. 167, describes the movement in these words, ". . . under its thousand guises and fictions, Communism is a universally organized force of evil—the mystical body of Satan—that through zealous and indefatigable apostles strives to capture the human soul." Albert Galter, ed., *The Red Book of the Persecuted Church* (Westminster, Md.: Newman Press, 1957), details the persecution of Catholics under Communist regimes.

2. For an authoritative history of the spread of communism in the postwar world, see Hugh Seton-Watson, *Neither War Nor Peace: The Struggle for Power in the Postwar World* (New York: Frederick A. Praeger, 1960). The following books and pamphlets are representative samplings of Catholic literature on communism: F. J. Sheed, *Communism and Man* (New York: Sheed & Ward, 1938), and John LaFarge, *Communism and the Catholic Answer* (New York: American Press, 1936), though published in the 1930s, were still widely read in the 1950s. The National Catholic Welfare Conference published, under its auspices, a pamphlet on communism in 1947: John F. Cronin, S.S., *Communism: A World Menace* (Washington: NCWC, 1947). Bp. Fulton Sheen, op. cit., and Richard James Cardinal Cushing, *Questions and Answers on Communism* (Boston: St. Paul Editions, 1941), were among the members of the hierarchy who wrote on the topic. Waldemar Gurian, the editor of the scholarly Catholic journal, *Review of Politics*, contributed many books on this subject, among them, *Bolshevism: An Introduction to Soviet Communism* (Notre Dame, Ind.: University of Notre Dame Press, 1952), and *Soviet Imperialism: Its Origin and Tactics* (Notre Dame, Ind.: University of Notre Dame Press, 1953). Among Catholic theologians who wrote on communism were Cyril D'Arcy, *Communism and Christianity* (New York: Devin-Adari Co., 1957), and the French Catholic Jesuit Henri Chambre, whose *Christianisme et Communisme* was translated for American audiences by R. F. Trevett, *Christianity and Communism* (New York: Hawthorne Books, 1960).

3. J. C. Hurewitz, *Soviet-American Rivalry in the Middle East* (New York and London: Frederick A. Praeger, 1969), p. 5.

4. *America*, 82 (March 18, 1950): 684.

5. On Israeli relations with Moscow after statehood, see Avigdor Dagan, *Moscow and Jerusalem* (London, New York, and Toronto: Abelard-Schuman, 1970), pp. 28–46; Kenneth W. Bilby, *New Star in the Near East* (Garden City, N.Y.: Doubleday, 1950), pp. 219 f., and the *NYT* reports on settlements affecting the Russian Orthodox Church in Israel, September 13, 1948, p. 4, and February 11, 1949, p. 11. See also the Catholic international quarterly, *Unitas*, 1 (Winter 1949): 79, for further discussion on the appointment of Leonid and the transfer of property.

For the image of the Jewish settler as a Communist, see supra, pp. 24–25. One of the more graphic examples of the resuscitation of this image in 1948 is found in *CW*, 166 (March 1948): 498 f. That this opinion was held by respectable Catholic clergy in

Israel is confirmed by James G. McDonald, *My Mission in Israel, 1948–51* (New York: Simon & Schuster, 1951), p. 219.

6. Walter Z. Laqueur, *The Soviet Union and the Middle East* (New York: Frederick A. Praeger, 1959), pp. 264–80, 295–314; Pierre Rondot, *The Changing Patterns of the Middle East* (New York: Frederick A. Praeger, 1962), pp. 13–22, 147–68.

7. *AAS*, 33 (June 2, 1951): 497–528. See also the commentary in Renè-Pierre Millot, *Missions in the World Today* (New York: Hawthorne Books, 1961), pp. 21–24. On the status of Catholic minorities in the Middle East before 1948, see A. H. Hourani, *Minorities in the Arab World* (London: Oxford University Press, 1947), and for post-1948, see Etteldorf, op. cit.

8. G. C. Anawati, "The Roman Catholic Church and Churches in Communion with Rome," in *Religion in the Middle East: Three Religions in Concord and Conflict*, ed. A.J. Arberry (Cambridge: Cambridge University Press, 1969), 1: 365, 415. For an assessment of Fr. Anawati, see Etteldorf, op. cit., p. 172.

9. Ibid., pp. 60–62, 74, 83–85. A survey of the precarious situation of Catholics in the Middle East after the Suez War, particularly in Egypt and Syria, is given in *Unitas*, 9 (Spring 1957): 34–40. Also, "Majorities and Minorities in the Middle East," *Israel Economist*, 25 (February 1969): 38 f.

10. Catholic churches in the Middle East include the Roman Catholic Church (or Latin rite) as well as various churches of the Eastern rite which are in communion with Rome. The latter include the Greek Catholics (Melkites), Maronites, Syrian Catholics, Chaldeans, Gregorian (Armenian) Catholics, Catholic Copts, and Catholic Ethiopians. For a brief summary of the origins and religious history of these various Eastern rite churches, see Anawati, op. cit., pp. 347–417. Statistical tables of population distribution are given in ibid., pp. 418–22. Among the Catholic communities in Israel, the Greek Catholic is the most numerous, although the Latins maintain the greatest number of institutions.

11. In the 1930 census of the mandatory government, which classified Christians according to their churches, the figures for Orthodox Christians were more than double the Catholic total. In the registration of the population in January 1949, Catholics totaled 16,630 while the Orthodox total dropped to 11,764. The Catholic population continued to grow, and according to Etteldorf's statistics, the Catholic total was over 28,000 in 1958. Etteldorf, op. cit., p. 38. Another change in the population pattern post-'48 was the rise in the ratio of Christians to Moslems, from an estimated one to seven prior to the state to a one-to-four ratio afterwards. Chaim Wardi, ed., *Christians in Israel: A Survey* (Jerusalem: Israeli Ministry of Religious Affairs, October 1950), pp. 30 f.

12. Wardi, op. cit., pp. 7–10; Saul Colbi, *Short History of Christianity in the Holy Land* (Jerusalem: Am Hassefer, 1965), pp. 54–62; *CNI*, 6 (December 1955): 21.

13. See Yehoshua Freudenheim, *Government in Israel* (Dobbs Ferry, N.Y.: Oceana Publications, 1967), pp. 85–87, 99–104, for an elucidation of the *millet* system within the legal framework, and pp. 110 f., regarding later changes in the jurisdiction of religious courts. Wardi, op. cit., pp. 31–33; Colbi, op. cit.

14. For a perceptive and sensitive clarification of the problems confronting Christian

Arabs, see Alice Eckardt and A. Roy Eckardt, *Encounter with Israel* (New York: Association Press, 1970), pp. 122–27.

Herbert Wiener records very candid conversations he had with Catholic clergy in Israel on the question of missionary efforts. A number of the religious seemed to be willing to forgo active proselytizing in favor of an "apostolate of the presence." *The Wild Goats of Ein Gedi* (Garden City, N.Y.: Doubleday, 1961), pp. 63–70. In 1953 an attempt to outlaw Christian missionary schools was rejected by Israel's legislature. This tolerance was in sharp contrast to the restrictions against Christian missionary efforts in neighboring Moslem countries. See the pamphlet published by the Catholic Students Mission Crusade, *Middle East in Five Hours* (Cincinnati: CSMC, 1957), pp. 9, 22, and Etteldorf, op. cit., pp. 23, 61, 167.

15. *National Catholic Almanac, 1955,* ed. Felician A. Foy, O.F.M. (Paterson, N.J.: St. Anthony's Guild, 1955), p. 495.

16. Supra, pp. 87–88.

17. *Register,* November 27, 1955, p. 7.

18. Ibid., November 11, 1956, p. 3.

19. Ibid., November 25, 1956, p. 7.

20. *OSV,* March 25, 1956, p. 2; June 10, 1956, p. 2. "Another View on Israel" was not signed, but it appeared on the editorial page.

21. *SJR,* 50 (December 1957): 267; also ibid. (September 1957): 162 f.

22. *Ave M,* 83 (May 19, 1956): 4.

23. Ibid., 88 (August 23, 1958): 16.

24. *Pilot,* August 11, 1956, p. 5. *Pilot* ran a series of articles on the Suez crisis during the summer of 1956. While Nasser was treated with considerable skepticism and even dislike, the major issue at stake, and the issue which was believed to foment all the other crises, was the unresolved Arab-Israeli conflict. See particularly, ibid., August 4, 1956, p. 5; September 15, 1956, pp. 2 f.; October 20, 1956, p. 2.

25. His replacement, Augustine P. Hennessy, C.P., changed the tenor of the journal. Hennessy initiated a liberal and ecumenical approach. Fr. Edward Flannery, whose pro-Israel views were well known, was published in *Sign* in 1967, and Rabbi Abraham J. Heschel was elected one of Sign's "People of the Month" in 1968.

26. *Sign,* 36 (April 1957): 6.

27. The best summary of his theological beliefs concerning the Jews is found in a lengthy editorial, ibid., 39 (May 1960): 6. On the reforms of the sixties, see 41 (May 1962): 8, and 44 (August 1964): 33 f. Gorman had been labeled in the Catholic press as an "ultra-conservative." During the spring and summer of 1954, he devoted several editorials to a denial of this reputation, and finally defined himself as somewhere "between an ultra-conservative and an ultra-liberal," or, as he preferred to call himself, "a progressive conservative." Ibid., 34 (March 1954): 4; (May 1954): 4; (June 1954): 4.

28. For example of his Easter editorials, see ibid., (April 1956): 6; 36 (April 1957): 6. See also 32 (February 1953): 15–17, in which total support for Arab demands was most vigorously stated. For reader critiques of Gorman's unqualified praise of Nasser, see ibid., 36 (March 1957): 3 and 77.

29. Ibid., 35 (January 1956): 8; 36 (August 1956): 13–16 and (December 1956): 6; 37 (April 1958): 6; 38 (September 1958): 6.

30. For example, ibid., 36 (August 1956): 8, 13–16; 37 (September 1957): 61; 39 (February 1960): 14. Gorman frequently quoted Alfred M. Lilienthal and James Warburg.

31. *CMW,* 63 (November 25, 1955): 188.

32. Ibid., 63 (March 16, 1956): 609 f.; 64 (May 11, 1956): 138. See also the editorial in 65 (November 9, 1956): 141–42, which criticized the U.S. for having continually rebuffed Israel's requests for arms.

33. Ibid. (December 14, 1956): 276 f. The American attitude on the Suez crisis, formulated and directed by President Eisenhower and Secretary of State John F. Dulles, undoubtedly had an impact on American Catholic attitudes regarding Israel. It cannot be expected that American Catholics would oppose their country's foreign policy on an issue which did not affect them directly. This fact should be appreciated in the interpretation of the views of those Catholic journals which were hostile to Israel at the time. For American foreign policy during the Suez crisis, see Herman Finer, *Dulles Over Suez* (Chicago: Quadrangle Books, 1964).

34. Ibid., 65 (February 1, 1957): 454 and (March 8, 1957).

35. The American Friends of the Middle East (AFME), founded through the efforts of columnist Dorothy Thompson, concentrated on publicizing the Arab cause to the American public. For the storm of protest raised by Cogley's speech, see *NYT,* January 29, 1954, p. 8.

36. *Proceedings,* Second Annual Conference of AFME. January 28–29, 1954, pp. 39 f.

37. *CMW,* 65 (December 14, 1956): 284; see also a concurring report by William Pfaff, former associate editor, in ibid., 67 (November 8, 1957): 145 f.

38. Charles Keenan, the managing editor, described the day-by-day procedure of putting out the weekly in an article in celebration of the periodical's fortieth anniversary year. *America,* 80 (February 19, 1949): 544 f. The task of the editor-in-chief was to make the final decision on choice of topics.

39. Ibid., 86 (February 16, 1952): 528; 87 (April 5, 1952): 4; 88 (January 17, 1953): 420 and (February 21, 1953): 553; 79 (June 13, 1953): 293 f.

40. Ibid., 111 (May 29, 1954): 245 f.

41. Ibid., 114 (February 18, 1956): 550.

42. Ibid., 89 (May 30, 1953): 233; 90 (October 31, 1953), 120 and (January 9, 1954), 376–78; 92 (March 19, 1955): 636; 94 (January 28, 1956): 464. For a reliable account of Arab terrorism and Israeli reprisals, see Ernest Stock, *Israel on the Road to Sinai, 1949–1956* (Ithaca, N.Y.: Cornell University Press, 1967), pp. 71–83.

43. Ibid., 90 (March 27, 1954): 681 f. (letter); 91 (April 3, 1954): 3 (news comment); 96 (February 2, 1957): 495 and (February 23, 1957): 575 (editorials); 94 (February 11, 1956): 522; and 96 (March 16, 1957): 665 (Parsons's column). Parsons was the editor-in-chief of *America* from 1925 to 1936, during which time the periodical directed much of its attention to questions of social justice.

44. For an excellent review of the involvement of American Catholics in the ecu-

menical movement, see John B. Sheerin, "American Catholic Ecumenism," in *Contemporary Catholicism in the United States,* ed. Philip Gleason (Notre Dame, Ind.: University of Notre Dame Press, 1969). On the definition and development of ecumenism in Catholic thought, see Gregory Baum, O.S.A., *That They May Be One* (Westminster, Md.: Newman Press, 1958), pp. 102–34.

45. *CW,* 167 (July 1948): 289 f.
46. Ibid., 168 (October 1948): 6–13.
47. Ibid., 169 (May 1949): 109–14. For the next seven years *CW* published no articles on the Arab-Israeli conflict. When, in 1955, *CW* began again to comment on the Middle East, the articles were noteworthy for their generally objective analysis and their total lack of polemic.
48. Ibid., August 1949, pp. 326–29. Zolli was the former rabbi of Rome who converted to Catholicism in 1945.
49. *CW,* 173 (June 1951): 173–77; 177 (June 1953): 208–13, (April 1954): 12–15; 180 (October 1954): 54–59; (November 1954): 116–20; (January 1955): 288–92. Sheerin came out openly in defense of Israel after the 1967 war, when, as he admitted, he first realized what Israel meant to American Jewry. He exhorted his readers, too, to recognize "the strong bonds of kinship and interdependence uniting American and Israeli Jews" in order that the Catholic-Jewish dialogue could go on without "slackening momentum." Ibid., 195 (August 1967): 260–63.
50. See n. 49. See also a very candid statement on the confusion in the minds of American Catholics on Israel (particularly as evidenced during the Six-Day War) and the effect Israel has on dialogue: Robert Drinan, "Israel: Theological Implications for Christians," *Conservative Judaism,* 22 (Spring 1968): 28–35. For Catholic press responses following the war, see Eugene Rothman, "Rome and Jerusalem: The Uncertain Voice of the American Catholic Press," *Midstream,* 17 (April 1971): 33–42.
51. *CMW,* 674 (April 13, 1956): 63 f. Fr. Edward H. Flannery, "Anti-Zionism and the Christian Psyche," *JES,* 6 (Spring 1969): 173–84, analyzes this correlation in depth.
52. Formed in 1945 through the merger of the American Palestine Committee and the Christian Clergy for Palestine. For a recent discussion on its formation, see Doreen Bierbrier, "The American Zionist Emergency Council: The Analysis of a Pressure Group," *AJHQ,* 60 (September 1970): 93–95.
53. The reluctance of Fr. Ford to take a publicly pro-Zionist stand can be easily understood when one considers the numerous problems he encountered as a result of his public espousal of liberal issues. He suffered reprimands from both Cardinals McIntyre and Spellman, and his resignation from the Columbia University chaplaincy and from Corpus Christi Church was a direct result of his refusal to abdicate his sponsorship of the National Committee to Combat Antisemitism. See George Barry Ford, *A Degree of Difference* (New York: Farrar, Straus & Giroux, 1969), pp. 97–113. For some measure of the depth of Ford's feelings for the Holy Land and for Jewish aspirations there, see ibid., pp. 39–42, where he describes his 1923 visit to Jerusalem.

Both Rev. Karl Baehr and Dr. Carl Hermann Voss, directors of the ACPC, praised Ford's genuine interest and participation in the committee. And Dr. Voss was particularly grateful for letters of introduction to Jacques Maritain and Cardinal Tisserant which Fr. Ford prepared for him. Personal interviews with Karl Baehr, July 10, 1972, and Carl H. Voss, October 26, 1972.

54. On the involvement of American Protestant clergy in the ACPC, see Herzl Fishman, "American Protestantism and the State of Israel, 1937–1967" (Ph.D. diss., New York University, 1971), pp. 98–137.

55. Thomas Sugrue, *Watch for the Morning* (New York: Harper, 1950).

56. Despite confinement to a wheelchair and the severe pain he endured, Sugrue participated actively on the Speakers' Bureau of the ACPC. The heroic efforts of Sugrue were conveyed to me by Dr. Carl Hermann Voss. Personal interview, October 27, 1972.

Sugrue's effectiveness as a Catholic spokesman may have been impaired by his friction with the Church, which began in 1951 and continued to his death. Sugrue's difficulties with the Church began with two critical articles published in *Christian Herald* and later incorporated in his *A Catholic Speaks His Mind on America's Religious Conflict* (New York: Harper & Brothers, 1952).

57. *Christians and Israel*, 2 (March 1963): 3. See also Bishop's report on Israel in *CMW*, 66 (September 6, 1957): 566–69. Mrs. Bishop's perspectives on Israel were clarified for me in a personal interview on November 14, 1972.

Claire H. Bishop's activities in fostering Catholic-Jewish understanding are manifold. Among these activities was her role on the Speakers' Bureau of the ACPC and as a Danforth Lecturer on Christian-Jewish Relations. She is also credited with the introduction of Jules Isaac's *Jesus and Israel* to the American public. She contributed the introduction to the American publication of Isaac's *The Teaching of Contempt*.

58. The address was published in pamphlet form by the Institute, *Why Judaeo-Christian Studies?* (1954). See p. 28. Msgr. Oesterreicher's contributions to a theological reinterpretation of Judaism will be dealt with more extensively in the next chapter, p. 115–16.

59. See, particularly, Edward H. Flannery, "Theological Aspects of the State of Israel," *Bridge,* 3 (1958).

60. *NYT,* May 26, 1971, p. 43. See also the commitment expressed in "A Statement of Conscience," in *Brothers in Hope* vol. 5 of the *Bridge* (February 1970), pp. 291–95; "Salute to Israel," *Teshuvah,* Institute Paper no. 1 (1970); and *The Rediscovery of Judaism* (Institute of Judaeo-Christian Studies, 1971), pp. 37 f.

61. *NYT,* May 26, 1971, p. 43.

62. *Bridge,* 5 (February 1970): 241.

63. Published under the title of *The Anguish of the Jews* (New York: Macmillan Co., 1965).

64. A. Roy Eckardt, "Christian Perspectives on Israel," *Midstream,* 18 (October 1972): 46. Flannery's most recent article on Israel is in *America,* 126 (May 27, 1972). His running debate with Abp. Joseph T. Ryan, in defense of Israel, is reported in Judith Banki, ed., "Compendium of Christian Statements and Documents Bearing on Christian-Jewish Relations," mimeographed (Interreligious Affairs Department–American Jewish Committee, n.d.), pp. 48 f. Msgr. Francis J. Lally, former editor of the *Pilot,* noted the influence of Fr. Flannery's commentary on Israel upon diocesan editors. Personal communication, August 3, 1972. See also Fr. Flannery's "A State-

NOTES 167

ment of Conscience," cited in n. 60. For additional references, see bibliography.

65. It should be noted, however, that individual bishops have come out openly in support of Israel's continued existence. Particular attention should be taken of the activities and statements of Richard Cardinal Cushing of Boston. In combating both anti-Semitism and anti-Zionism, he was unequivocally outspoken. Doreen Bierbrier, op. cit., p. 94, n. 37, claims that the cardinal (then archbishop) agreed to be one of the sponsors of the pro-Zionist American Christian Conference when it met in Boston in 1945. (She gives no documentation for this claim, however.) Rev. Karl Baehr, director of the ACPC, also recalled that Cushing wrote personal letters urging members of his diocese to attend ACPC lectures and conferences. Personal interview, July 10, 1972. In a forthright address to an Interfaith Assembly in Massachusetts on March 13, 1969, he denounced the arguments usually directed against Israel by her detractors. He maintained that it was false to say that Israel is not the rightful owner of Palestine, that Israel is indifferent to the Arab refugees, that Israel has expansionist designs or is guilty of atrocities or terror. He refuted the arguments one by one and emphasized that "the State of Israel must have its rightful place among the family of nations, and it must be allowed to develop in dignity and honor." A leaflet of excerpts of the address, *The Arab-Israel Conflict: Basic Facts,* was published by the American-Israel Friendship Committee, N.Y., for limited distribution. See also, on Cushing's interventions at the Second Vatican Council, Vincent A. Yzermans, *American Participation in the Second Vatican Council* (New York: Sheed & Ward, 1967), pp. 586–87.

CHAPTER VII

1. Augustin Cardinal Bea, *The Church and the Jewish People,* trans. Philip Loretz (London: Geoffrey Chapman, 1966), p. 13. See also Bea's addresses to the council in app. 2, pp. 154–72.

2. Supra, pp. 9–15.

3. See n. 5. For the reiteration of this theme during the Second Vatican Council, see "Dogmatic Constitution on the Church," II, 9, in *Documents of Vatican II,* ed. Walter M. Abbot, S.J. (New York: America Press, 1966), pp. 24 f.

4. For a history of the formation of these Christian attitudes, see James Parkes, *The Conflict of the Church and the Synagogue* (Cleveland and New York: World Publishing Co., Meridian Books, 1961), pp. 100–106 and 157–68; Edward H. Flannery, *The Anguish of the Jews* (New York: Macmillan Co., 1965), pp. 44–63. For selected documents and commentary, see Karl Heinrich Rengstorf and Siegfried von Kortzfleish, eds., *Kirche und Synagoge,* vol. 1 (Stuttgart: Ernst Klett Verlag, 1968), and A. Lukyn Williams, *Adversus Judaeos* (Cambridge: Cambridge University Press, 1935).

5. The history and background of the Vatican statement on the Jews have been ably recorded by Arthur Gilbert, *The Vatican Council and the Jews* (Cleveland and New York: World Publishing Co., 1968). Many accounts have been written of the council proceedings. Some of the more detailed reports are those of Xavier Rynne (pseud.).

See particularly *The Third Session: The Debates and Decrees of Vatican Council II,*

September 14 to November 21, 1964 (Farrar, Straus & Giroux, 1965). A day-to-day account was kept by the NCWC. In response to requests of the American hierarchy, the account of the third session was edited and published as a "temporary source book." Floyd Anderson, ed., *Council Daybook, Vatican II, Session 3* (Washington: NCWC, 1965).

6. The excerpts from the "Dogmatic Constitution" are taken from the translation in ibid., sess. 3, pp. 309–12.

7. Ibid., p. 315.

8. The opposition tactics of Arab and Middle Eastern prelates and the maneuvers of the conservative clergy to block, or at least weaken, the statement are documented in Gilbert, op. cit., pp. 77 f., 85, 92 f., 138 f., 151 f., 155, 172–74, and 192. Gilbert also provides, in apps. A–D, pp. 262–79, full texts of all four versions.

See also the admission of Bea that the emendations in the final version were undertaken to meet the objections raised by conservative and Middle Eastern clergy. Bea, op. cit., p. 25.

9. For the full text in translation, see *Documents of Vatican II*, pp. 663–67.

10. Gilbert, op. cit., p. 141.

11. Ibid., p. 149.

12. Msgr. Vincent A. Yzermans, ed., *American Participation in the Second Vatican Council* (New York: Sheed & Ward, 1967), pp. 586 f.

13. Ibid.

14. For the full text of his intervention, see ibid., pp. 587–89.

15. Ibid., p. 590.

16. Ibid., p. 582.

17. Ibid., pp. 582 f.

18. For a review of the secretariat's accomplishments, see *Vatican Council II's Statement on the Jews: Five Years Later,* compiled by the Foreign Affairs and Interreligious Affairs Department of the American Jewish Committee (February 1971), pp. 5–9. Thirty-five dioceses have official committees to deal with Catholic-Jewish relations. Particularly active dioceses are Brooklyn, Albany, Atlanta, Baltimore, Boston, Rockville Centre, Philadelphia, Detroit, and Galveston-Houston. In 1967 the secretariat established a full-time office at Seton Hall University with Fr. Edward Flannery as executive secretary. Since January 1972 the office has been housed in the building of the National Conference of Catholic Bishops in Washington, D.C.

See also, Rabbi Marc H. Tanenbaum, "A Survey and Evaluation of Christian-Jewish Relationships since Vatican Council II," mimeographed (Address delivered at a joint seminar of the Institute of Judaeo-Christian Studies and the American Jewish Committee, October 26, 1970).

19. Supra, pp. 88–89.

20. Bea, op. cit., pp. 159, 164, 167, and 170.

21. This realization was most succinctly expressed by the editor of *Catholic World,* Fr. John B. Sheerin, in *CW,* 195 (August 1967): 260–63. Also, Robert F. Drinan discussed the impact of this revelation upon Catholics in "The State of Israel: Theological Implications for Christians," *Conservative Judaism,* 22 (Spring 1968): 28–35.

22. *Newsletter* published by the Secretariat for Catholic-Jewish Relations for the years 1968–1971, passim.

23. The full text appeared in the Baltimore diocesan weekly, the *Catholic Review,* December 12, 1969, pp. 1+.

24. Ibid.

25. Rev. Edward H. Flannery, "A Survey of Catholic-Jewish Relations 1970" November 17, 1970.

26. Quoted in Judith Banki, comp. and ed., "Compendium of Christian Statements and Documents Bearing on Christian-Jewish Relations," mimeographed (Interreligious Affairs Department of the American Jewish Committee, May 1972), pp. 13 ff.

27. It is important to see in this respect the running debate in *JES* which followed the publication of Edward Flannery's article, "Anti-Zionism and the Christian Psyche." See, particularly, the responses of Flannery, *JES,* 7 (Winter 1970): 110–16, and (Fall 1970): 796–802.

28. Msgr. John M. Oesterreicher, *The Rediscovery of Judaism* (pamphlet published by the Institute of Judaeo-Christian Studies, Seton Hall University, 1971), p. 37. See also, Oesterreicher, "The Theologian and the Land of Israel," *Bridge,* 5 (February 1970): 237 f.

29. "A Theology of Judaism: A Christian Perspective," mimeographed (Address delivered to a joint seminar of the Institute of Judaeo-Christian Studies and the American Jewish Committee, October 26, 1970).

30. Ibid., pp. 12 f.

31. Ibid., p. 14.

32. Ibid., pp. 16–18. The selected quotations do injustice to Fr. Rijk in reducing a complex theological challenge to a simplistic solution. However, my purpose here is only to point out the direction of new theological trends, not to analyze them.

33. "The Theological Dimensions of the State of Israel," mimeographed (Delivered on October 28, 1970).

34. Ibid., pp. 22–24. Already in 1964, Fr. Edward H. Flannery noted the emergence of a new thesis in the Church which proposed the idea of a "doctrine of two covenants." *Unitas,* 16 (Summer 1964): 150 f. Flannery assumed, however, that the new theology could not be expected to replace the universal missionary Church "for a long time to come."

35. Monika Hellwig, "Christian Theology and the Covenant of Israel," *JES,* 8 (Winter 1970): 48.

36. Ibid., p. 47.

37. Ibid., p. 50. There is room to conjecture that the original meaning of "Jesus is the son of God" or "Jesus is divine" may have been poetic statements whose exact meaning is now elusive.

38. Ibid., p. 51. Hellwig enlarges on these themes in a highly suggestive dissertation, "The Proposal towards a Theology of Israel as a Religious Community Contemporary with the Christian" (Ph.D. diss., Catholic University of America, 1968).

39. Supra, p.17. The persistence of the "old theology" should not be underestimated or overlooked. One salient example is a memorandum drawn up by Catholic

and Protestant clergy participating in a World Conference for Christians on Palestine in May 1970. Entitled "What is Required of the Christian Faith Concerning the Palestine Problem," the memorandum read: ". . . the Jewish people is prophetic, not a nation or a people, but 'a witness of God among the nations.' . . . the Jewish race was chosen to serve the Salvation of Humanity and not to establish itself in any particular religious or racial way . . . . From the Christian point of view it is clear from this that the creation of an exclusively Jewish State of Israel goes directly against God's plan for the Jews and the World." *Christians, Zionism and Palestine* (Beirut: Institute for Palestine Studies, 1970), pp. 73 f.

Bibliography

CATHOLIC PERIODICALS AND NEWSPAPERS

America   w. (1909–)
American Benedictine Review   q. (1950–)
American Catholic Quarterly Review   q. (1876–1924)
American Ecclesiastical Review   m. (1889–)
Ave Maria   w. (1865–)
CAIP News   m. (1929–1967; with intermittent suspensions of publication)
Catholic Action   m. (1919–1953)
Catholic Biblical Quarterly   q. (1939–)
Catholic Digest   m. (1936–)
Catholic Historical Review   q. (1915–)
Catholic Mind   m. (1903–)
Catholic Worker   m. (1933–)
Catholic World   m. (1865–)
Central-Blatt and Social Justice Review   m. (1908–; since 1940, *Social Justice Reivew*)
Christian Social Action (Christian Front)   m. (1936–1942)
Columbia   m. (1921–)

Commonweal w. (1924–)
Cross Currents q. (1950–)
The Crusader's Almanac q. (1884–)
Eastern Churches Quarterly q. (1936–; since 1964, *Eastern Churches Review*)
Extension m. (1906–)
Homiletic and Pastoral Review m. (1901–)
Michigan Catholic w. (1872–)
Missions (title varied: *Catholic Missions; Annals of Propagation of the Faith*) bim. (1906–)
National Catholic Almanac (titles varied) a. (1904–; since 1970, *The Catholic Almanac*)
The (Chicago) *New World* w. (1892–)
The (Boston) *Pilot* w. (1829–)
Priest m. (1945–)
The Register w. (1905–) syndicated
Review of Politics q. (1939–)
Shield m.; later q. (1922–1969?)
SIDIC tri-annual (1967–)
Sign m. (1921–)
Our Sunday Visitor w. (1912–) syndicated
The (Brooklyn) *Tablet* w. (1908–)
Theological Studies q. (1940–)
Thought q. (1926–)
The (Los Angeles) *Tidings* w. (1871–)
Unitas q. (1949–)

****

Christian News from Israel (published by the Israeli Government Ministry of Religious Affairs, Department of Christian Communities) m. (1949–)
National Catholic News Service Bulletins
Religious News Service Bulletins (interdenominational)

ORGANIZATIONAL REPORTS, PAMPHLETS, AND LEAFLETS

America Israel Friendship Committee. *The Arab-Israel Conflict: The Basic Facts*. Excerpts from an address delivered by Richard Cardinal Cushing at the Fifth Annual Interfaith Assembly, Somerville, Mass., March 13, 1970. (Leaflet)

American Council for Judaism. *Christian Opinion on Jewish Nationalism and a Jewish State*. With a foreword by Morris S. Lazaron. Philadelphia, 1944. (Pamphlet)

American Jewish Committee. "The American Jewish Committee: Christian Press Comment on the Beirut Airport Raid and the Iraqi Trials and Executions." Edited by Judith H. Banki. Mimeographed. New York, n.d.

―――. *Christian Reactions to the Middle East Crisis: New Agenda for Interreligious Dialogue*. Edited by Judith H. Banki. New York: Institute of Human Relations, January 1968.

―――. "Compendium of Christian Statements and Documents Bearing on Christian-Jewish Relations." Edited by Judith H. Banki. Mimeographed. New York: Interreligious Affairs Department, May 1972.

―――. *Christians Support Unified Jerusalem*. New York: Interreligious Affairs Department, October 1971. (Pamphlet)

―――. *The Tel Aviv Massacre: A Survey of Reaction to the May 30th Tragedy*. Edited by Inge Gibel. New York: Interreligious Affairs Department, July 1972. (Pamphlet)

―――. *Vatican Council II's Statement on the Jews: Five Years After*. New York: Foreign Affairs and Interreligious Affairs Departments, February 1971. (Pamphlet)

American Jewish Congress. *Hitler's Black Record*. New York, March 1943. (Pamphlet)

――― *Hitler's Ten Year War on the Jews*. New York, September 1943. (Pamphlet)

American Palestine Committee. "The American Palestine Committee: What Is It?" Mimeographed. New York, n.d. [ca. 1941].

―――. "The Christian Point of View on Palestine." Mimeographed. New York, 1946.

Archdiocese of New York, Diocese of Rockville Centre and Diocese of Brooklyn. *Guidelines for Catholic-Jewish Relations*. November 1969. (Pamphlet)

Catholic Near East Welfare Association: McMahon, Thomas J. *Job and Jacob*. New York, n.d. [ca. 1945]. (Pamphlet)

―――. *Only the Meek*. New York, 1949. (Pamphlet)

———. *The Pope and the Palestine Tragedy.* New York, 1950. (Pamphlet)
———. *Not by Bread Alone.* New York, 1951. (Pamphlet)
———. *Sufficient unto This Day.* New York, 1953. (Pamphlet)
———. *Hills of the Morning.* New York, n.d. [ca. 1954]. (Pamphlet)
Silver Thread: Twenty-five Years of the Catholic Near East Welfare Association. New York, November 1951. (Pamphlet)
Catholic Student Mission Crusade. *Middle East in Five Hours.* Cincinnati, 1957. (Pamphlet)
Institute for Judaeo-Christian Studies:
Oesterreicher, John M. *The Rediscovery of Judaism.* South Orange, N.J., 1971. (Pamphlet)
———. *Why Judaeo-Christian Studies?* South Orange, N.J., 1954. (Pamphlet)
National Council of Catholic Men. "The Religious Significance of Israel." Transcript of the Catholic Hour radio program, December 31, 1967. (Leaflet)
Zionist Organizations:
American Public Opinion and British Policy in Palestine. Washington: American Zionist Bureau, October 1939. (Pamphlet)
Great Britain, Palestine and the Jews: A Survey of Christian Opinion. London: Zionist Organization, 1919. (Pamphlet)

DOCUMENTS

Abbot, Walter M., ed. *Documents of Vatican II.* New York: America Press, 1966.
Acta Apostolicae Sedis. Commentarium Officiale. 11, 12, n.s. 15, n.s. 16, n.s. 33, Rome: Typis Polyglottis Vaticanis.
Blet, Pierre, Angelo Martini, and Burkhardt Schneider, eds. *Actes et Documents du Saint Siege relatifs à la second guerre mondiale.* 5 vols. Vatican: Libreria Editrice Vaticana, 1965–69.
Higgins, Rosalyn. *United. Nations Peacekeeping 1946–1967.* Vol. 1. *Middle East: Documents and Commentary.* London: Oxford University Press, 1969.

Huber, Raphael M., ed. *Our Bishops Speak, 1919–1951*. Milwaukee: Bruce Publishing Co., 1952.

Hurewitz, J. C. *Diplomacy in the Near and Middle East: A Documentary Record*. 2 vols. Princeton, N.J.: Van Nostrand, 1956.

United Nations. *Official Records of the First Special Session of the General Assembly, Resolutions*. A/364; Annexes A/364/Add.3.

―――. *Official Records of the Second Session of the General Assembly. Ad Hoc Committee on the Palestine Question*. A/519 Annexes 19, 19a.

―――. *Official Records of the Fourth Session of the General Assembly: Ad Hoc Political Committee*. Annex I, A/973; A/AC.

United States, Congress, House. Committee on Foreign Affairs. *Establishment of a National Home in Palestine: Hearings on H. Con. Res. 52*. 67th Cong., 2d sess., 1922.

―――. Committee on Foreign Affairs. *Resolutions Relative to the Jewish National Home in Palestine: Hearings on H. Res. 418 and H. Res. 419*. 78th Cong., 2d sess., February 8–16, 1944.

―――. Committee on Foreign Relations. *International Refugee Organization: Hearings on S. J. Res. 77*. 80th Cong., 2d sess., 1947.

―――. Committee on Foreign Affairs. *Palestinian Refugees: Hearings on S. J. Res. 153*. 81st Cong., 2d sess., February 16–17, 1950.

UNPUBLISHED MATERIAL

American Jewish Committee Archives. Vertical Files under the headings: Catholic-Jewish Relations; Israel–Catholic Church; Israel–Christian Church; Israel-Christians; Israel–Holy Places—AJC; Israel–Holy Places—Israeli Government; Israel-Jerusalem; Israel–Jerusalem–Catholic Church; Israel-Jerusalem-Internationalization; Middle East and Christian Churches.

American Zionist Archives. American Zionist Emergency Committee–Executive Meetings (1941–1944); American Christian Palestine Committee.

Catholic Near East Welfare Association. Executive Committee Meetings—Minutes, August 27, 1948 to November 17, 1955; Pontifical Mission for Palestine—Annual Reports, 1949–1954; Statement of Msgr. Thomas J. McMahon for the House Committee on Foreign Affairs and his remarks before the House Committee, July 26, 1951 (typed transcript).

Elizur, Judith N. "The Image of Israel in Protestant Eyes." Ph.D. dissertation, Harvard University, 1972.

Fishman, Hertzel. "American Protestantism and the State of Israel, 1937–1967." Ph.D. dissertation, New York University, 1971.

Goldblatt, Charles Israel. "American Attitudes to the Balfour Declaration, 1917–1922." Master's essay, Columbia University, 1963.

Hellwig, Monika. "The Proposal towards a Theology of Israel as a Religious Community Contemporary with the Christians." Ph.D. dissertation, Catholic University of America, 1968.

Klein, Charlotte. "The Theological Dimensions of the State of Israel." Mimeographed. Address delivered to a joint seminar of the American Jewish Committee and the Institute of Judaeo-Christian Studies, October 28, 1970.

National Archives. Myron Taylor to State Department, 1943–1944. 867N.01/6-2443.

Oder, Irwin. "The United States and the Palestine Mandate," 1920–1948: A Study of the Impact of Interest Groups on Foreign Policy." Ph.D. dissertation, Columbia University, 1956.

Rijk, Cornelius. "A Theology of Judaism: A Christian Perspective." Mimeographed. Address delivered to a joint seminar of the American Jewish Committee and the Institute of Judaeo-Christian Studies, October 26, 1970.

Tanenbaum, Marc H. "A Survey and Evaluation of Christian-Jewish Relationships since Vatican Council II." Mimeographed. Address delivered to a joint seminar of the American Jewish Committee and the Institute of Judaeo-Christian Studies, October 27, 1970.

Thering, Sister Rose Albert. "The Self-Concept Potential in Religious Texts." Ph.D. dissertation, St. Louis University, 1961.

Wentz, F. K. "The Reactions of the Religious Press in America to the Emergence of Nazism." Ph.D. dissertation, Yale University, 1954.

BIBLIOGRAPHY

BOOKS

Abell, Aaron I. *American Catholicism and Social Action: A Search for Social Justice 1865–1950.* Garden City, N.Y.: Hanover House, 1960.

Adler, Cyrus, and Aaron M. Margalith. *With Firmness in the Right: American Diplomatic Action Affecting Jews, 1840–1945.* New York: American Jewish Committee, 1946.

Adler, Selig. *The Isolationist Impulse.* London and New York: Abelard & Schuman, 1957.

———. *The Uncertain Giant: 1921–1941, American Foreign Policy Between the Wars.* New York: Macmillan Co., 1965.

Alon, Gedalia. *A History of the Jews in Palestine during the Mishnaic and Talmudic Epochs.* 2 vols. Tel Aviv: Hakibbutz Hameuchad, 1954. (Hebrew)

Anderson, Floyd, ed. *Council Daybook. Vatican II, Session 2.* Washington: National Catholic Welfare Conference, 1965.

Andrews, Fannie Fern. *The Holy Land under the Mandate.* 2 vols. Cambridge: Houghton Mifflin Co., 1931.

Antonius, George. *The Arab Awakening.* Philadelphia: J. B. Lippincott and Co., 1939.

Arberry, A. J., ed. *Religion in the Middle East: Three Religions in Concord and Conflict.* 2 vols. Cambridge: Cambridge University Press, 1969.

Attwater, Donald. *The Christian Churches of the East.* 2 vols. Milwaukee: Bruce Publishing Co., 1948.

Azcárate y Flóres, Pablo de. *Mission in Palestine, 1948–1952.* Washington: Middle East Institute, 1966.

Badeau, John S. *The American Approach to the Arab World.* New York: Harper & Row, 1968.

Baehr, Karl. *In Search of Brotherhood in the Holy Land.* Rev. ed. New York: Interfaith and University Committee, 1969.

Barbour, Neville. *Nisi Dominus.* London: George G. Harrup, 1946.

Baron, Salo W. *The Social and Religious History of the Jews.* 2d ed. rev. vol. 1. Philadelphia: Jewish Publication Society, 1958.

Bauer, Yehuda. *Flight and Rescue: Bricha.* New York: Random House, 1970.

———. *From Diplomacy to Resistance: A History of Jewish Palestine 1939–1945.* Philadelphia: Jewish Publication Society, 1970.

Baum, Gregory. *The Jews and the Gospel.* Westminster, Md.: Newman Press, 1961.

———. *That They May Be One.* Westminster, Md.: Newman Press, 1958.

Baumgartner, Appolinaris William. *Catholic Journalism: A Study of Its Development in the United States, 1789–1930.* New York: Columbia University Press, 1931.

Bea, Augustin Cardinal. *The Church and the Jewish People.* Trans. Philip Loretz. London: Geoffrey Chapman, 1966.

Belloc, Hilaire. *The Battleground: Syria and Palestine.* London and Philadelphia: J. B. Lippincott Co., 1936.

Berger, Elmer. *The Jewish Dilemma.* New York: Devin-Adair Co., 1945.

Bernadotte, Count Folke. *To Jerusalem.* Trans. Joan Bulman. London: Hodder & Stoughton, 1951.

Bilby, Kenneth W. *New Star in the Near East.* Garden City, N.Y.: Doubleday, 1950.

Billington, Ray. *The American Crusade, 1800–1860: A Study of the Origins of American Nativism.* Chicago: Quadrangle Books, 1964.

Borochov, Ber. *Nationalism and the Class Struggle: A Marxian Approach to the Jewish Problem.* New York: Young Poale Zion Alliance of America, 1935.

Bourne, Francis Cardinal. *Occasional Sermons.* London: Sheed & Ward, 1930.

Bovis, H. Eugene. *The Jerusalem Question, 1917–1968.* Stanford, Calif.: Hoover Institution Press, 1971.

Brown, Francis J., and Joseph S. Roucek, eds. *One America: The History, Contributions, and Present Problems of Our Racial and National Minorities.* New York: Prentice-Hall, 1952.

Burr, Nelson Rollin. *A Critical Bibliography of Religion in America.* 2 vols. Princeton, N.J.: Princeton University Press, 1961.

Burrows, Millar. *Palestine Is Our Business.* Philadelphia: Westminster Press, 1949.

Callahan, Daniel, ed. *Generation of the Third Eye.* New York: Sheed & Ward, 1965.

———. *The Mind of the Catholic Layman.* New York: Charles Scribner's Sons, 1963.
The Catholic Catechism. Ed. Peter Cardinal Gasparri. Eng. Trans. Hugh Pope, O.P. New York: P.J. Kenedy, 1932.
Chesterton, G. K. *The New Jerusalem.* London: Hodder & Stoughton, 1921.
Cianfarra, Camille. *The Vatican and the War.* New York: E. P. Dutton, 1944.
Claude, Inis, Jr. *National Minorities: An International Problem.* Cambridge: Harvard University Press, 1955.
Code, Joseph B. *The Spanish War and Lying Propaganda.* New York: Paulist Press, 1938.
Cohen, Israel. *The Zionist Movement.* London: F. Muller, 1945.
Cohen, Naomi. *Not Free to Desist: A History of the American Jewish Committee, 1906–1966.* Philadelphia: Jewish Publication Society, 1972.
Colbi, Saul. *Christian Churches in Israel.* Jerusalem: Israel Economist, 1969.
———. *Short History of Christianity in the Holy Land.* Jerusalem: Am Hassefer, 1965.
Collin, Bernardin. *Les Lieux Saints.* Paris: Presses Universitaires de France, 1962.
Connaughton, M. S. *The Editorial Opinion of the Catholic Telegraph of Cincinnati on Contemporary Affairs and Politics, 1871–1921.* Washington, 1943.
Cronin, John F. *Communism: A World Menace.* Washington: National Catholic Welfare Conference, 1947.
Crossman, Richard. *Palestine Mission: A Personal Record.* New York and London: Harper & Bros., 1947.
Crum, Bartley C. *Behind the Silken Curtain.* New York: Simon & Schuster, 1947.
Dagan, Avigdor. *Moscow and Jerusalem: Twenty Years of Relations between Israel and the Soviet Union.* London, New York, and Toronto: Abelard-Schuman, 1970.
Davis, Moshe, ed. *Israel: Its Role in Civilization.* New York: Harper & Bros., 1956.
Demann, Paul. *The Jewish Faith.* Trans. P. J. Hepburne-Scott. New York: Hawthorn Books, 1961.

De Novo, John A. *American Interests and Policies in the East: 1900–1939*. Minneapolis: University of Minnesota Press, 1963.

Donovan, C. F. *The Story of the Twenty-Eighth International Eucharistic Congress Held at Chicago, Illinois, United States of America from June 20–24, 1926*. Chicago, 1927.

Draper, Theodore. *Israel and World Politics: Roots of the Third Arab-Israeli War*. New York: Viking Press, 1968.

Ebersole, Luke E. *Church Lobbying in the Nation's Capital*. New York: Macmillan Co., 1951.

Eckardt, A. Roy. *Christianity and the Children of Israel*. New York: King's Crown Press, 1948.

———. *Elder and Younger Brothers: The Encounter of Jews and Christians*. New York: Charles Scribner's Sons, 1967.

———, and Alice Eckardt. *Encounter with Israel: A Challenge to Conscience*. New York: Association Press, 1970.

Egan, Maurice F., and John B. Kennedy. *The Knights of Columbus in Peace and War*. New Haven: Knights of Columbus, 1920.

Elath, Eliahu. *Israel and Her Neighbors*. Cleveland and New York: World Publishing Co., 1957.

Ellis, John Tracy, *American Catholicism*. 2d. rev. Chicago: University of Chicago Press, 1969.

———. *The Life of James Cardinal Gibbons*. Vol. 2. Milwaukee: Bruce Publishing Co., 1952.

———. *A Select Bibliography of the History of the Catholic Church in the United States*. New York: Declan X. McMullen Co., 1947.

Elston, D. R. *Israel: The Making of a Nation*. London: Oxford University Press, 1963.

Esco Foundation for Palestine. *Palestine: A Study of Jewish, Arab and British Policies*. 2 vols. New Haven: Yale University Press, 1947.

Ettinghausen, Richard. *A Selected and Annotated Bibliography of Books and Periodicals in Western Languages Dealing with the Near and Middle East*. Washington: Middle East Institute, 1952.

Ettledorf, Raymond. *The Catholic Church in the Middle East*. New York: Macmillan Co., 1959.

Fahey, Denis. *The Kingship of Christ and the Conversion of the Jewish Nation*. Dublin: Regina Publications, 1953.

Falconi, Carlo. *The Popes of the Twentieth Century: From Piux X to John XXIII*. Trans. Muriel Grinrod. London: Weidenfeld & Nicholson, 1967.
Feige, Gregory. *The Church and the Jews*. New York: Paulist Press, 1937.
Feinstein, Marnin. *American Zionism, 1884–1904*. New York: Herzl Press, 1965.
Fenton, John H. *The Catholic Vote*. New Orleans: Hauser Press, 1960.
——. *Salt of the Earth: An Informal Profile of Richard Cardinal Cushing*. New York: Coward-McCann, 1965.
Finer, Herman. *Dulles Over Suez*. Chicago: Quadrangle Books, 1964.
Fink, Reuben, ed. *America and Palestine*. New York: American Zionist Emergency Council, 1944.
——, ed. *The American War Congress and Zionism*. New York: Zionist Organization of America, 1919.
Finley, James F. *James Gillis, Paulist*. Garden City, N.Y.: Hanover House, 1958.
Finn, Brendan A. *Twenty-Four Cardinals*. Boston: Bruce Humphries, 1947.
Fisher, Sydney N., ed. *The Middle East: A History*. 2d ed. New York: Alfred A. Knopf, 1969.
Flannery, Edward H. *The Anguish of the Jews: Twenty-Three Centuries of Anti-Semitism*. New York: Macmillan Co., 1965.
Flynn, George Q. *American Catholics and the Roosevelt Presidency*. Lexington: University of Kentucky Press, 1968.
Ford, George Barry. *A Degree of Difference*. New York: Farrar, Straus & Giroux, 1969.
Forrestal, James V. *The Forrestal Diaries*. Ed. Walter Millis with the collaboration of E. S. Duffield. New York: Viking Press, 1951.
Freudenheim, Yehoshua. *Government in Israel*. Dobbs Ferry, N.Y.: Oceana Publications, 1967.
Friedman, Philip. *Their Brothers' Keepers*. New York: Crown Publishers, 1957.
Friedrich, Carl J. *American Policy toward Palestine*. Washington: Public Affairs Press, 1956.
Fuchs, Lawrence H., ed. *American Ethnic Politics*. New York: Harper & Row, 1968.

———. *John F. Kennedy and American Catholicism.* New York: Meredith Press, 1967.

———. *The Political Behavior of American Jews.* Glencoe, Ill.: Free Press, 1956.

Galter, Albert, ed. *The Red Book of the Persecuted Church.* Westminster, Md.: Newman Press, 1957.

Gannon, Robert I. *The Cardinal Spellman Story.* New York: Doubleday, 1962.

Gilbert, Arthur. *A Jew in Christian America.* New York: Sheed & Ward, 1966.

———. *The Vatican Council and the Jews.* Cleveland and New York: World Publishing Co., 1968.

Glazer, Simon. *The Palestine Resolution: A Record of Its Origin.* Kansas City: United Synagogue of Kansas City, 1922.

Gleason, Philip, ed. *Contemporary Catholicism in the United States.* Notre Dame: University of Notre Dame Press, 1969.

Glick, Edward B. *Latin America and the Palestine Problem.* New York: Theodor Herzl Foundation, 1958.

Glock, Charles Y., and Rodney Stark. *Christian Beliefs and Anti-Semitism.* New York and London: Harper & Row, 1966.

Grabill, Joseph L. *Protestant Diplomacy and the Near East: Missionary Influence on American Policy, 1810–1927.* Minneapolis: University of Minnesota Press, 1971.

Graham, Robert A. *Vatican Diplomacy.* Princeton, N.J.: Princeton University Press, 1959.

Granados, Jorge-Garcia. *The Birth of Israel.* New York: Alfred A. Knopf, 1949.

Greeley, Andrew. *The Catholic Experience: An Interpretation of the History of American Catholicism.* Garden City, N.Y.: Doubleday, 1967.

Gurian, Waldemar. *Bolshevism: An Introduction to Soviet Communism.* Notre Dame: University of Notre Dame Press, 1952.

———, and M. A. Fitzsimons, eds. *The Catholic Church in World Affairs.* Notre Dame: University of Notre Dame Press, 1954.

Haber, Julius. *The Odyssey of an American Zionist.* New York: Twayne Publishers, 1956.

Halperin, Samuel. *The Political World of American Zionism.* Detroit: Wayne State University Press, 1961.

Halpern, Ben. *The Idea of a Jewish State*. Cambridge: Harvard University Press, 1961.
Hanna, Paul L. *British Policy in Palestine*. Washington: American Council on Public Affairs, 1942.
Hargrove, Katherine T. *The Star and the Cross: Essays on Jewish-Christian Relations*. Milwaukee: Bruce Publishing Co., 1966.
Hay, Malcolm. *Foot of Pride: The Pressure of Christendom on the People of Israel for 1900 Years*. Boston: Beacon Press, 1950. (Republished as *Europe and the Jews*, 1960.)
Herberg, Will. *Protestant, Catholic, Jew: An Essay in American Religious Sociology*. New York: Doubleday, 1956.
Herr, Dan, and Joel Wells, eds. *Through Other Eyes*. Westminster, Md.: Newman Press, 1965.
Hertzberg, Arthur. *The Zionist Idea: A Historical Analysis and Reader*. New York: Harper Torchbooks, 1966.
Herzl, Theodor. *The Complete Diaries of Theodor Herzl*. Ed. Raphael Patai and trans. Harry Zohn. Vol. 4. New York: Herzl Press; London: Thomas Yoseloff, 1960.
Higham, John. *Strangers in the Land*. New Brunswick, N.J.: Rutgers University Press, 1955.
Hirschman, Ira A. *The Embers Still Burn*. New York: Simon & Schuster, 1949.
Holborn, Louise W. *The International Refugee Organization; A Specialized Agency of the U.N.: Its History and Work, 1946–1952*. London, New York, and Toronto: Oxford University Press, 1956.
Hollis, Christopher, and Ronald Brownrigg. *Holy Places: Jewish, Christian and Muslim Monuments in the Holy Land*. New York: Frederick Praeger, 1969.
Horowitz, David. *State in the Making*. Trans. Julian Meltzer. New York: Alfred A. Knopf, 1953.
Hourani, A. H. *Minorities in the Arab World*. London: Oxford University Press, 1947.
Hurewitz, J. C. *Middle East Dilemmas*. New York: Harper & Bros., 1953.
———, ed. *Soviet-American Rivalry in the Middle East*. New York: W. W. Norton, 1950.
———. *The Struggle for Palestine*. New York: W. W. Norton, 1950.

Hyamson, Albert M. *Palestine under the Mandate*. London: Methuen, 1950.

Isaac, Jules. *Has Anti-Semitism Roots in Christianity?* Trans. Dorothy Parkes and James Parkes. New York: National Conference of Christians and Jews, 1961.

———. *The Teaching of Contempt: Christian Roots of Anti-Semitism*. Trans. Helen Weaver. New York: McGraw-Hill Book Co., 1965.

Israeli Government. *Jerusalem 1948–1951: Three Years of Reconstruction*. Jerusalem, 1951.

Janowsky, Oscar, ed. *The American Jew: A Reappraisal*. Philadelphia: Jewish Publication Society, 1964.

Joseph, Dov. *The Faithful City*. New York: Simon & Schuster, 1960.

Journet, Charles. *Destinées d'Israël*. Paris: Egloff, 1945.

Kallen, Horace M. *Judaism at Bay*. New York: Bloch Publishing Co., 1932.

———. *Zionism and World Politics*. Garden City, N.Y.: Doubleday, Page & Co., 1921.

Kaplan, Deborah. *The Arab Refugee Problem*. Trans. Misha Louvish. Jerusalem: Rubin Mass Press and Jerusalem Post Press, 1959.

Khadduri, Majdia D., ed. *The Arab-Israeli Impasse*. Washington: R. B. Luce, 1968.

Khouri, Fred J. *The Arab-Israeli Dilemma*. Syracuse, N.Y.: Syracuse University Press, 1968.

Kimche, Jon. *The Second Arab Awakening*. New York, Chicago, and San Francisco: Holt, Rinehart & Winston, 1970.

———, and David Kimche. *The Secret Roads: The Illegal Migration of a People, 1938–1948*. New York: Farrar, Straus & Cudahy, 1955.

Kinsel, Paschal, and Leonard Henry. *The Catholic Shrines in the Holy Land*. New York: Farrar, Straus & Young, 1951.

Kirk, George. *Survey of International Affairs, 1939–1946: The Middle East in the War*. Oxford: Oxford University Press, 1952.

———. *Survey of International Affairs: The Middle East, 1945–1950*. New York and London: Oxford University Press, 1954.

Koestler, Arthur. *Promise and Fulfillment*. New York: Macmillan Co., 1949.

Kung, Hans. *The Council, Reform and Reunion.* Trans. Cecily Hastings. New York: Sheed and Ward, 1961.
LaFarge, John. *An American Amen: A Statement of Hope.* New York: Farrar, Straus & Cudahy, 1958.
———. *Communism and the Catholic Answer.* New York: America Press, 1936.
———. *The Manner Is Ordinary.* New York: Harcourt, Brace, 1954.
Landau, Jacob, M. *The Arabs in Israel: A Political Study.* New York: Oxford University Press, 1969.
Lapide, Pinchas E. *The Last Three Popes and the Jews.* London: Souvenir Press, 1967.
Laqueur, Walter Z. *Communism and Nationalism in the Middle East.* New York: Frederick A. Praeger, 1956.
———. *The Middle East in Transition.* New York: Frederick A. Praeger, 1958.
———. *The Soviet Union and the Middle East.* New York: Frederick A. Praeger, 1959.
Laurentin, René, and Joseph Neuner. *Commentary on the Declaration of the Relation of the Church to Non-Christian Religions.* Glen Rock: Paulist Press, 1966.
Lauterpacht, Elihu. *Jerusalem and the Holy Places.* London: Anglo-Israel Press, 1968.
Learsi, Rufus [Israel Goldberg]. *The Jews in America: A History.* New York: Ktav, 1972.
Lenczowski, George. *The Middle East in World Affairs.* Ithaca, N.Y.: Cornell University Press, 1952.
———, ed. *United States Interests in the Middle East.* Washington: American Enterprise Institute for Public Policy Research, October 1968.
Lewis, Bernard. *The Middle East and the West.* New York: Harper & Row, 1966.
Lieberman, Chaim. *Strangers to Glory: An Appraisal of the American Council for Judaism.* New York: Rainbow Press, 1955.
Lilienthal, Alfred M. *What Price Israel?* Chicago: Henry Regnery Co., 1953.
Lorch, Natanel. *The Edge of the Sword: Israel's War of Independence,*

1947–1949. New York: G. P. Putnam's Sons, 1961.

McAvoy, Thomas T. *A History of the Catholic Church in the United States*. Notre Dame: University of Notre Dame Press, 1969.

McDonald, James G. *My Mission in Israel, 1948–1951*. New York: Simon & Schuster, 1951.

Manuel, Frank E. *The Realities of American-Palestine Relations*. Washington: Public Affairs Press, 1949.

Marden, Charles F. *Minorities in American Society*. New York: American Book Co., 1952.

Maritain, Jacques. *A Christian Looks at the Jewish Question*. New York and Toronto: Longmans, Green, 1939.

———. *Redeeming the Time*. London: Centenary Press, 1943.

Marlowe, John. *Rebellion in Palestine*. London: Cresset Press, 1946.

———. *The Seat of Pilate*. London: Cresset Press, 1959.

Marty, M. E., ed. *The Religious Press in America*. New York: Holt, Rinehart & Winston, 1963.

Masse, Benjamin L., ed. *The Catholic Mind through Fifty Years, 1903–1953*. New York: America Press, 1953.

Maynard, Theodore. *The Catholic Church and the American Idea*. New York: Appleton-Century-Crofts, 1953.

Meinertzhagen, Richard. *Middle East Diary, 1917–1956*. London: Cresset Press, 1959.

Meistermann, Barnabas. *Guide to the Holy Land*. Rev. ed. London: Burns, Oates & Washbourne, 1923.

Meyer, Isidor S., ed. *Early History of Zionism in America*. New York: American Jewish Historical Society and Theodor Herzl Foundation, 1958.

Miller, David Hunter. *My Diary at the Conference of Paris with Documents*. Vols. 4 and 5. New York: Printed for the author by the Appeal Printing Co., 1924.

Millot, Rene-Pierre. *Missions in the World Today*. New York: Hawthorne Books, 1961.

Moore, Edmund A. *A Catholic Runs for President: The Campaign of 1928*. Gloucester, Mass.: Peter Smith, 1968.

Morgan, Thomas B. *Speaking of Cardinals*. New York: G. P. Putnam's Sons, 1946.

Morse, Arthur. *While Six Million Died: A Chronicle of American*

Apathy. New York: Random House, 1968.
Mott, Frank Luther. *American Journalism: A History, 1690–1960*. 3rd ed. New York: Macmillan Co., 1962.
Myers, Gustavus. *History of Bigotry in the United States*. 2d ed. rev. New York: Capricorn Books, 1960.
Nathan, Robert R., Oscar Gass, and Daniel Creamer. *Palestine: Problem and Promise, An Economic Study*. Washington: Public Affairs Press, 1946.
O'Ballance, Edgar. *The Arab-Israeli War, 1948*. London: Faber & Faber, 1956.
O'Brien, David. *American Catholics and Social Reform*. New York: Oxford University Press, 1968.
O'Connell, William Cardinal. *Recollections of Seventy Years*. Boston and New York: Houghton Mifflin Co., 1934.
Oesterreicher, John M., ed. *The Bridge: Judaeo-Christian Studies*. 5 vols. New York: Pantheon Books, 1955–70.
———, ed. *Brothers in Hope*. Vol. 5 of *The Bridge: Judaeo-Christian Studies*. New York: Herder & Herder, 1970.
O'Neill, Charles, ed. *Ecumenism and Vatican II*. Milwaukee: Bruce Publishing Co., 1964.
Parkes, James. *The Conflict of the Church and the Synagogue: A Study in the Origins of Anti-Semitism*. London: Soncino Press, 1934. Reprint. New York: Meridian Books, 1961.
———. *A History of Palestine from 135 A.D. to Modern Times*. New York: Oxford University Press, 1949.
Pattee, Richard. *This Is Spain*. Milwaukee: Bruce Publishing Co., 1951.
Peretz, Don. *Israel and the Palestinian Arabs*. Washington: Middle East Institute, 1958.
Pernot, Maurice. *Le Saint-Siège, L'Eglise Catholique et la Politique Mondiale*. 2d ed. Paris: Librairie Armand Colin, 1929.
Pinson, Koppel, ed. *Essays on Antisemitism*. 2d ed., rev. and enl. New York: Conference on Jewish Relations, 1946.
Pisani, Lawrence F. *The Italian in America*. New York: Exposition Press, 1957.
Poliakov, Leon. *Harvest of Hate*. Syracuse, N.Y.: Syracuse University Press, 1954.

Proudfoot, Malcolm J. *European Refugees: 1939–52, A Study in Forced Population Movement.* London: Faber & Faber, 1957.
Putz, Louis, ed. *The Catholic Church, U.S.A.* Chicago: Fides Publishers Association, 1956.
Rackauskas, Constantine. *The Internationalization of Jerusalem.* Washington: Catholic Association for International Peace, 1957.
Rengstorf, Karl Heinrich, and Siegfried von Kortzfleisch. *Kirche und Synagoge, Handbuch zur Geschichte von Christen und Juden.* Vol. 1. Stuttgart: Ernst Klett Verlag, 1968.
Revusky, A. *Jews in Palestine.* New York: Vanguard Press, 1935.
Rondot, Pierre. *The Changing Patterns of the Middle East.* New York: Frederick A. Praeger, 1962.
———. *Les Chrétiens d'Orient.* Paris: J. Peyronnet, 1955.
Rynne, Xavier [pseud.]. *The Third Session: The Debates and Decrees of Vatican Council II, September 14 to November 21, 1964.* New York: Farrar, Straus & Giroux, 1965.
Safran, Nadav. *From War to War: The Arab-Israeli Confrontation, 1948–1967.* New York: Pegasus, 1969.
———. *The United States and Israel.* Cambridge: Harvard University Press, 1963.
Sakran, Frank C. *Palestine Dilemma: Arab Rights versus Zionist Aspirations.* Washington: Public Affairs Press, 1948.
Samuel, Viscount Herbert. *Memoirs.* London: Cresset Press, 1945.
Sayegh, Fayez. *The Palestinian Refugees.* Washington: AMARA Press, 1952.
Schechtman, Joseph. *The Arab Refugee Problem.* New York: Philosophical Library, 1952.
———. *The Refugee in the World.* New York: A. S. Barnes, 1963.
———. *The United States and the Jewish State movement: The Crucial Decade, 1949–1959.* New York: Herzl Press, 1966.
Serafian, Michael [pseud.]. *The Pilgrim.* New York: Farrar, Straux & Co., 1964.
Shaughnessy, Gerald. *Has the Immigrant Kept the Faith? A Study of Immigration and Catholic Growth in the United States, 1790–1920.* New York: Macmillan Co., 1925.
Sheed, F. J. *Communism and Man.* New York: Sheed & Ward, 1938.
Sheen, Fulton J. *Communism and the Conscience of the West.* In-

dianapolis and New York: Bobbs-Merrill Co., 1948.
———. *This Is the Holy Land*. Garden City, N.Y.: Doubleday, 1962.
Sherman, Charles B. *The Jew within American Society: A Study in Ethnic Individuality*. Detroit: Wayne State University Press, 1965.
Shuster, George N. *The Catholic Spirit in America*. New York: Dial Press, 1927.
Sokolow, Nahum. *History of Zionism, 1600-1918*. 2 vols. London: Longmans, Green, 1919.
Stedman, Murray S., Jr. *Religion and Politics in America*. New York: Harcourt, Brace & World, 1964.
Stein, Leonard. *The Balfour Declaration*. New York: Simon & Schuster, 1961.
Stock, Ernest. *Israel on the Road to Sinai, 1949-1956: With a Sequel on the Six-Day War, 1967*. Ithaca, N.Y.: Cornell University Press, 1967.
Stokes, Anson Phelps, and Leo Pfeffer. *Church and State in the United States*. Rev. ed. New York, Evanston, and London: Harper & Row, 1950.
Stoloff, Rose N. *Cooperatives and Collectives in Palestine*. New York: League for Labor Palestine, 1935.
Strong, Donald S. *Organized Anti-Semitism in America: The Rise of Group Prejudice during the Decade 1930-1940*. Washington: American Council on Public Affairs, 1941.
Sugrue, Thomas. *Watch for the Morning*. New York: Harper, 1950.
Sykes, Christopher. *Crossroads to Israel*. Cleveland and New York: World Publishing Co., 1968.
———. *Two Studies in Virtue*. New York: Alfred A. Knopf, 1953.
Synan, Edward A. *The Popes and the Jews in the Middle Ages*. New York: Macmillan Co., 1965.
Syrkin, Nahman. *Essays on Socialist Zionism*. New York: Young Poale Zion Alliance of America, 1935.
Thomas, Hugh. *The Spanish Civil War*. New York: Harper & Bros., 1961.
Trachtenberg, Joshua. *The Devil and the Jews*. New Haven: Yale University Press, 1943.

Trevor, Daphne. *Under the White Paper.* Jerusalem: Jerusalem Press, 1948.
Truman, Harry S. *Memoirs.* 2 vols. Garden City, N.Y.: Doubleday, 1955–56.
Tull, Charles J. *Father Coughlin and the New Deal.* Syracuse, N.Y.: Syracuse University Press, 1965.
United Arab Republic. *The Problem of the Palestinian Refugees.* Cairo: Information Department, 1964.
Vester, Bertha Spafford. *Our Jerusalem.* Garden City, N.Y.: Doubleday, 1950.
Vollmar, Edward R. *The Catholic Church in America.* 2d ed. New York: Scarecrow Press, 1963.
Voss, Carl H. *The Palestine Problem Today: Israel and Its Neighbors.* Boston: Beacon Press, 1953.
Warburg, James P. *Crosscurrents in the Middle East.* New York: Atheneum, 1968.
Ward, Leo R., ed. *The American Apostolate.* Westminster, Md.: Newman Press, 1952.
Wardi, Chaim, ed. *Christians in Israel: A Survey.* Jerusalem: Ministry of Religious Affairs, 1950.
Weigel, Gustave. *Catholic Theology in Dialogue.* New York: Harper & Row, 1961.
Weiser, Francis X. *The Holy Land.* Collegeville, Minn.: Liturgical Press, 1965.
Weizmann, Chaim. *Trial and Error: The Autobiography of Chaim Weizmann.* New York: Harper & Bros., 1949.
Welles, Sumner. *We Need Not Fail.* Boston: Houghton Mifflin Co., 1948.
Weyl, Nathaniel. *The Jew in American Politics.* New Rochelle, N.Y.: Arlington House, 1968.
Wiener, Herbert. *The Wild Goats of Ein Gedi.* Garden City, N.Y.: Doubleday, 1961.
Williams, A. Lukyn. *Adversus Judaeos: A Bird's-Eye View of Christian Apologiae until the Renaissance.* Cambridge: Cambridge University Press, 1935.
Williams, Michael. *The Catholic Church in Action.* Rev. ed. Zsolt Aradi. New York: P. J. Kenedy, 1957.

Wiltgen, Ralph M. *The Rhine Flows into the Tiber.* New York: Hawthorne Books, 1967.
Wischnitzer, Mark. *To Dwell in Safety.* Philadelphia: Jewish Publication, 1948.
Wise, Stephen S. *Challenging Years.* London: East and West Library, 1951.
Wood, James E., ed. *Jewish-Christian Relations in Today's World.* Waco, Tex.: Baylor University Press, 1971.
Wright, Quincy. *Mandates under the League of Nations.* Chicago: University of Chicago Press, 1930.
Yzermans, Vincent A. *American Participation in the Second Vatican Council.* New York: Sheed & Ward, 1967.
Zander, Walter. *Israel and the Holy Places of Christendom.* London: Weidenfeld & Nicolson, 1971.

ARTICLES

Adler, Selig. "The Palestine Question in the Wilson Era." *Jewish Social Studies* 10 (October 1948): 303–334.
Allinsmith, Wesley, and Barbara Allinsmith. "Religious Affiliation and Politico-Economic Attitude: A Study of Eight Major U.S. Religious Groups." *Public Opinion Quarterly* 12 (Fall 1948): 377–389.
Berkhof, H. "Israel as a Theological Problem in the Christian Church." *Journal of Ecumenical Studies* 6 (Summer 1969): 329–347.
Bierbrier, Doreen. "The American Zionist Emergency Council: The Analysis of a Pressure Group." *American Jewish Historical Quarterly* 60 (September 1970): 82–105.
Binchy, D. A. "The Vatican and International Diplomacy." *International Affairs* 22 (January 1946): 47–56.
Burton, William L. "Protestant America and the Rebirth of Israel." *Jewish Social Studies* 26 (October 1964): 203–214.
Chapman, Emanuel. "The Catholic Church and Anti-Semitism." *Social Frontier* 5 (January 1939): 108–111.
Cohen, Naomi W. "Reform Rabbis and Zionism." *Publication of the American Jewish Historical Society* 40 (July 1951): 361–394.

Crossan, Dominic. "Anti-Semitism and the Gospel." *Theological Studies* 26 (June 1965): 193–199.

Démann, Paul. "The Jews and Christian Doctrine Teaching." *Lumen Vitae* 4 (January 1949): 67–82.

———. "Signification de l'Etat d'Israel." *Cahiers Sioniens* 5, no. 1 (March 1951): 32–43.

Drinan, Robert F. "Israel: Theological Implications for Christians." *Conservative Judaism* 22 (Spring 1968): 28–35.

Eckardt, A. Roy. "Christian Perspectives on Israel." *Midstream* 18 (October 1972): 40–50.

Flannery, Edward H. "Anti-Zionism and the Christian Psyche." *Journal of Ecumenical Studies* 6 (Spring 1969): 173–184.

———. "Theological Aspects of the State of Israel." In *The Bridge,* Vol. 3, ed. John M. Oesterreicher, pp. 301–324. New York: Pantheon Books, 1958.

Glick, Edward B. "The Vatican, Latin America and Jerusalem." *International Organization* 11 (Spring 1957): 213–219.

Handy, Robert T. "Studies in the Interrelationship between America and the Holy Land: A Fruitful Field for Interdisciplinary and Interfaith Cooperation." In *Jewish-Christian Relations in Today's World,* ed. James E. Wood, Jr., pp. 105–123. Waco, Tex.: Baylor University Press, 1971.

———. "Zion in American Christian Movements." In *Israel, Its Role in Civilization,* ed. Moshe Davis, pp. 284–297. New York: Harper & Bros., 1956.

Hastings, Martin. "United States—Vatican Relations." *Records of the American Catholic Historical Society* 69 (1958): 20–55.

Heer, Friedrich. "The Catholic Church and the Jews Today." *Midstream* 17 (May, 1971): 20–31.

Hellwig, Monika. "Christian Theology and the Covenant of Israel." *Journal of Ecumenical Studies* 12 (Winter 1970): 37–51.

Iglesias, S. Munoz. "Origen de la creencia vulgar en las pretendidas profecías sobre la no restauración política de Israel." *Estudios Biblicos* 10 (1951): 403–433.

Journet, Charles. "The Mysterious Destinies of Israel." In *The Bridge,* Vol. 2, ed. John M. Oesterreicher, pp. 35–90. New York: Pantheon Books, 1956.

Langmuir, Gavin I. "Majority History and Post-Biblical Jews." *Jour-

nal of the History of Ideas 27 (September 1966): 343–364.
McAvoy, Thomas. "The Catholic Church in the United States between the Two Wars." *Review of Politics* 4 (October 1942): 409–431.
Minerbi, Y. "The Vatican and Zionism." *Molad* 27 (May–June 1971): 139–149. (Hebrew)
Mohn, Paul. "Jerusalem and the United Nations." *International Conciliation,* no. 464 (October 1950).
Nevins, Albert J. "A Profile of the Catholic Press." In *Twentieth Century Catholicism,* vol. 3, ed. Lancelot Sheppard, pp. 29–50. New York: Hawthorn Books, 1966.
Oder, Irwin. "American Zionism and the Congressional Resolution of 1922." *Publication of the American Jewish Historical Society* 45 (September 1955): 35–47.
Pernot, Maurice. "La Question de Palestine." *L'Esprit International* 12 (October 1938): 571–582.
Poliakov, Leon. "The Vatican and the 'Jewish Question.'" *Commentary,* 10 (November 1950): 439–449.
Robbins, Richard. "American Jews and American Catholics: Two Types of Social Change." *Sociological Analysis* 26 (Spring 1965): 1–18.
Rosenau, W. "Cardinal Gibbons and His Attitude toward the Jewish Problem." *Publication of the American Jewish Historical Society* 31 (1928): 219–224.
Rothman, Eugene. "Rome and Jerusalem: The Uncertain Voice of the American Catholic Press." *Midstream* 17 (April 1971): 33–42.
Sheehan, Edward R. "American Catholicism." *Dublin Review* 239 (Spring 1965): 337–376.
Sheerin, John B. "American Catholics and Ecumenism." In *Contemporary Catholicism in the United States,* ed. Philip Gleason, pp. 71–95. Notre Dame, Ind.: University of Notre Dame Press, 1969.
———. "Development of the Catholic Magazine in the History of American Journalism." *U.S. Catholic Historical Society—Historical Records and Studies* 45 (1953): 5–13.
Sklare, Marshall, and Benjamin B. Ringer. "A Study of Jewish Attitudes toward the State of Israel." In *The Jews, Social Patterns of an American Group,* ed. Marshall Sklare. Glencoe, Ill.: Free Press, 1958.
Sokolow, Florian. "Nahum Sokolow and Pope Benedict XV. *Zion,* 1

(January–February 1950): 48–52.

Voss, Carl H. "Christians and Zionism in the United States." *Palestine Year Book* 2 (1946): 493–500.

Wilson, Evan, M. "The Internationalization of Jerusalem." *Middle East Journal* 23 (Winter 1969): 1–13.

Zacharewicz, Misaela. "The Attitude of the Catholic Press to the League of Nations." *Records of the American Catholic Historical Society* 68 (1957): 46–50.

Index

Acta et Decreta, 3
Aide Memoire, 61
America, 5, 20, 36, 39, 41, 46, 50–51, 54, 56, 59, 66, 68–69, 74–75, 83–84, 99–102, 124 n.33, 133 n.8-n.9, 141 n.95, 144 n.–n.9, 153 n.28, 155 n.49, 156 n.54, 159 n.71, 159 n.75, 160 n.89, 164 n.38, 166 n. 64, 168 n.43
American Catholic Historical Society, 123 n.19
American Catholic Quarterly Review, 23–24
American Christian Palestine Committee (ACPC), 65, 104, 165 n.52, 165 n.53, 166 n.56–n.57, 167 n.65
American Council for Judaism, 66, 99, 149 n.51
American Ecclesiastical Review, 7, 160n.86
American Friends of the Middle East (AFME), 100, 164 n.35
American Jewish Committee, 76–77, 152 n.25, 158 n.61, 166 n.64, 168 n.18
American Jewish Historical Quarterly, 165 n.52
American Zionist Emergency Committee (AZEC), 58, 146 n.20
Anawati, G. C., 94
Anglo-American Committee of Inquiry on Palestine, 59–61, 63
Antonious, George, 19
Assaf, Michael, 75
Assemani, Abraham, 62–63, 147 n.32
Auspicia Quaedam, 61, 80, 151 n.4
Ave Maria, 5, 20–22, 26, 35, 52, 97, 138 n.66, 152 n.25

Baldus, S.A., 45–46

Balfour Declaration, 2, 17–18, 21–25, 27–28, 33, 40–43, 47, 50, 53, 77
Barlassina, Louis, 25, 28, 128 n.10, 135 n.34
Baum, Gregory, 11
Baumgartner, Apollinaris W., 6, 122 n.6
Bea, Augustin, 10, 107, 114, 168 n.8
Benedict XV (Pope), 17, 24–25, 31, 77–78, 119, 153 n.30
"Biltmore Program," 58
Bishop, Claire Huchet, 65, 104, 166 n.57
Bishops Emergency Drive, 86
Blackfriars, 160 n.87
Bonaventure Simon, 79, 154 n.38
Bookman, 18
Bourne, Francis, 24–25, 36–37, 129 n.25
Bridge (Brothers in Hope), 105, 160 n.88, 166 n.59–n.60, 169 n.28
Bruya, Anthony, 62–65, 76, 147 n.29

Cahiers Sioniens, 160 n.88
Catholic Action, 6, 155 n.49, 156 n.54, 159 n.71
Catholic Association for International Peace (*CAIP News*), 6, 124 n.27, 143 n.4, 152 n.23
Catholic Biblical Quarterly, 7, 159 n.75
Catholic Central Verein, 6, 73, 97, 141 n.93, 148 n.43
Catholic Digest, 8, 160 n.90
Catholic Historical Review, 26
Catholic Hour, 157 n.61
Catholic Messenger, 123 n.15
Catholic Mind, 7, 124 n.33, 148 n.41, 159 n.72
Catholic Near East Welfare Association (CNEWA), 64–65, 82–85, 147 n.37,

148 n.41, 156 n.52–n.53, 158 n.61, 159 n.70–n.71, 159 n.75
Catholic Press Association, 5, 123 n.13, 124 n.20
Catholic Review, 121 n.2, 169 n.23
Catholic Standard, 3
Catholic Students Mission Crusade, 163 n.14
Catholic Telegraph, 128 n.9
Catholic Worker, 7, 46, 54, 73, 138 n.74, 141 n.97, 144 n.9, 150 n.63
Catholic World, 5, 20, 22, 27, 36–37, 50, 59, 66–68, 73, 88, 103, 124 n.33, 129 n.21, 133 n.8–n.9, 139 n.78, 150 n.58, 161 n.5, 165 n.47, 165 n.49, 168 n.21
Central-Blatt, 6, 50–51, 124 n.24, 138 n.67. *See also Social Justice Review*
Central Union. *See* Catholic Central Verein
Cerny, Edward A., 88
Cerretti, Bonaventura, 34
Chesterton, G. K., 37, 134 n.21
Christian Council on Palestine. *See* American Christian Palestine Committee
Christians Concerned for Israel (American Christian Association for Israel), 104
Christian News From Israel, 157 n.60
"Christian Union of Palestine", 63, 75, 80
Chrysostom, John, 13
Cicognani, Amleto G., 61–62
Civiltà Cattolica, 15
Code of Canon Law (1919), 34
Cogley, John, 100, 164 n.35
Coleran, James, 141 n.95
Columbia, 6, 155 n.49, 157 n.61, 159 n.72, 160 n.90
Committee for Justice and Peace in the Holy Land, 73
Commonweal, 4, 6–7, 39, 41–43, 46, 51–53, 56, 59–60, 68, 74, 99–100, 103–4, 123 n.15, 133 n.10, 135 n.27, 138 n.71, 138 n.74, 144 n.9, 146 n.9, 146 n.21, 151 n.14, 152 n.20, 153 n.28, 155 n.49, 164 n.32, 164 n.37
Communism, Church view of, 44–46, 51–52, 56, 66–67, 91–94, 144 n.8, 161 n.1–n.2, 161 n.5; Jew as Communist, 46, 51, 67, 92, 161 n.5
Conciliation Commission, 83
Congar, Yves, 88–89, 113–14, 160 n.87
Congregation de Propaganda de Fide, 8
Conservative Judaism, 165 n.50, 168 n.21
Coughlin, Charles, 46, 132 n.45, 138 n.74
Crabites, Pierre, 42
Crum, Bartley C., 65, 148 n.44
Crusader's Almanac, 5, 124 n.22, 147 n.29
Cushing, Richard, 82, 111–12, 155 n.49, 161 n.2, 167 n.65

Day, Dorothy, 7
Dearborn Independent, 35, 133 n.9
"Declaration on the Relationship of the Church to Non-Christian Religions," 108
Deedy, John G., 3, 122 n.6, 122 n.11
Delmarva Dialog, 123 n.14
Displaced persons, 55–60, 145 n.11–n.12, 145–46 n.17–n.18
"Dogmatic Constitution on the Church," 108
Drinan, Robert, 165 n.50, 168 n.21

Ecclesiastical Review, 20
Ellis, John Tracy, 8
Evangelii praecones, 94
Evian Conference, 49, 140 n.89
Extension, 20, 45, 138 n.68

Fascists, 47
Federation of Catholic Societies, 34
Fishman, J. L. (Maimon), 76
Flannery, Edward H., 71, 105–6, 115, 128 n.9, 150 n.3, 158 n.61, 160 n.88, 163 n.25, 165 n.51, 166 n.64, 168 n.18, 169 n.27, 169 n.34
Ford, George Barry, 65, 104, 149 n.45, 165 n.53

Gasparri, Peter (Cardinal), 29, 31, 61, 130 n.35, 153 n.30
George-Picto, Charles, 77

INDEX

Ghergossian, James, 75
Gibbons, James, 19, 25, 133 n.9
Gillis, James, C.S.P., 73, 103, 139 n.78, 150 n.58
Goldstein, David, 73–74, 151 n.13
Gori, Alberto, 75, 153 n.27
Gorman, Ralph, 68, 73, 98–99, 142 n.101, 144 n.8, 146 n.18, 163 n.27–n.28
Graham, Robert A., 157 n.61
Griffin, Bernard William, 150 n.57
Guilt of deicide, 14, 52, 54, 110, 112, 127 n.68
Gurian, Waldemar, 7, 161 n.2

Haggear, Gabriel-Grégoire, 26
Hallett, Paul H., 96
Hay, Malcolm, 13, 125 n.47
Hayes, Patrick Joseph, 39
Hellwig, Monika, 118–19, 169 n.38
Hennessy, Augustine P., 163 n.25
Herzl, Theodor, 1, 153 n.30
Herzog, Yaakov, 155 n.52
Heschel, Abraham J., 163 n.25
Holmes, John Haynes, 41
Holocaust, 54–57, 60, 71, 84
Homiletic and Pastoral Review, 7
Hughes, Arthur, 85, 147 n.26, 153 n.27, 159 n.70
Hunt, Godfrey, 20

In Multiplicibus, 81–82
International Congress of the Catholic Press, 3
International Eucharistic Congress, 34
International Organization, 121 n.3
Isaac, Jules, 14, 125 n.47
Israel Economist, 162 n.9
Israel, Ministry of Religious Affairs, Department for Christian Communities, 76, 94–95

Jewish Chronicle, 30
Jewish Daily Bulletin, 136 n.49
John XXIII (Pope), 98, 106
Journal of Ecumenical Studies (JES), 118, 165 n.51, 169 n.27

Kearney, Vincent S., 101–2
Keenan, Charles, 164 n.38

Klein, Charlotte, 117–18
Knights of Columbus, 6, 34, 45, 155 n.49
Ku Klux Klan, 35

La Farge, John ("The Pilgrim"), 41, 136 n.43, 144 n.9
Lally, Francis J., 3, 123 n.14, 166 n.64
Leipzig, Francis P., 113
Les Missions Catholiques, 26
Leven, Stephen A., 113
Ludlow, Robert, 150 n.63

McDonald, James G., 82, 155 n.52
MacDonald Paper of 1939, 33, 41, 47
McIntyre, James Francis, 165 n.53
McMahon, Francis E., 65, 148 n.44
McMahon, Thomas J., 64–65, 76–77, 82–87, 148 n.38, 148 n.42, 152 n.22, 154 n.40, 155 n.51–n.53, 157 n.57, 159 n.70
Magnes, Judah L., 136 n.50
Maritain, Jacques, 65–66
Maurin, Peter, 7, 141 n.97, 151 n.12
Menace, 35, 133 n.9
Mesitermann, Barnabas, 37
Meyer, Albert, 112
Michigan Catholic, 5, 138 n.71, 141 n.97
Midstream, 165 n.50, 166 n.64
Mit brennender Sorge, 143 n.4
Molad, 121 n.3, 153 n.30
Month, 22, 134 n.18

National Catholic Almanac, 122 n.9
National Catholic News Service (NCNS), 26–28, 62, 73, 76, 85, 151 n.16, 159 n.70
National Catholic Reporter, 123 n.15
National Catholic War Council, 34
National Catholic Welfare Conference (NCWC) (National Catholic Welfare Council), 6, 9, 34, 40, 43, 64, 125 n.41, 136 n.55, 139 n.74, 149 n.45, 152 n.25, 155 n.49, 155 n.51, 159 n.71, 161 n.2, 168 n.5. *See* Catholic Action
National Conference of Catholic Bishops, 115, 125 n.41, 168 n.18
National Conference of Christians and Jews, 152 n.25
National Council of Catholic Men, 53

Nevins, Albert J., 122 n.6
New Palestine, 134 n.26
New World, 5, 22, 30, 36, 132 n.46, 135 n.36
New York Post, 148 n.44
New York Times, 26, 45, 105, 157 n.61, 159 n.70
Nostra Aetate, 107, 110, 113, 115, 118–19

O'Connell, William Henry, 131 n.44
Oesterreicher, John M., 104–6, 115–16, 157 n.61
O'Gara, James, 71
O'Keefe, Henry, 23, 129 n.21
O'Rourke, John, 69
Osservatore Romano, 39–40, 46, 61, 73
Our Sunday Visitor, 5, 7, 22, 39, 56, 86, 97, 133 n.10, 143 n.5, 152 n.22

Parkes, James, 13–14, 125 n.47
Parsons, Wilfred, 102, 164 n.43
Passfield Paper of 1930, 33, 41, 43, 136 n.42
Pattee, Richard, 97, 160 n.90
Paul VI (Pope), 157 n.61
Paulding, C. G., 68–69, 150 n.63
Peel Commission, 48, 51, 77, 140 n.84
Pfaff, William, 164 n.37
"Pilgrim, The". See LaFarge, John
Pilot, 3, 5, 29, 36, 39, 56, 88, 123 n.13, 123 n.18, 131 n.44, 151 n.13, 160 n.83
Pius IX (Pope), Quanta Cura, 137 n.57
Pius X (Pope), 1, 8, 153 n.30
Pius XI (Pope), 64; Divini Redemptoris, 137 n.58; Mit brennender Sorge, 143 n.4
Pius XII (Pope), 31, 81–82, 87, 94, 143 n.4, 147 n.25, 155 n.52; Auspicia Quaedam, 61, 80; Evangelii praecones, 94; In Multiplicibus, 81; Redemptoris Nostri, 81–82
Pontifical Mission for Palestine, 87
Praeparatio Evangelica, 108–10
Priest, 7, 159 n.72
Providence Visitor, 152 n.25

Quanta Cura, 137 n.57

Quotidiano, 73, 151 n.11

Redemptoris Nostri, 81–82
Reedy, John, 97
Refugees, 85–86, 158 n.64, 159 n.75
Register, 5, 87–88, 96–97, 152 n.27, 155 n.49, 159 n.71
Review of Politics, 7, 161 n.2
Rihani, Ameen, 18–19, 128 n.6
Rijk, Cornelius, 116–18, 169 n.32
Riots of 1929, 31, 33, 37–40, 42, 47
Ritter, Joseph, 112–13
Roosevelt, Kermit, 73
Rummel, Joseph, 146 n.20
Ryan, John A., 149 n.45
Ryan, Joseph T., 158 n.61, 166 n.64

Scanlon, Patrick, 123 n.13, 132 n.45, 139 n.75
Secretariat for Catholic-Jewish Relations (Sub-commission on Catholic-Jewish Relations), 113, 115, 168 n.18; Newsletter, 169 n.22
Secretariat for Promoting Christian Unity, 1, 106–8, 114–15
Serédi, Jusztinián György, 143 n.5
Seton Hall University, Institute of Judaeo-Christian Studies, 150, 166 n.58, 166 n.60; Seton Hall University Conference (1970), 116–18, 168 n.18
Shaw Commission, 41–42, 135 n.39
Sheean, Vincent, 42, 136 n.49
Sheen, Fulton J., 160 n.90, 161 n.2
Sheerin, John B., 103, 122 n.6, 128 n.9, 165 n.49, 168 n.21
Shehan, Lawrence, 1, 114–15
Sign, 5, 51–52, 54, 59, 65, 67–68, 72–73, 98–99, 133 n.10, 138 n.66, 138 n.69, 142 n.101, 144 n.8, 146 n.18, 159 n.73, 160 n.81, 160 n.90, 163 n.25, 163 n.27–n.28
Simpson report, 41, 136 n.42
Six-Day War, 114, 165 n.49–n.50
Smith, Matthew, 87–88, 96
Social Frontier, 138 n.74
Social Justice Review, 73, 97, 124 n.24. See Central-Blatt
Sociological Analysis, 125 n.45, 139 n.75

Sokolow, Nahum, 17, 31, 77, 153 n.30
Spellman, Francis, 82–83, 85, 148 n.42, 159 n.70–n.71, 165 n.53
Suez crisis of 1956, 100, 103, 164 n.33
Sugrue, Thomas, 104, 166 n.56
Sykes, Mark, 24, 77

Tablet, 5, 21, 26–27, 29–31, 35, 40, 46, 51–52, 56, 72, 123 n.13, 129 n.25, 132 n.45, 135 n.36, 139 n.75, 142 n.100
Taylor, Myron, 61
Teshuvah, 166 n.60
Theological Digest, 8
Theology Digest, 8, 160 n.87
Third Arab Congress in Haifa, 25
Third Plenary Council of Baltimore, 3, 132 n.3
Tidings, 5, 21–23, 25–26
Thompson, Dorothy, 164 n.35

Uhler, John E., 150 n.58
Unitas, 161 n.5, 162 n.9, 169 n.34
United Nations Special Committee on Palestine (UNSCOP), 61, 65, 69, 79, 148 n.42

U. S. Catholic Conference, 124 n.17, 125 n.41, 158 n.61
U. S. Catholic Historical Society—Historical Records and Studies, 122 n.6

Vatican Council, Second, 2, 89, 98, 103, 107–13, 116–19
Vergani, Antonio, 76–77
Voss, Carl Hermann, 149 n.45, 165 n.53, 166 n.56

Wauchope, Arthur, 140 n.80
White Paper (1922), 28, 31, 33, 62, 78
White Paper (1939), 47, 49–51, 60, 140 n.88, 141 n.95, 146 n.20
Wiener, Herbert, 163 n.14
Williams, Michael, 6, 144 n.9
Witness, 31, 151 n.13
Woodhead Report, 48
World Conference for Christians on Palestine, 170 n.39

Zionism, 22–25, 27–30, 33–34, 41, 43, 53, 55–70, 86–87, 99, 103
Zionist Organization of America, 27–28
Zolli, Eugenio, 103, 165 n.48